The
RISE
of the
RICH

The RISE *of the* RICH

A New View of Modern World History

Peter Gran

SYRACUSE UNIVERSITY PRESS

First Edition 2009

09   10   11   12   13   14   6   5   4   3   2   1

The paper used in this publication meets the minimum requirements
of American National Standard for Information Sciences—Permanence
of Paper for Printed Library Materials, ANSI Z39.48–1984.∞™

For a listing of books published and distributed by Syracuse University Press,
visit our Web site at SyracuseUniversityPress.syr.edu.

ISBN-13: 978-0-8156-3171-2   ISBN-10: 0-8156-3171-5

Library of Congress Cataloging-in-Publication Data

Gran, Peter, 1941–

The rise of the rich : a new view of modern world history / Peter Gran.

— 1st ed.

p. cm.

Includes bibliographical references and index.

ISBN-13: 978-0-8156-3171-2 (hardcover : alk. paper)

ISBN-10: 0-8156-3171-5 (hardcover : alk. paper)

1. History, Modern.   2. Rich people—History.   3. Upper class—History.
4. Social classes—History.   5. Social history.   6. Economic history.   7. World
politics.   I. Title.

D210.G66 2008

909.08—dc22

2008045870

CONTENTS

Peter Gran is professor of history at Temple University. He is author of *Islamic Roots of Capitalism: Egypt, 1760–1840* and *Beyond Eurocentrism: A New View of Modern World History*, both published by Syracuse University Press.

ACKNOWLEDGMENTS

THIS WORK, which has been ongoing with a few interruptions since the late 1990s, has benefited from the help of many individuals and a number of institutions and funding bodies. It gives me pleasure here to be able to express a word of appreciation for what they did.

My own institution, Temple University, and my own department, the History Department, have been of considerable help not only in terms of granting me release time but also in supplying me with technical information on different points, space to present my ideas, and some kind words of encouragement. Our former dean Susan Herbst, our former chairman Richard Immerman, and our current chairman, Prof. Andrew Isenberg, as well as Mark Haller and Arthur Schmidt among other colleagues, come quickly to mind. I would also like to thank the university for a study leave and for summer research funding and the University Grants Office for helping me secure a Fulbright. I would also like to thank our librarians in Paley Library who spent much time helping me gain access to material. I would also like to acknowledge the help I received from my students, both undergraduates and graduates, in class discussions, and formally thank one of them, Brandon Edwards, for his help preparing the bibliography.

Since coming to Temple, I have been affiliated with the University of Pennsylvania Middle East Center and enjoyed many of its activities over the years. Prof. Robert Vitalis, the center's previous director, cotaught a course with me on American Orientalism, a subject that appears in this book. For this and other kindnesses I thank him.

I worked on this book in tandem with a project on Egyptian history. This project was supported by grants in this time period as well, and these grants afforded me the leisure to think about both projects. And, as the reader will observe, quite a bit of Egyptian history finds its way into the present book. I would thus like to thank the Fulbright Foundation for one grant, the National Endowment for the Humanities for another, the Social Science Research Council for another, and the American Research Center in Cairo for hosting me on different occasions.

The World History Center, which existed until fairly recently at Northeastern University, gave me several opportunities to present the argument of the Rise of the Rich, and I am grateful to its students and colleagues and especially its guiding spirit, Prof. Patrick Manning. The World History Association conferences gave me further opportunities.

Several other institutions invited me to conferences or otherwise gave me a chance to present my ideas and gave me some feedback. I would like to begin by thanking Prof. Dora Kanoussi for an invitation to the Gramsci Center in Puebla for a memorable week that clarified a lot for me concerning Gramsci today. I would like to thank Profs. Wolfgang Haug and Thomas Weber of the *Historisch-Kritisches worterbuch des marxismus* (Berlin) for inviting me to write on Marx's views on the Egyptian peasantry and then for their criticisms. I would like to thank Prof. Tuomo Melasuo of the Tampere Peace Research Institute (TAPRI) for his invitations to Tampere and his hospitality as well as for the opportunity to come in contact with the struggle to combat the racism against Arabs through the Euro-Mediterranean dialogue. Visits to TAPRI gave me the chance to work on the issue of hegemony in relation to the Mediterranean. Professor Hiroshi Kato invited me for a stay and a chance to lecture through the Islamic Studies Project in Tokyo, and there I was able to try to relate the hegemony-model approach to different countries. Koichi Ohara of the Japanese branch of the International Gramsci Society (also in Tokyo) invited me to lecture on the hegemony in Japan.

Several other individuals invited me for visits and lectures as this project progressed. I would like to thank Prof. Roger Owen at the Center for Middle East Studies at Harvard University for a chance to discuss the Oriental-despotism model today, the UCLA Humanities Center and Prof. Hala Halim for a chance to participate in a Nations and Identities Conference, Prof. Joey Beinin for a workshop on globalization and Islam at Stanford University, Prof. Robert Vitalis for an invitation to speak about the "Southern

Question" in Egypt at the University of Pennsylvania Middle East Center, and Prof. Jonathan Berkey for a stay at Davidson College and a chance to discuss the issue of the non-West in the Western Civilization course.

I would like to also thank Profs. Nick Hopkins and Reem Saad of the American University in Cairo (AUC) for introducing me to a number of experts on upper Egypt in a conference in Aswan, this subject being important for my argument about the Southern Question. Prof. Enid Hill, also of AUC, invited me to a workshop on method that led to a collected work of which she was the editor; it was my first chance to apply hegemony analysis to all of the countries of the Middle East. My chapter in the proceedings of the conference was often useful thereafter in teaching and lies buried in the present book, especially in Chapter 4. Three other institutions in Cairo have also often invited me for various stays and provided me opportunities to lecture and to discuss my work and related matters. I would like to mention how indispensable they have been in my life and work. Dr. Ghislaine Alleaume, the previous director of Le Centre d'Etudes et de Documentation Economiques, Juridiques, et Sociales (CEDEJ), went out of her way to encourage my work through a conference in December 1998 at CEDEJ on my books, and on other occasions over the years she brought me into direct contact with contemporary French thought on the issue of Napoléon's invasion of Egypt in 1798 and with the question of how it was being interpreted. This too figures in the present book. I would also like to thank Prof. Jabir Asfour of the Supreme Council of Culture for translating and publishing my work *Beyond Eurocentrism* in 1998 and for inviting me to a series of conferences on cultural issues thereafter that did much to broaden my horizons. I would like at this point to thank Prof. Emad Abu Ghazi who in his work at the council helped and encouraged my work as well. I come now to the opportunity to thank the Egyptian Society for Historical Studies. This society was led for a long time by the late Prof. Raouf 'Abbas. He and Professor Nelly Hanna, an AUC professor and Professor 'Abbas's collaborator in the society and in the ongoing Ottoman Seminar, have strongly supported my work and encouraged me since the late 1960s and early 1970s down to the present day. For pretty much everything I have written I owe them a word of thanks. This indebtedness is most especially true for Professor Hanna, who carefully read an earlier draft of this work.

In terms of getting through the editing, a timely invitation by Dyala Hamza to visit the Zentrum fur Moderner Orient in Berlin coupled with the hospitality of Wissenschaftskolleg zu Berlin, where I was the official guest of Dr. Samah Selim and Dr. George Khalil, allowed this book to come to light. I am very grateful to them all.

Two other close colleagues have spent much time talking to me about this project. They are Prof. Amira Sonbol at Georgetown University and Prof. Rifa'at Abou El Haj at SUNY-Binghamton. Both have shared my discomfort over the years at the resurgence of Orientalism in the academy.

Syracuse University Press has supported my work for a long time and most particularly Mary Selden Evans, who has been endlessly encouraging with the most wonderful, lighthearted humor. This work also greatly benefited from suggestions of three outside readers, all of whom I wish to recognize for their help.

My family is by this time used to how much longer everything I do takes than I say it will—at least I hope so. Their approval of my endeavors means more to me than I can express.

INTRODUCTION

THIS BOOK is a contribution to the rethinking of modern world history. It introduces the outline of a new metanarrative, one that I call the "Rise of the Rich," which attempts to overcome some of the difficulties currently confronted by historians in interpreting modern and contemporary world history through the commonly used metanarrative of the "Rise of the West," owing to the latter's imprecision. The book attempts, in other words, a paradigm challenge. However, it is not a conventional paradigm challenge, one that involves tinkering with the details of the existing edifice; rather, this one requires a fairly substantial amount of rebuilding. Adopting the Rise of the Rich as a paradigm has so many implications that point toward unresearched themes that it necessarily takes the form of an agenda book.

I present the rationale for this undertaking in the first half of the book. I argue that the main paradigm in the discipline of history, the Rise of the West, has reached a point where it can no longer assimilate new knowledge effectively. It is, in effect, imprecise. What is therefore required is a paradigm shift. In the second half of the book I provide a rough sketch of modern history reorganized according to the paradigm of the Rise of the Rich.

The Rise of the West, as its very name indicates, is Eurocentric. Many historians have been aware of this fact for a long time. In fact, there is now a trend to right past wrongs by encouraging a wider inclusion of materials from around the world. Although this book shares in that trend, it differs in its insistence that the problem of Eurocentrism along with other forms of imprecision will not go away until the discipline of history finds some new way of organizing its basic metanarrative; there is no salvaging the Rise of the West, even assuming a greater degree of cosmopolitanism. One must confront Eurocentrism in a theoretical sense, not simply paper it over. The

Rise of the West creates a rising West, a stagnant Orient, and a people without history, serving to marginalize most people in the world. The challenge is to find a way to write world history so that Middle Eastern countries are not Oriental, Africans are not people without history, and Western history has a place, if not one that is continuously rising. How can one meet this challenge without falling into polycentrism and losing a reasonable sense of the narrative of power? The Rise of the Rich is an attempt to solve this problem.

To introduce a new paradigm involves confronting the one that exists, as paradigms tend to simply keep rejuvenating themselves unless they are confronted. If they are challenged with new facts, nothing much is likely to change. New facts encourage an almost continual superficial process of rejuvenation. Thus, at least until now, whenever the Rise of the West has been confronted by new facts, as it has been a number of times, it has emerged more or less intact and perhaps even a bit stronger. The West in some sense could always be found to be rising and expanding; the idea of the Orient could somehow always be rearranged but held on to, and it could always be made to be static. Thus, one could eliminate Japan and China from the idea of the Orient if need be and still have an Orient. The revolution in social history could be acknowledged, but elites could still be said to have made history and most people could still be said to be without history. Such observations are, of course, not meant to discourage empirical challenges but rather to draw the reader's attention to the probability that few would conclude from reading an empirical work that one needs to rethink the paradigm issue implied by it unless it also includes a good deal of argumentation. One could go further and suggest that the common acceptance of the Rise of the West as a metanarrative even works to block out what does not agree with it. If, for example, an empirical work uncovers some unexpected set of details, the typical reader will likely simply retreat upon encountering it, as I will demonstrate with illustrations from African and Middle Eastern studies.

The Rise of the West paradigm exaggerates the importance of all things Western at the expense of the Third World—even of the Third World ruling classes. The ordinary Westerner is made to play a larger role in world history than even the leader of a Third World country. This position is both intellectually implausible and educationally questionable. Should we teach

Western students that they have such power and importance? Is it a good idea to teach Third World students that their only hope is to become Westernized, which means supporting their ruling class because the ruling class is the most Westernized class in the country?

WHAT IS MEANT BY "RISE OF THE RICH"?

The Rise of the Rich is used here in two different senses. They overlap, they inspire each other, but they are different. The Rise of the Rich is a paradigm that can explain world history, and it is also an empirical insight about an important phenomenon in world history, one that has been generally overlooked, perhaps because of the obstacles put in its way by the logic of the Rise of the West paradigm. The Rise of the Rich as a paradigm is given priority in the first two chapters, the empirical phenomenon in the later ones.

As an empirical phenomenon, the Rise of the Rich is an important trend of the past few centuries; it is a coalescing of the world's powerful and dominant elements. Coalescence here is termed *Rise* and the world's powerful and dominant elements and their hangers-on *the Rich*. The process of coalescing, as we will find, has social, political, and economic dimensions.[1]

Modern history, that is, history from the sixteenth century onward, witnessed the development of a set of troubled but intimate relations of national ruling classes and hegemonic elements around the world, groups whose shared class interests led them toward promoting market development but whose interrelationships were otherwise often fraught with many problems. If nothing else, there was always a great deal of competition for a bigger slice of the pie. This group was and is the Rich, which we can observe today in what appears to be the autumn of its power as it tries in one country after another to reinforce the existing hegemonic strategies through rule by emergency legislation and by acceding to a world policeman.

The use of the term *Rich* has certain advantages in a paradigm discussion over a number of other terms more commonly in use. Though not unfamiliar in a literal sense, it has not been developed as a metaphor and does not play any significant role in theory or even in the conventional repertoire of terms used in the study of history.[2] If, conventionally, the terminology of Western history is related to the idea of expansion and the terminology of Third World history is related to the idea of victimization as a result of this expansion, then the Rise of the Rich as an alternative narrative of power has the advantage of allowing the researcher to analyze history in a more objective fashion, as noted.[3]

Paradigms have both polemical and scientific dimensions. The Rise of the West claims in a rather polemical way that what it represents is science and that other traditions are simply ideological.[4] For the Rise of the Rich, the polemical dimension lies in the claim that the Rise of the West when applied to world history fails to do what it says it will do, that is, it fails to explain how the past brings us to the present, or how the different aspects of history interrelate. If it did, problems such as Eurocentrism very likely would take care of themselves. What has made this discrepancy between what is claimed and what is accomplished so apparent has been the rise of social history. In an age when the historian is knowledgeable about social history, how can he or she still rely on a paradigm in which two-thirds of humanity is outside of history?

One might think that to a degree the problem of Eurocentrism has already been dealt with, even along the lines proposed here.[5] After all, there is a whole tradition of studies built around such terms as *world elite*,[6] *world ruling caste,* and *world class.*[7] However, if one looks closely at this tradition, one finds the main use of all these terms is as a way to describe Westerners. When it comes to the Third World power structures, what one invariably finds in such formulations are references to allies, accommodators, or unequal partners of the West. Following the Rise of the Rich approach, by way of contrast, Third World rulers are taken to be coproducers of the modern world order. Third World ruling classes are collaborators with Western ruling classes in the oppression both of the Third World mass population and of its Western counterpart. It is this alliance that has made the counterhegemonic struggle on the national level so difficult and frustrating for nations caught in the world market.[8]

• • •

ACADEMIC BOOKS come out of particular contexts. Knowledge of these contexts usually explains a fair amount about a book's rationale. In this section I will explain how, despite the profound attachment to the Rise of the

West paradigm in countries such as the United States,[9] one can still launch an argument such as this one, the reasons being both the unusual nature of world history as a field in American academia and the fact that the United States as a country is entering a period of crisis that is calling into question many of its core assumptions.[10]

What the reader doubtless may also know about the field of world history is that it is very American. In fact, at this point, writing and reading about world history appear to be virtually American pastimes. Few of the books being produced are of interest in Third World countries or even in Europe. As this situation is not typical of other fields, especially other fields in history, one might ask what it is about this body of literature that accounts for this fact.

Looking back over the past thirty years at how the field of world history arose in the United States, some tentative answers to these questions begin to emerge. As the American economy became more internationalized in the 1970s, the field of world history arose, taking over the function of the older field of Western civilization in many universities while still retaining a very positive view of the United States and other Western countries. This emphasis on Western identity might explain the relative lack of interest of some foreign readers. It might also explain one of the main features of the field, its resistance to the idea of a paradigm or paradigm conflict or theoretical debate. One might wonder, then, what is the rationale for choosing such a field as one's point of entrance into a paradigm challenge?

Here one must keep in mind yet another feature of world history: that the field's very nature is public, that is, it is a field as much in the society as it is in the university. World history in the United States is mandated by many state governments as far down as the secondary level. It thus reflects the culture of the public far more than does the work of historians in most other fields. Although a book on world history is of course by definition a wide-ranging affair, it is thus also one that in practice is typically organized with a very specific audience in mind and for that reason the author is obliged to know what the audience expects from such a book. What it means for a field to be in the public domain in a period of growing social crisis is an interesting question, i.e., how can an author know what an audience would expect. Suffice to note at this point, therein lies one part of the justification of choosing the field of world history as the place to engage conventional wisdom: crisis forces a society to rethink itself.

The likelihood of a paradigm challenge, I am imagining, also has a connection to the niche that the field has or does not have in the academy. A field whose practitioners perceive themselves to have a secure niche is a field unlikely to strike out in new directions. For some world historians, world history appears to have such a niche, one in which the instructor never wants for students; for others, however, the sense is more of being hemmed in by state legislatures and textbook companies and being marginalized in university life and not considered real contributors to knowledge—in other words, having no niche at all. For the latter, one could assume that some might want to rethink their subject and its curious history.

Examining the field as it developed since the 1980s, one notices that it never looks back before that period in time and that it eschews any close connection with the historiography of the other parts of the discipline of history that do of course look back. For a field in a professional history department today, this makes it fairly distinctive. Most historians take their specialty to have arisen in the nineteenth century and to have developed from that point forward; world historians look back at a field that began in their view in the 1980s.

In its present incarnation at least, the field of world history arose with postmodernism in the wake of a revolution in social history that failed, one that was then muzzled by being turned into social-cultural history. In its early stage, world history had to adjust to the "cultural turn" and then to "postcolonial studies" and to find its bearings within them. In this endeavor, the professors of world history proved successful, and they certainly benefited from making these adjustments. The coming of the "cultural turn" served to undermine several of the field of world history's most important rivals, comparative history, comparative literature, comparative politics, political economy, and historical sociology.

In staking out the idea of a paradigm challenge as the goal of the book, the logical place to begin would be with what is meant by *paradigm*, as such terms get used in many ways. As was already mentioned, the idea of the paradigm or paradigm challenge is a subject of importance in most academic disciplines but not in identity-related fields, such as world history. The reason is that the whole premise of these fields is that there is not supposed to be any doubt about the material, so even the idea of a paradigm is a bit alien, at least in normal times. Paradigms are found along with paradigm challenges in fields such as sociology, literature, and philosophy, fields that allow for doubt and relativity. In addition, I now need to add that the most common understanding of the paradigm and paradigm challenge even in those fields is not necessarily the one that is most useful for our purposes. Here, what I mean is the idea of the paradigm according to Thomas Kuhn, an author widely known in the United States for his work on paradigms and especially for his concern with the quick rise of a triumphant new paradigm over an old established one. Kuhn was not so concerned with paradigm conflict or with the possible coexistence of multiple paradigms in a particular knowledge area, as we are here. He believed, to the contrary, that a better paradigm would simply eliminate a worse one.[11]

From the vantage of a discipline such as history taken as a whole, Kuhn was perhaps mistaken to believe that one paradigm could eliminate another so easily, simply because it was better. Fields such as history usually sustain several competing paradigms.[12] As a result, in history what one is advised to do is present one's approach as cogently as possible and hope the reader finds it contains what others lack. In my case, I hope there might exist some interest in how the "West" can be reinterpreted so that it does not distort world history by requiring the services of an "Orient" as an other. Some readers, I hope, will want to know how regions such as the Middle East might look if they had not been designated to perform this service,[13] or relatedly how to deal with the media's campaign to promote re-Orientalization—for example, the "clash of civilizations."[14] In no way, though, do I mean to imply that all historians have these concerns or should have them.

A corollary to these last two points, one that also bears on the use of history for the purpose of a paradigm challenge, is the observation that it is high-prestige fields that have paradigm conflicts and low-prestige ones that do not. By the mid-1980s it was apparent that the prestige of history was at a very low ebb in the American academy. Many had begun to look at history as a whole more as heritage than as science. Under such conditions, the question comes back again, how is one to launch a paradigm challenge entirely from within any branch of history? What came to mind first was that what was intended was not an ordinary paradigm challenge, and second, here to repeat the earlier point, world history occupied the odd location within the field of history as insider and outsider both to the discipline and even to the academy, so third, the broader context of crisis in the United States could make such an attempt on the part of someone in world history plausible. Under present conditions, world historians will be among the first to come in contact with the winds of change in the society.

• • •

ALL BOOKS in history, world history included, are judged in terms of their sources. What kind of sources should a world history book such as this one make use of if it attempts to go beyond the conventional subject matter and discuss paradigms? This turned out to be a thorny question.

Through the 1970s historians assumed that sources could generally be divided between primary (archival or original) and secondary (published or derivative). A world history text would be based on secondary sources. In this sense, it would be derivative. In the 1980s this matter became more complicated as Foucauldians, postmodernists, and others came to critically assess the idea of the primary source.[15] Still, the distinction survived, although more as something to be argued than to be assumed. This work reflects this post-1980s situation.

In the 1980s, the choice of sources and how they are understood came to reflect yet another concern that must be acknowledged: professional sensibilities.[16] Here I have in mind in particular the distaste, for example, for conspiracy narratives. Over the past generation or two, historians, and rightly so in my view, have become concerned about the growing reliance in the media on conspiracy thinking. If one wants to claim, as I do, a collaboration among the world's dominant elements, part of the evidence for which is based on structural inference, it could lead to problems. In anticipation of possible confusion, it is important to make clear that I am assuming that structural logic may induce certain choices, but that this is different from conspiracy. The two often look much the same without actually being the same. The important difference is that structural logic is a part of the norm of complex societies, and conspiracy to the best of our knowledge is something that is contrived at one moment or another. To avoid confusing the two, the best approach seems to be one of working from the most widely accepted sources—for example, documents in international relations (IR) and diplomatic history. Of course, such material is rather staid, but it is solid and objective. To this material I have added the usual repertoire from social history, social science, and social theory. Investigative journalism plays a much larger role.

The issue for historians is also manner of presentation. All books are, of course, potentially documents or are potentially secondary sources. What seemed appropriate was to construct long endnotes spelling out different intellectual positions on subjects, these sometimes replacing the traditional endnote that cites a fact on a page of a particular book. By proceeding this way, the text can keep its focus on a few main lines of thought, while the notes convey some idea of sources and where other things might fit. For example, one might want to concentrate in the text, as I do, on the Rise of the Rich. At the same time, this subject, like any other empirical theme, has a context. There is clearly more to world history than what is related to it, however important it may be for explaining world power and however neglected it may have been by scholars in the past. The long endnotes allow me to make this point.

The agenda book being a somewhat ill-defined genre, an author faces not only the problem of content, style of argument, and sources but the problem of form as well. There is no one prescribed form for an agenda book.[17] Historians in general prefer narratives. This was absolutely the case through the 1970s. Thereafter, this preference became a bit less pronounced, but even today it still represents something of a norm for a teaching-driven field such as world history. For agenda books, unfortunately, narrative cannot be considered the major option. One might even suggest that if one could write a narrative, one would not consider an agenda-book approach. To put it another way, a narrative implies some kind of relative finality that for an agenda book is necessarily lacking. What a successful use of the narrative presupposes is the existence of a fair degree of consensus concerning many aspects of a subject to be treated, the narrative allowing the author to acknowledge the consensus and to focus on subordinate issues that may still be unresolved. The narrative, thus, clearly has its place. There are times when there is consensus, and there are times when teaching requirements make the narrative quite helpful. I emphasize this point as I believe my view may need further justification. As many historians from the 1970s and 1980s onward have argued, and correctly, the very development of the field of history has all but made the narrative obsolete. One thinks here of the revolution in gender analysis and of the growth of a concern with the literary form of historical writing. These innovations served to challenge the logic of narrativity.

Whatever one's opinion about these developments or about the use of the narrative on pragmatic grounds, the present book, as noted before, does not lend itself to much narrative. For this reason, the reader will find that in order to deal with sequence and process, I have relied on a common form of approximation of the narrative, one drawn from middle-level historical sociology. Middle-level historical sociology allows an author the freedom to tell a story but to do so in a somewhat looser way, to make asides, present multiple currents, and do so to an extent that would be disruptive were all these elements to exist in a conventional narrative. At the same time, the author is also free from the chaos of particulars that face the writer of narrative history. The use of historical sociology, then, has advantages, but it also has its disadvantages. It is an inferior choice to the narrative in that often enough it fudges one main area of responsibility of historians: addressing the subject of power and thereby clarifying who has it and how it is being used or resisted. In the case of this work, the reader will find a concerted effort to overcome this problem, despite the reliance on historical sociology.[18]

Finally, I have suggested that a paradigm change requires a crisis and that American society is increasingly entering into one. A paradigm change is not simply an ivory tower event. Fields such as world history that are very much rooted in the classroom are likely to be among the first to reflect the crisis the society itself is experiencing. It is on this basis that I believe an attempt to confront the Rise of the West paradigm in world history is justified.

• • •

THIS BOOK is organized in three main overlapping parts. The first part takes a fairly critical look at liberalism and Marxism as the worldviews that serve as the underpinnings of the Rise of the West paradigm today, the second sketches out what the Rise of the Rich might look like in early modern and modern history, and the third shows how the Rise of the Rich adds to the study of the contemporary United States.

We begin with a discussion of the crisis in liberal and Marxist historiography, a crisis we hypothesize first made apparent by the revolution in social history and then by the continuing growth of knowledge thereafter. What appears to be the case is that neither worldview can absorb this newer knowledge because of their commitment to the metanarrative of the Rise of the West.

In the second part we try to anticipate what the Rise of the Rich would look like over time and discuss world power since the birth of modern capitalism. This section is divided into two chapters, one covering the early modern period, the other covering the modern period. For the study of the early modern period, the main issue is how to account for the origins and early development of the modern capitalist system on a world scale without falling into Eurocentrism or polycentrism. I approach this task by addressing the more specific question of how groups emerged in different countries and grew powerful using the market once the capitalist mode of production came into being. Pursuing this tack, I find that these groups mainly relied on mercantilism as their form of political economy, and this dependence was the case all over the world. Mercantilism took a number of different forms, but all of them shared one particular feature: their reliance on bilateral relations. The growth of the institution of bilateral relations between Western commercial powers and Third World rulers was one of the central features of the early history of capitalism.

For the period of contemporary history, that is, the period after 1850, the most common form of political economy was the capitalist nation-state; mercantilism receded. The rulers of these nation-states continued to rely on bilateral relations, but the new and very important tool for increasing power in this period was multilateralism. Multilateralism allowed for the imposition of a much expanded domestic market on more and more countries and with greater security, resulting in far greater wealth for the ruling classes and dominant elements than had theretofore been possible.

As one moves closer to the present, we find indications that the Rich are handicapped not only by the nation-state as a political system but even by capitalism as an economic system, the latter threatening their well-being by its inability to develop redistributive mechanisms. Capitalism, it appears, can keep accumulating, but that is all it can do. Given a capitalist system, the Rich, it is suggested, have therefore developed as much as they can. Given the existence of the nation-state, the Rich are not able to progress to being a class "for itself," because, as Lenin wrote in his classic on imperialism a century ago, rivalries are bound to continue so long as there are nation-states.

In the third part of the book I take up the question of why the Rise of the Rich makes sense even for a part of history one would take to be the prime beneficiary of the Rise of the West paradigm, namely, contemporary America. We find that by switching to the Rise of the Rich, one can explain aspects of U.S. history that one cannot when working from the Rise of the West paradigm. Here I focus on the subject of foreign political influence in U.S. politics and decision making. I look at the institution of the foreign lobbyist, a group that is integral to understanding foreign influence. Foreign lobbyists in Washington have had a profound impact on the domestic political economy of the United States, yet given the way the dominant paradigm works their activities are scarcely ever noticed. On the other hand, if one starts from the idea of the Rise of the Rich, it would be intuitive that there would need to be brokers to work out the details of the relations among different hegemonic groups in the world.

Chapter 1, "Modern World Economic History Between Liberalism and Political Economy," raises the dilemma for the world historian of functioning either within the framework of contemporary liberalism or Marxism, and of applying their concepts to the study of world economic history. What we find is that not only are there empirical problems in a growing number of cases, but there is also the problem for the historian of falling into presentism when one tries to use them. Yet these concepts contain much that is highly suggestive. The chapter takes up as an example the concept of transnationalism. It is a concept which has many interesting possibilities. And for that reason, it has many ardent supporters, even among historians, as well as within the wider scholarly community. There is, for example, a particularly strong commitment to the use of this concept on the part of advocates of the European Common Market and others as well as trying to theorize political economy beyond the nation-state.

I also take a brief look at contemporary Marxist economic history and find it arriving for the most part at the same results as those of New Liberalism, albeit using its own language and method. Though it appears as a sweeping critique of liberalism, on close examination one finds the critique is at most a limited one, one defined as it is by the framework created by liberalism. What I then find is that an economic domain is assumed to exist and to be what is meant by materialism; this domain is assumed to hold the key to understanding history. Where New Liberalism tends toward a utopian teleology, Marxism tends toward dystopia. As a result, in Marxism as in liberalism there is quite some distance—in fact too much distance—between the broader metaphysic and its application in studies of the actual history of different countries.

In Chapter 2, "Modern World Political History Between Liberalism and Political Economy," I focus on the political aspect of modern history in the mirror of New Liberalism and on the problems this approach creates, for itself and for Marxism.

New Liberal political theory, I find, in effect boils down to a number of interrelated concepts added on to the old liberalism. Among these concepts one might reasonably single out two as being exceedingly important to a student of world history: New Social Movements (NSMs) and subalternity, concepts that recur in numerous writings yet are difficult for a historian to use, even to coexist with, given the importance of time, sequence, and specificity of place to historical analysis. New Social Movements, for example, implies a mysterious spontaneity, and subalternity implies some sort of preexisting cultural essence. Neither arise nor fit into predictable structures at given times and places, nor can they be explained in any very precise way. The prominence of these concepts as a part of this political theory along with those ideas already mentioned puts liberalism today to a degree in opposition to history as a discipline. At the very least, it creates problems for historians trying to do precise analyses through liberalism. It almost seems that liberalism as a worldview is today more at home with chronology, genealogy, or heritage than with history, that it has truly reached the "end of history." To illustrate this point, I provide an extended discussion of an example of what is taken to be either a new social or a subaltern movement, one widely studied in contemporary liberal scholarship: the Zapatista movement of southern Mexico. First, I summarize the prevailing Marxist and New Liberal interpretations of the Zapatista movement as a New Social Movement. What I find is that if one takes this approach, the Zapatistas would be only an incidental part of Mexican history and its dynamics. If the Zapatista movement is put in a political economy framework in the sense preferred here, on the other hand, the Mexican nature of the movement is what stands out. This illustration makes it clear how much follows from one's initial choice of metanarrative. Following a Rise of the Rich approach, one would tie the Zapatista movement to its namesake, Emiliano Zapata, and to the old but still ongoing problems of the land system. Following the Rise of the West, one might emphasize simply the charisma of the contemporary leader, Subcommandante Marcos.

Having laid a foundation for the claim that the traditional Rise of the West history, whether as liberalism or as Marxism, does not explain modern history very well, I argue that the Rise of the Rich is currently the most promising alternative. The question then becomes one of what would modern world history look like as the Rise of the Rich? Chapters 3 and 4 prejudge what the resulting "narrative" might resemble, assuming such research.

Chapter 3, "The Rise of the Rich in Early Modern Times," begins the attempt to portray what the new paradigm would look like as a way to study early modern world history for the period 1550 to 1850, that is, the period proceeding from the birth of modern capitalism to the creation of the capitalist nation-state. To do so I take up three elements of the rise of modern capitalism of obvious importance that is scarcely mentioned in standard accounts. First, I consider the role of diplomacy and of the new bilateral diplomatic relations. Bilateral diplomatic relations contributed in an important sense to the spread of a new style of market, and this new style market, with its strategic consumerism, I then argue, should be considered a key to understanding how there was a modern history. As the reader may recall, there were several failed transitions to capitalism in world history, mainly the result of a lack of market. In this case, bilateral relations played a big role in helping to overcome that problem.

A second factor explaining the development of the capitalist mode of production is that of primitive accumulation, or plunder. For example, the plundering of New World gold and silver played a major role in the rise of capitalism and by extension of the modern world as a whole. Thus, one might claim, as I do, that primitive accumulation is both integral to capitalism and not something separate from it. Capitalism was never simply a form of economy, much less a form of economy based on goods in a market freely and legally exchanged, as one might imagine from reading Adam Smith. If it were, it would have stagnated. What saved it was pillage. Pillage was truly profitable. The rate of return on pillage was far greater than the rate of return on trade or manufacturing. If there had not been plunder alongside strategic consumerism, even the "British" experience of early modern history could easily have wound up as another footnote in the history of failed transitions to capitalism.

I then turn to consider a third element in the rise of capitalism, focusing on an important group of people found around the world, the group most intimately concerned with diplomacy and plunder. This group is termed the "New Men." The New Men were a very dynamic element within the Rich or seeking to join the Rich. What their activities make clear is the link between the larger subject of the Rise of the Rich and plundering. Although much of the Rise of the Rich involved adjustments by existing ruling classes to the new order, these were never the whole picture, nor are they today. A range of evidence both from early modern and modern history suggests that New Men have existed for several centuries; as a group they have been facilitating trade diplomacy and plunder, and without them it is difficult to imagine capitalism succeeding and progressing as it has.

In sum, to identify modern history with the capitalist mode of production and the capitalist mode of production in a sense with revolution still seems warranted, assuming one puts one's emphasis on that which was actually new and revolutionary. Where much previous scholarship emphasized the bourgeois revolutions of the seventeenth, eighteenth, and nineteenth centuries in Western countries, the even more revolutionary feature of capitalism is the extraordinary triumph of a small group on a world scale who came to dominate the political economy of the planet.

It might also be noted that sources for the study of the early modern period exist. Treaties could serve as an example of them. Depending on one's paradigm, either Europe or capitalism was expanding. In other words, treaty documents are simply trade agreements, or alternatively, they reveal the solidification of the relationships of the Rich. For our purposes, it was of course the latter that seemed more persuasive. What one finds in these treaties are examples of the well-known kinds of hegemonies in contact with one another, each imposing its will on the other, each following its own logic, each ruler doing so seemingly at the expense of many of his own compatriots, but at the same time each reflecting a certain concern for a need to maintain the appearance of respecting the domestic status quo and to thereby conceal certain of their dealings. The decision to emphasize the use of Middle Eastern material in this section is meant to serve a double function: first, to illustrate the general phenomenon of bilateralism and, second, to highlight how a Rise of the Rich approach could overcome the problems of the Orientalist or liberal one when it comes to a consideration of the Middle East.

Is Europe, one might then wonder, all there is to history, the four hegemonies found in Europe being the ones reproduced elsewhere? The answer, it turns out, is yes and no. For one thing, I argue there is no one thing called Europe for a world historian. There are four main forms of political economy in Europe. Moreover, the forms of political economy found in Europe also exist around the world. This point has many ramifications. What is relevant for our discussion, though, is that the fact that there are these identifiable forms of political economy works to the advantage of researchers in the field of world history, as it frees them from the "tyranny of difference" of the old civilizational history with which Hegel struggled. Historical dynamics found around the world, we now understand, have specificities, *difference* becoming a term one can use more sparingly.

In Chapter 4, "The Age of Multilateralism: The World after 1850," I introduce contemporary history in the framework of the Rise of the Rich. The emphasis is on the capitalist nation-state. At this point, we leave bilateralism and mercantilism behind.

World history after 1850 witnessed the imposition of the capitalist nation-state on the world's peoples. For it to have occurred, rulers needed safeguards and fall-back positions. Half the ruling classes in the world would not have attempted it without a colonial system backing them up. In the face of such challenges, the international system nonetheless continued to evolve and to find ever more ways to offer its support, the period witnessing a great growth in the number of treaties agreed to by all or at least by most of the states.

This growth of treaties was astonishing; it appears to have had ramifications for the lives of millions. One would think the treaties and what gave rise to them would thus be a matter of common discussion, but given the factor of paradigm logic most of these treaties are rarely discussed outside of the technical literature of particular fields. Nonetheless, what one can infer is that as a result of these treaties, rulers at least found themselves in a more and more secure situation. Thus, while rulers by 1900 may have been confronting the growing threat of a world war, as regards their more personal well-being such an eventuality was less and less threatening. If one takes a skeptical view, one might suggest that the level of risk that could be contemplated in matters of confrontation rose as it became clear that the personal safety of the ruler was going to be ensured regardless of the outcome. One thinks of the unprecedented carnage of World War I and the wars that followed and wonders if what we call "total war" would have occurred had there not been this multilateralism.

The age of multilateralism also saw the continuation of old forms of oppositional struggle but also the birth of new one. For the early modern period, historians have traditionally assumed that the most important political opposition movements were the ones striving for inclusion in the new political order—for instance, the middle class in the Bourgeois Revolution. Another assumption is that the Bourgeois Revolution would inevitably take place, and once it had it was irreversible. Next would come the struggle of the workers. And although this struggle for inclusion has continued on up to recent times, increasingly this whole historical sequence now seems open to question given what has happened to the middle and working classes in recent decades. In effect, the struggle for inclusion in the political order was to a large extent defeated by the Rise of the Rich. The middle and working classes in many places are much weaker and less included today than they were even a half century ago.

Although historians, especially those scholars drawn to the Rise of the West paradigm, interpret modern history as moving toward an "end of revolution" and even an "end of history," it is interesting that today's rulers do not seem to share this view. Rulers today exhibit a fear of their subjects. This fear has resulted in a turn to rule by emergency legislation in an increasing number of states around the world. This shift would suggest in all probability a need for a retheorization of the subject of opposition. There must be more to it than historians in the past have detected.

In Chapter 5, "The Rise of the Rich Paradigm Applied to the Contemporary United States," I address the question of whether the Rise of the Rich paradigm has a line of argument and a body of sources to back it up sufficient to compete in a context where the Rise of the West is already well established, taking what I supposed would be a fair case, that of the contemporary United States. The United States is a lead country; it benefits from claiming to embody Westernness. What would a student of U.S. history or of world imperialism gain by dropping the Hegelian paradigm?

What I show in this chapter is that readily available empirical evidence suggests that contrary to what one would expect following Hegel, Third World ruling classes manage to successfully pursue their objectives in contemporary America and do so at the expense of the Western middle and working classes and even at the expense of segments of the American ruling class itself. Third World ruling classes are thus not simply compradors who deal on the local level with worldwide Western interests and take orders. They may appear that way at times, but on the whole they are actually much more powerful than a true comprador class would be, as evidenced by the fact that they frequently have their means of influence where their vital interests are concerned. This point brings us back again to the generally neglected figure of the foreign lobbyist.[19]

To make optimal use of the available secondary literature, I have surveyed the record of foreign lobbyists in Washington, D.C., from the post–World War II era to the present. This world, we learn, is one of insider dealing and bribery. The rich bribe each other in business and politics; lobbyists arrange the deals and pay the bribes. Of course, bribery is illegal. It clearly is not something tolerated on the level of civil society. When such practice is drawn to the attention of Congress, as it has been more than once, further legislation is passed but seemingly to no avail.

Can one then understand power in the United States today and ignore the role of the foreign lobbyist? Following the Rise of the West paradigm, apparently one can. However, if one approaches the subject in terms of the Rise of the Rich, then the relationship between lobbyists representing foreign interests and local politicians appears to be an integral part of history, leading one to the not uninteresting conclusion that a lobbyist working for a foreign state could impose changes on the United States in the interest of a client, perhaps even major changes. And it seems logical to hypothesize that a lobbyist is most likely to be the one to do such things, because a diplomat would be rather conspicuous in such a role. Nor is this situation purely hypothetical. I note cases where foreign ruling classes, working through formal diplomacy and more informally through lobbyists, have managed to compel American factories to move to different parts of the country, thereby creating the Rust Belt in cities such as Detroit and Pittsburgh, as well as managing to get rid of unwanted workers by having them emigrate to the United States. As these trends involved risks for those involved, one must conclude that lobbyists made possibly illegal offers to American politicians, which the latter appear to have accepted, the risks thereby becoming tolerable. Without doubt in recent decades, the stakes were enormous. Over the course of the 1980s the United States lost control of important parts of its economy and a not insignificant part of its tax base as jobs went overseas. Without foreign lobbyists in Washington, the facts suggest it would never have occurred. In sum, it is hard to escape the thought that by labeling Britain or the United States a great power, as we tend to do in writing world history, we close our eyes to the nitty-gritty of actual power relations inside those great powers and by extension the power possessed by Third World ruling classes, among others.

• • •

MY HOPE in writing this book, here to conclude, is not to persuade the reader of my contention that the narrowness and Eurocentric nature of the old Rise of the West model makes it undesirable. This contention is almost routinely found in current scholarship in the field of world history and does not need to be dwelled on here. Rather, I hope to persuade the reader that overcoming these problems requires a change in the metanarrative of history, that is, the characterization of the narrative of power,[20] and that the Rise of the Rich is one worthy of their consideration.

The
RISE
of the
RICH

1

MODERN WORLD ECONOMIC HISTORY BETWEEN LIBERALISM AND POLITICAL ECONOMY

ALTHOUGH MANY IN THE FIELD of world history are aware of the shortcomings of the Rise of the West paradigm, the main trend remains one of trying to preserve it, possibly by reforming it as opposed to abandoning it for something better. In this chapter I look at the attempts at reformism by turning to world economic history as it is now being developed in New Liberalism.[1] To reduce the subject of New Liberalism to manageable proportions, I focus in this chapter on one concept associated with it, one that is of particular importance for a study of world history: transnationalism. Transnationalism, one finds, is serving to justify for New Liberalism some fairly major revisions in the familiar periodization of world history, and as we shall see it performs other functions as well.

I will then briefly consider Marxist economic thought. And, again, contrary to what one might suspect in practice today, neither in its metanarrative of world history nor in its methodology is it much different from liberalism. Not only, then, do both liberalism and political economy share in the Rise of the West, but they share a great deal more as well. I then ask if Marxism, once an alternative to positivism and liberalism, became absorbed by it. If so, is reform of Marxism still a possibility?

TRANSNATIONALISM AND ITS DIVERSE USAGES

Commentators on the world economy basing their work on the use of the term *transnationalism* were among the first to point to the increasingly international and fragmented nature of contemporary capitalism, the term thereafter taking on a life of its own, developing a number of different but related meanings, thereby gaining significance for writers in many fields beyond economics, narrowly conceived.[2] In the process, transnationalism became a very important concept in world economic history, conveying not just a way to pursue the study of history beyond the nation-state but a way to link the subject of world history to other fields of scholarship with similar concerns. Thus, we find that whereas transnationalism initially introduced simply the idea of going beyond the nation-state or of functioning in the framework of globalization,[3] as it developed it came to serve as a point of departure for research on numerous issues related to it, among which are the "knowledge society," transnational feminism, the postindustrial economy, the idea of the diasporic self, and of migration. To these topics one could add two other uses to which the concept of transnationalism is also currently being put, one by religionists who perceive solidarities extending beyond the nation-state, as in Pan-Islam, and the other by researchers who find the European Common Market to be an example of what is meant by going beyond the nation-state. After examining these various usages, I conclude by examining the impact that the term in its expanded sense is now having on the writing of world history and find it to be considerable.

An article written in the year 2000 on transnational corporations (TNCs) introduced the basic idea of transnationalism, asserting that TNCs own or control a quarter of the world's productive assets.[4] Given their size, TNCs dominate oligopolistic situations, as for example in the oil and the car and truck manufacturing industries. Given their size and power, TNCs are able to operate outside their country of origin and are thus typically characterized by having operations in two more countries. Their management decisions are based on regional or global market possibilities as opposed to national concerns. In effect, the TNC is independent not only of national history but indeed of any cause and effect that a historian could easily introduce. When one looks at the matter more closely, the two parts of this definition are clearly of different orders of magnitude, and it is the second one that appears to be the really problematic one for the historian. A corporation could operate in several countries and its manager could be affected by global market conditions, but the nature of its decision making could not necessarily be inferred from these facts alone. From the perspective of a more traditional cause-and-effect history, the country where the dominant shareholders, the home office, and the CEO is located would be a potentially important influence to consider when it comes to analyzing the nature of its decision making; other factors would be just considerations. In fact, in practice it might even be difficult to determine if a company is truly transnational. As the article admits, it is not uncommon for a parent company in the original country to influence overseas subsidiaries, so the issue of whether a company is transnational or ultimately nation-based remains a bit unclear.

The history of TNCs, the authors assert, goes back a century, but the number, size, and scale of their operations greatly increased after 1970. The turning point came with the introduction of the computer. The introduction of the computer, or the computer revolution, as it is called, was so important that it in effect obliterated what went before it. Computer technology facilitated not only the growth of but also the autonomy of the corporation vis-à-vis national politics. This new autonomy led to a change in priorities, in decision making, and even in market logic. Increasingly in recent years, large investments were directed by TNCs to Third World countries, as these countries were low-wage zones with few regulatory laws; often these investments took place at the expense of the core societies. Scholars investigating this capital flight have been wondering how it could be taking place. What would happen to the Rise of the West if it continued? New Liberal theory provides an answer. By linking outsourcing to the idea of corporate autonomy or transnational market logic, the writer in the New Liberal tradition associates it with the Rise of the West. The actual decline of traditional Western society can then be explained in terms of market rationality, New Liberalism thereby resolving what had been for the older liberalism a complete contradiction. However, one does note some fairly important changes that have occurred in the process. The idea of the Rise of the West is now much more associated with corporations than with countries or cultures; it has become deterritorialized. This leads to another consideration.

Why is it among New Liberals, then, that one now finds a preoccupation with Eurocentrism? Why is it that many of the critics of Eurocentrism are New Liberals? A moment's reflection makes one aware that this too is perfectly logical. If the majority of the "territory-based" Americans and Europeans are losing their claim to be "Westerners" because they are not part of transnationalism, one has to expect a reaction on their part, perhaps a rise of populist nationalism and Eurocentric xenophobia. Liberals will need a critique of these trends if they are to retain their stance of being the voice of reason and progress.

Yet, while the idea of corporate transnationalism is an interesting one in a theoretical sense for some and a practical one for others, some would still doubt its long-term utility. Is one really demonstrating corporate transnationalism, that is, the autonomy of the corporation? Can one prove that corporations are not being pushed by politicians of particular countries? Indeed, might it not have been the latter who were the real beneficiaries of the internationalization of capitalism and part of the impetus for it? TNCs, the article states, are often well known for their manipulation of political processes, an example being their ability to get the United States to intervene to protect company interests. But this point begs the question. It remains to be shown that the U.S. defense of corporate interests results from the manipulation of the political process or if corporations are outside the political process. If all manner of people show up at shareholder meetings or influence bankers to extend or withhold credit, even the existence of "business autonomy" as an assumption, much less transnational autonomy, would seem to be one that is open to question. If there is such autonomy, what would it mean? The article under consideration attempts to answer this question, drawing our attention to the fact that one of the main ways in which TNCs generate income is to sell goods and services back and forth within a given company, one branch to another around the world at below-market prices. Such a practice, the authors rightly contend, implies corporate autonomy, that is, a considerable degree of freedom from political constraints. And this situation no doubt exists. Here one thinks of Enron. Enron was perhaps an extreme example of such autonomy, but Enron executives were actually making corrupt use of buying and selling practices common in TNCs the world over in the past generation. An estimate, the article cites, is that by 1960 one-third of the world's trade was intracompany. If this statistic is right, then presumably, if one knew fair market value for the commodities traded, one could figure out how much countries lost in terms of tax revenue as a result of these practices.

Clearly, it was and is a lot. Still, the question exists of whether these practices indicate autonomy or simply are part of a phase in history in which states are not exerting their regulatory functions because of class interests.

In Chapter 5, here to look ahead, I recount the well-known tale of how during the 1980s U.S. automobile companies fought a losing fight in Washington to keep Detroit as an automobile production center. Washington did not come through for them. Was the reason for this business autonomy or more a matter of politics? Where does the one end and the other begin?

The larger concern here is that New Liberalism's insights come at a certain price, even for mainstream history. Can one have transnationalism and still have the historical narrative of the Rise of the West at the same time?[5] Too much autonomy of the corporate elite, and one no longer has that narrative. Or is transnationalism so useful for liberalism that the latter can live without the traditional narrative of modern history, settling for the idea of the "end of history" and a return to the chronicle? These issues remain unresolved.

The concept of transnationalism is also tied up with assumptions about the workforce. Can one show that not only is there a transnational managerial world but there is also a "new worker," one who is working for this transnational economy? Does there today exist in effect a new deterritorialized working class, one that produces without reference to the country it lives in (belongs to?), examples perhaps being producers of virtual reality or of a visual economy? The question would lead one to think, as one writer puts it, that deterritorialization was an actual historical development, that when cinema emerged out of industrial capitalism, for example, it led to a reorganization of the subject by the image. This in turn led to a change in the capital-logic and hence of labor and of accumulation as a result of the visuality.[6] Such a line of thought allows one to conceive of a development in the movie industry's workforce leading into the age of the computer and the knowledge worker, a movement beyond the nation-state toward transnationalism.

But what kind of society would have a deterritorialized working class? One writer concerned with this issue, Sheldon Ungar, argues that so far this question has generated three separate ideas of what such a society would be, no one of which, he acknowledges, has yet to be borne out empirically.

These ideas are, first, a society valorizing the well-informed citizen; second, a society organized to facilitate the creation of knowledge-centered citizens; and third, a knowledge society marked by the role of the Internet in providing its basis. Ungar concludes that a society in which there is a high degree of specialization of knowledge in the workplace is probably in fact a knowledge-averse society. As time progresses, in such a society, professions define their specializations in narrower and narrower terms, the weight of new publications leading to reading reluctance, the ordinary person no better informed than a generation ago about general matters despite college attendance, the use of the computer outside of work driven by a desire to listen to music more than to attain new knowledge.[7] Ungar leaves the reader, however, with a sense that the idea of the deterritorialized worker is an important issue for contemporary liberalism, not one to be lightly discarded.

In his conclusion, Ungar identifies Steven Brint as the theorist perhaps most determined to demonstrate empirically the existence of the "knowledge economy." This seems worthwhile pursuing to get at the underpinnings of transnationalism. In turning to one of Brint's recent articles, we find that he takes quite a low-key view of the matter for someone introduced as the scholar most determined to demonstrate its existence. He appears aware of the reservations on the part of most social scientists for the use of the term *knowledge society,* as reflected in the continuing preference for the term *industrial* or *advanced industrial society,* the term *knowledge society* lacking a precise meaning. Given this situation, Brint proceeds by looking at four different scholarly views of a knowledge society, attempting to locate from among them one common empirical terrain. Some downscaling of expectations, he suggests, is necessary, as the knowledge-based economy is not in any sense the preponderant part of today's existing economy, nor one even particularly confined to any one sector in today's society.[8] What is left unquestioned even after some downscaling is whether knowledge-based economy theory or transnationalism more generally can compete with the traditional theory of American imperialism or even the IR theories of the older liberalism?

For a number of theorists of a more classical liberal or political economy bent, what is actually going on is more neonationalism than transnationalism.

American-based corporations own much of the world's economy, and their policy is to impose crises on vulnerable countries so they can buy up their remaining assets cheaply. The information technology sector is not a basis for a new economy but a highly speculative domain, one where most of the firms have gone under. Moreover, it has been shown that Europe is surging ahead in terms of its economy with far less use of computers than is found in the United States. In short, are we not moving to another round of interimperialist wars and perhaps some new attempts at socialism? Here, parts of liberalism, especially the old liberalism, converge with the political economy version of the imperialism theory.[9] Both raise the specter that we appear to somehow have moved back to the Gilded Age of the late nineteenth century, a time of crisis, and that New Liberalism with its presentism has got it all wrong. Still, one wonders whether from a Left or Right perspective if the world today is what it was in 1900. Has there really been no change? Here the New Liberal theorists have the better of it. Let us consider this point.

Although there are certainly important similarities between the days of McKinley and Bush—for instance, both were periods of finance capitalism—there also are differences. Today, one finds large-scale foreign investment in the United States to which one must add a consideration of the size of the debt in the hands of foreigners. This situation has no precedent. As a result of the debt, the United States is now vulnerable to sudden shifts in foreign investment, all the more so given that some of this investment is now in critical sectors.[10] A familiar question of recent years has been what if the Chinese change their policy of buying U.S. Treasury Notes? We thus cannot return to nineteenth-century America and use it as a model, even with regard to economic matters. Too much has changed, and too many things would be left unexplained. For example, a finance-capitalism approach alone would not explain why there has been a high level of foreign investment in recent years, despite the fact that foreign corporations have generally been outperformed by domestic ones in the American context, often making them losing—even failing—ventures, yet for whatever reasons they choose not to leave. This question certainly attracts attention.

What has been hypothesized in some recent scholarship is a desire on the foreigners' part for American expertise. This motive has been shown to be present in only a small number of cases, though. Various studies, moreover, have shown that the capacity to transfer expertise is not so great, making any expertise gained of limited value. At the same time, it is well known that the French government considered it important for Renault to be in the United States, so Renault stayed. It seems obvious that in this case politics was involved.[11] Unless the case of Renault is a complete exception to the rule, here we find national politics defining business interests, not the reverse. Where does that observation leave transnationalism and the TNC?

Although this point cannot be resolved at the moment, what is possible to note is the continuing widening use of the term *transnationalism* by scholars in many other fields, who appear to take the economic basis of the concept for granted. Thus, we find that feminist scholars, in particular the ones associated with transnational feminism, are introducing yet another dimension of the contemporary use of the term *transnationalism*. According to their theorization, the breakdown of the production-centered economy and the rise of the knowledge- and service-based postindustrial economy after 1970 created a context in which women had a stronger claim on economic and political power. From this point, the man was no longer the sole or even necessarily the most important breadwinner. Would it not stand to reason that this transformation of roles would lead to a rise in women's power? In some cases, it obviously did. The problem for women, transnational feminists argue, had been the production-based economy backed as it was by the nation-state. This setup had favored the male breadwinner. The priority for women, then, must be to get beyond the constraint of the nation-state, upholding as it does all the older forms of modernism, all the old binaries of men and women in terms of roles to be performed and rewards to be received for performing them. To get beyond the nation-state, transnational feminism emphasizes gender in connection with travel, this focus being an attempt to subvert the state and to expedite the coming of a new stage of history and economy.[12]

Transnational analysis, feminists found, conveys the "uneven and dissimilar circuits of capitalism and culture" that they experience, doing so better than did the older feminist analyses based on what was called the international economy. The latter term rests on an assumption about the existing world as one of nation-states, whereas transnationalism captures, in addition, the mood of resignation, which feminists find realistic, accepting the conclusion at least for the time being that there is "no such thing as a feminism free of asymmetrical power relations." So it is that a specifically transnational feminist praxis, as these writers term it, is one "involving forms of alliance, subversion, and complicity within which asymmetries and inequalities can be (acknowledged but) critiqued." Is it not the case that the nation-state is a male and patriarchal project, one deceiving both Western women and others, and local Third World feminisms are simply forms of codependency with the state? Should one uncritically accept the view that women ought to use migration from the Third World to get away from religious persecution? After all, coming to the West is not a utopian solution. Though this argument persuades some, others disagree. Should women not fight for a secure country in which to live? If they have to flee, must religion be their identity, and if so must identity be destiny?

Without passing judgment on the positions adopted, one could still suggest that no decisive critique of internationalism as a concept has been made by transnational feminism to this point. Transnational feminist practice in fact suggests coming to terms both with the neoliberal state and with the existing geometry of the world market. States are a bad thing, especially for women, but like markets they are inevitable. The solution for feminists appears to be transnational alliances of women in the interstices, the implication being that there is a state system, a core, and a periphery that one cannot get rid of and even the states of the periphery are too strong to confront. Thus, life under transnationalism seems to require a matter of "interstitiality," which in turn seems to be a form of praxis inclining women's movements to avoid making alliances with other oppressed groups or coming out in the open, instead relegating them to the margins.

THE APPLICATION OF TRANSNATIONALISM
TO MIGRATION AND DIASPORAS

Many transnationalist writers, among them transnationalist feminists, share in common a certain preoccupation with the issue of migration. Though it is widely recognized by such writers that migrants have often suffered irreparably from the forced or semiforced migrations caused by globalization, such migration is still thought to be the price to be paid for the development believed to be taking place. From this strategic compromise, however, arise many ambiguities. Does one praise the virtues of migration because it got you a maid? Is this development?

What is clear in any case is that a greater scholarly awareness of migration does appear to follow the advent of transnationalist thinking than was the case earlier when the emphasis was more on immigration or emigration than on migration. What is not clear in New Liberal theory is what is so new about migration or reverse migration or even what is necessarily so transnational about it.[13]

The largest known migrations of our times have not been transnational at all for the most part, being the movement of millions of people from the countryside to the towns and cities of their own countries over the past century. It would appear that the justification for emphasizing specifically transnational migration appears to be its size in recent years in certain places. And indeed in recent years, there have been a large number of people migrating across certain borders, which for many observers dramatizes the need for new theorization about the subject. However, for some, especially in the circles of transnationalist theory, the direction this theorizing has been going leads them to find the relevant point less in the size of today's migrations than in the fact that these migrations are coming at a time of advanced communication technology. This technology allows for a sustained transnational link between where people came from and where they are now, a link no doubt made affordable by the number of people involved. Communication technology, one could hypothesize, may be (and no doubt is) helping people who are undergoing the stress of transition to a new life. Yet although such technology is in use today, one wonders if it predictably keeps in place religious and racial migratory groups as diasporas no matter who the people involved are or where they happen to be. Here New Liberalism seems to be a bit out on a limb. Recent research is raising questions about whether empirically it makes sense to speak of people's beliefs and behavior conforming to ethnic racial diasporas of the sort one would expect. It would seem sometimes they do and sometimes they do not.

As early as the late 1990s, a study of Peruvians living in Paterson, New Jersey, found that whereas some of these immigrants conformed to the transnational linkage idea, others were more defined by local issues arising from the dynamics of American life. A study of Chinese in the UK carried out in the same period likewise suggested much variability. Links assumed to be diasporic turned out on close examination often to be class-based ties as opposed to ethnic ones, and often enough political ones as well.[14] This point reminds us that the multiple messages transmitted from a country such as China or Peru might well be antithetical to one another—they might or might not promote ideas of the unity of race, religion, or national origin.

In yet other recent studies, the idea of migration as being something transhistorical, that is, something characterized by "flow, fluidity, and mobility," has been challenged by a researcher who charges that such a characterization serves to obscure the class and racial position of the migrant. The actual situation of poor Mexicans coming across the U.S. border is quite different from the position of the middle-class European migrant coming to the United States. Border crossing, this author insists, ought as a result to be a subject in its own right and not subsumed under generalized descriptions of migration. The Rio Grande is not always all that fluid.[15]

THE APPLICATION OF TRANSNATIONALISM TO PAN-ISLAM AND 9/11

Another constituency inside and outside of the academy that has recently seen much of value in transnational theorizing has been religionists and others interested in the "Pan-" movements. Transnationalism with its emphasis on the computer, migration, and diaspora issues is a way to explain the rise of powerful pan- movements, such as Pan-Islam.

It is common enough to find writers in this domain who begin from the premise that political Islam, as it is called, is a global movement independent of the policy of states, the states having been in any case something artificially imposed on Muslim people. Again, empiricism may not sustain these points too well. The idea of the state *(al-Dawlah)* in the Islamic context goes back to the period of the rightly guided caliphs of the seventh century and some would claim even a bit earlier, to the Constitution of Madina

in the lifetime of the Prophet Muhammad. The inherently diasporic nature
of the overseas Muslim is also open to some question. Well-studied examples of Muslim communities in all parts of the world reveal examples of
deep integration within states over a long period of time. Thus, although
the idea of diaspora fits with the theory of transnationalism, it may or may
not fit with what is known about Muslims in Indian history, African history, Southeast Asian history, earlier American history, and so forth, where
syncretism and assimilation are a bit closer to the mark than the notion
of separate and unchanging identities. Nonetheless, the idea of Muslim
diasporas has gained considerable salience since 9/11, after which the common perception became that "political Islam" if not Islam itself was transnational and the enemy of the West. Arguably, it is the subject of 9/11 more
than any other in recent times that has legitimated the transnationalist type
of explanation in the public mind, at least the diaspora part of it.

Few academic writers have yet to try a more traditional historical type
of inquiry about 9/11 to see if it could provide an alternative explanation, and indeed it is not easy; researchers who try to go in this direction
are stigmatized as conspiracy theorists. Yet fairly well-written works of a
quite nonconspiratorial sort show that members of the Bush family and of
the Sa'ud dynasty were friends and that Usama bin Ladin was not exactly
a stranger to either. More than one book studies the American use of
the Mujahidin in the Afghan war; the interconnections of the Pakistani,
Saudi, and American collaborators in that time period; and the blowback that followed. Despite evidence of this sort, evidence that might cast
doubts on a transnationalist type of explanation, all one can say is that
the subject remains to be worked on. It is as if researchers are mesmerized
by or perhaps essentially in agreement with the U.S. governmental decision to characterize this era as a war on Islamic terrorism, or perhaps they
are mesmerized by Usama bin Ladin's decision to use Muslims from all
over to attack the United States, scholars allowing this detail to persuade
them that there was a transnationalism in the form of Pan-Islamism.[16]
Still, the question remains if al-Qa'ida is a transnational organization that
is separate from the government of Pakistan. We will return to this topic
in Chapter 4.

THE APPLICATION OF TRANSNATIONALISM
TO THE EUROPEAN UNION

Whereas 9/11 or political Islam is what inspires the idea of transnationalism for some, especially in the United States, for others especially in Europe, transnationalism has gained similar credibility from the experience of the Common Market. Living in Europe one uses a single currency, the euro, travels at will, and can work in any country. Such experiences lead many observers in the direction of theorizing "beyond the nation-state" as well. Careful academic study of conditions prevailing in Europe, however, is reaching a rather different conclusion when it comes to explaining what is actually transpiring. In what is arguably the most important history of the Common Market to date, *The European Rescue of the Nation-State* (2d ed., 2000), Alan S. Milward argues that the creation and evolution of the Common Market involved the decisions of various states to vest responsibility in the market in order to strengthen themselves, and the states became stronger as a result of their participation in the market arrangement. Even in the case of the UK, which distanced itself from full membership, one finds, as Milward points out, an ongoing interest in seeking an association with the market for this reason. Thus, for example, for Belgium a big issue was how to phase out coal mining. In other countries some similar issue stood out. Each stood to gain from structural changes if there was some way to bring it about while at the same time letting the local politicians off the hook. For this reason, they signed the agreements. Today, the states and ruling classes find themselves in a good situation, while the new generation of workers is discovering there are no jobs.[17]

In sum, although transnationalism has come to mean many different things by virtue of the different directions that scholars have taken it,[18] its core meaning seems to be one based on the assumption of the existence of the TNC as the embodiment of market autonomy and of economic rationality in that market. From that set of ideas, much else seems to follow, including even the recasting of the periodization of world history, beyond the nation-state.

THE PERIODIZATION OF WORLD HISTORY
ACCORDING TO NEW LIBERALISM

For New Liberals the computer age is what makes modern history. The periodization of modern history should reflect this fact. Before the computer age the big differences in history were between civilizations and cultures more than they were between countries and time periods. World history was the record of these civilizations and cultures connected as they were by trade routes, these civilizations and cultures rising and falling over the millennia up until the age of the computer. For New Liberals, the European watershed of the sixteenth century that gave rise to capitalism in Britain is a blip on the radar screen, the world at that point dominated by the Asian market.

According to New Liberal analysis, most of the past is more like prehistory than a part of who we are today in any clear sense. Even a time period as seemingly recent as the Victorian era should be looked at as being part of some archaic phase, one in which there may have been some nationally based capital extended overseas but not in the sense of today's transnationalism. Following New Liberalism's preferred periodization, capitalism has in recent years achieved a revolutionary delinking from its respective nation-states. What is new in material terms, its protagonists would argue, is not the growth of overseas investment but the growth of a globally interlinked system of production that goes totally beyond the old overseas investment or "shallow penetration" typical of earlier capitalism. There is no comparison between the two. This globally interlinked production is so developed that it even has its own think tanks and policy centers, often supervised by the World Bank, the Group of Eight, and other such bodies that work to promote the interests of transnational capitalism. Transnationalism thus has its own culture and scholarship. And this culture and scholarship are highly focused. Their unfailing concern is how best to control the world economy. All scholars in this orbit share this objective, some doing so by putting more emphasis on maintaining the continuity of market logic, others by putting more emphasis on the need to confront the deepening economic crises in various countries noticeable since the 1990s. Here one might want to note that apparently since the 1990s, there have been divisions in transnational think-tank circles: on the one hand, there are the regulationists who are becoming more tentative about open-door policies, and, on the other, there are conservatives who see the open door as the only answer.

For historians attracted to New Liberalism, the field of world history thus needs a new periodization, one that would give due weight to transnationalism even if transnationalism as a phenomenon is only of quite recent vintage. However, as other historians have noted, this arrangement begs the question of what is due weight. If one adopts such a periodization, one overlooks parts of the available evidence even about transnationalism, evidence that serves to counterindicate the use of such periodization. For example, in the research of Mira Wilkins, the well-known business historian, one finds evidence of a type of company quite similar to today's transnational company that can be shown to have emerged in the nineteenth century: the early freestanding company.[19] In its time it too could be distinguished from the multinational company of that era, as the transnational company can today, by the fact that the founders had no plan from the beginning to operate at home. All the freestanding companies had was a headquarters in the country of origin, whereas most of its business activity was elsewhere. It is interesting, and perhaps not entirely coincidental, that most such companies arose under conditions of finance capitalism and most ran into problems and declined in the waning years of that period. From such evidence, it appears, one could make a claim about the existence of a transnational bourgeois element quite a long time ago.[20] Would New Liberal theorists explain this apparent anomaly as a meaningless part of prehistory also?

Although a specific answer to this point may elude us for the moment, one might predict that the problems transnationalism may have with world history are not going to last for long. In the past decade transnationalism has picked up a small but influential group of academic supporters, prominent among them a number of historians in the field of world history, a group interested in better rooting the idea of transnationalism in the long term of history.

In June 1996 the *American Historical Review* published a forum, "Cross-cultural Interaction and Periodization in World History." As

Professor Jerry Bentley wrote in the main article of this forum, if one periodizes world history around the details of the history of one country, it is not likely to work for others.[21] Bentley is no doubt correct; this problem had long bedeviled historians trying to extend the well-known periodization of Western history to other parts of the world. I believe a majority of today's world historians would agree that this quandary has been a weak point in the existing field. Bentley's solution, which he shares with a number of others in the World History Association, would be to create a periodization drawn from world trade history over the millennia, in this way preparing us for today's transnationalism. An important chapter would be "Cross-cultural Exchange on the Silk Roads."

Bentley's solution, in theory at least, resolves many problems and has gained wide acceptance. In practice, however, one might suggest it does so at a price. First, Bentley's solution of emphasizing trade and contact costs history a grounded conception of modernity for anything but the West. Without some weight placed on the modernity of political systems around the world, the West of the twentieth century becomes the unique embodiment of modern politics and the rest of world becomes simply a composite of civilizations reacting to the West as a result of contact. This representation seems to fall short of a "global perspective." Second, if a book in world history is to be essentially a panorama of civilizations animated by trade patterns, something of the complexity of human life and experience is lost. History risks becoming chronology.

Over time, Bentley correctly claimed, historians had become increasingly aware of the importance of trade as a part of history. They have found that trade is and always was more important than Marx found it to be in his discussion of merchant capitalism. In volume 1 of *Capital*, Marx, it may be recalled, claimed that before the capitalist mode of production, merchant capitalism was no more than the episodic long-distance trade in luxuries. According to Bentley, even where it was what Marx described, trade in luxuries should be seen as playing a role that was much wider and more historically important than simply supplying the means for idle consumption. For example, some recognition must be given to the role luxuries play in the stabilization of ruling groups. Rulers could give out or share luxuries as a part of buying support within their coteries. Bentley's point is well taken, although there is no way to know what percentage of luxuries served such a purpose. Second, according to Bentley, in the case of Asia and the Indian Ocean, what began as trade in luxuries expanded to include much else, to the point in certain instances that the role of trade was so pronounced as to reshape and integrate regions on an economic level along a trade route. What we call Indonesia today serves as an example. As such trade developed, new culture, new technology, and even new diseases spread. All these events could be said to characterize not just Indonesian history but much of the history of the rest of the Indian Ocean region as well. These points are Bentley's main claims, and he is careful not to overstate his case. Prior to 1492 trade-route history would not apply to the New World, sections of the Pacific, Africa, and so on, because they were outside the main long-distance trade routes. Bentley's schema thus unfolds in the Hegelian way, one civilization after another: age of complex societies, age of ancient civilizations, age of classical civilizations, a postclassical age, age of transregional nomadic empires, and the modern age. Given this periodization, he is as entitled to claim Hegel as his mentor as any other liberal, or for that matter as virtually any Marxist.

In conclusion, this section presented an outline of New Liberalism, emphasizing its economic side. This led to a focus on transnationalism, as this concept is the one that represents the link between New Liberal economics and world history. What appears is that transnationalism is a very problematic concept across the board, certainly in its application to world history. For New Liberal historians the past appears to be more of an inconvenience than a field of inquiry. It is only the near present of the computer age that truly matters. For New Liberals people in world history are also an inconvenience, as the critical features of world history are trade, technology, environment, and contact. What perhaps can be hypothesized is that New Liberal historiography provides a rationale for globalization, one that is superior to that of the traditional liberal historiography.[22]

THE POLITICAL ECONOMY TRADITION:
ITS WORLD HISTORY

A generation ago in his essay on Fordism, Antonio Gramsci identified the crisis of Marxism as arising from its dependence on liberalism.[23] The new praxis of the working class had become one of grabbing any and all pay raises possible and eschewing the struggle for control of the workplace or for power more generally. It was in this context that political economy as an intellectual tradition, one that was focused on the worker as proletarian, ran into problems. Indeed, it is at exactly this point where the crisis in political economy became visible in many countries, including the United States. The crisis was not the result of the collapse of the Soviet Union, which came many years later. Rather, the crisis in the United States in the 1930s occurred in the trade union movement in places such as Detroit. It was here that Marxism came to depend on liberalism.

Much had changed over the preceding fifty years. In 1884 Friedrich Engels had produced the classic Marxist statement of world history, *The Origin of the Family: Private Property and the State*. In it he theorized that the general phases of human history were the periods based on the developing dialectic of the human community, beginning with the tribal-communal mode of production and progressing through the slave to the feudal or tributary and on to the capitalist mode of production. Change, Engels theorized, came about when the ruling classes in each mode of production could no longer stop the struggle for liberation of the mass population. This struggle then led to revolution and ultimately to a new mode of production. Writers following Engels had applied his model in many contexts. Some had done so crudely, in a stage-ist way, as if still following Hegel, whereas others had tried in a more refined way, as Trotsky did in his theory of the combined and uneven nature of development with a conjuncturalist theory of history. By the interwar period, the Marxist tradition lacked continuators who could adjust it to the new conditions or even sustain its methodology, to return to the point about the changing nature of the trade unions. As a result, gradually, the unique epistemology of Marxism began to fall apart, and Marxist theory began to move toward liberalism. Those individuals aware of this crisis joined the Fourth International, with varying results.

By the 1970s the disarray of even the so-called New Left, the most important part of the Fourth International, could not be denied. At that point, the return of finance capitalism brought two elements within the Marxist theoretical framework that had been in relative harmony with each other into conflict, opening up, for better or worse, a rather glaring theoretical problem. The first of these elements was the assumption that new technology changing the relations of production would correspond with new classes rising to embody human progress, and the second was that the working class as the embodiment of the future would be the one to rise and control such technology.

The computer revolution represented an apparent example of such new technology. Thus far, however, as the discussion of Brint showed, the computer revolution has changed the relations of production without giving birth to specifically new classes. Thus far, moreover, it has been the capitalist class more than other classes that has gained from the development of the computer. Nonetheless, most in the political economy tradition would be inclined to liken the computer revolution to the Industrial Revolution of the eighteenth century, and perhaps they are correct to do so, despite the theoretical problems it leaves them with.

In the *Manifesto* and *Preface to the Critique of Political Economy,* Marx characterized the Industrial Revolution as the revolution solidifying the capitalist mode of production. In the wake of the Industrial Revolution, the old social structure, with its laws and mystifications, was pushed aside, Marx claimed, and a new class had arisen, which indeed appears to have been the case. The computer revolution of our own times seems, however, not to have had the same consequences. Rather, it seems to have facilitated the transition in capitalism from productive capitalism to finance capitalism and to capital flight. Production can be efficiently managed at this point from a great distance. In effect, capitalism has gained a second wind. As it did so, it broke the social contract in most countries, introducing a growing poverty and desperation around the world. Those individuals who retain the older Marxian optimism see in the protests against the World Trade Organization the birth of a globalization of struggle against capitalism, whereas others with a less optimistic view concede that capitalism has once again gained the upper hand and as a result may even be able to rule at least until the first major ecological disaster. The true pessimists see the present as a prelude for the introduction of capitalism to other planets, the Rich moving in due course to space stations as Earth becomes less habitable.

Marxism today, whether pessimistic or optimistic, remains concerned, as it has been for a generation or more, with the appearance of orthodoxy of its interpretations more than it does with the adequacy of its theoretical bases or with its ability to assimilate new knowledge or to interpret new situations. Critics routinely raise such matters, but they are ignored. Still, Marxism wants to be today what it no longer is, a scientific tradition. As economist and critic William Lazonick wrote some years ago in bemoaning the oversimplification of Marxist writing on British history,[24] the growth of the British economy to its position of preeminence was not the result of laissez-faire economics, as Marxists have been claiming, but the result of the power of the British state and military that could impose a global regime favorable to the British economy, an economy that for a certain period thus stood to gain from having an open market. It was, at least in Lazonick's view, a series of noneconomic decisions about the world that made the economy preeminent. Most economists, Marxists among them, overlook this point and naively or pragmatically accept the domain of the "economic" and function within it. A recent book, written by another economist, Salim Rashid, makes a similar criticism of the pretensions of the field of economics and by implication at least of Marxism. According to Rashid, Adam Smith brought no new ideas to economics beyond those of the common sense of his period, and what he added by way of innovation was actually inaccurate. The field that Smith supposedly founded was in effect not a field; it was simply popular culture. This strand of criticism is found as well in yet another work by an economist, Jean Gadrey, this time in reference to current claims made by economists about the future of the information-age economy. Apart from pundits who grab the attention of the media, Gadrey writes, few seriously think that the new information age has much that is new about it qua economics.[25] Interestingly, these critiques that are so useful for a rethinking of Marxism were written by liberals, not Marxists.

What orthodox Marxists do manage to salvage is a limited claim to historicism. For example, what New Liberals call globalization might better be termed neoliberalism. Globalization has no past referent and therefore no context, which makes for a very weak concept. Its identity is one largely built in terms only of how different it is from what went before.

Yet, even if neoliberalism is somewhat different today than in the late nineteenth century, the use of the term allows for a discussion of specificities and an analysis free from presentism. Where the historicism seems to break down, and this point should come as no surprise, is where the analysis would need to turn away from positivism and rely on a wider materialism.[26] This is something Marxism is still trying to recover.

AN EARLIER ATTEMPT AT A WIDER MATERIALISM: ANTONIO GRAMSCI

The main writer in the Marxist tradition in modern times who attempted to produce a wider materialist analysis was Antonio Gramsci. However, given what orthodoxy was and still is, his work has been viewed in a very selective and often distorted fashion, for which there are reasons, of course. To a degree, Gramsci brought this on himself. He was a critic of orthodox Marxism, and this affected his reputation in those circles. Thus, for example, because of decisions made by the Communist Parties in Italy and the Soviet Union, most of his work was not available even in Italian for many years after his death. This situation, of course, has now changed. His work now exists in Italian and in the past few years is beginning to appear in the other major languages of the world.

Today, the problem with Gramsci is one of access for a different set of reasons. Today, most commentators who write about him are liberals, many of them a part of the New Liberalism, and in their writings Gramsci comes to resemble less a founder of the PCI (the Italian Communist Party) than an antecedent of today's New Liberalism.[27] For this reason, most of Gramsci's thought is considered irrelevant by contemporary writers, because he lived back in the era of the "coherent nation-state." The reasons for valuing him today have more to do with his eye for various subordinate details of how hegemonies rule, what role intellectuals play, the nature of civil society, and so on than for his reliance on a wider materialism.[28]

In taking the opposite perspective, as I do in making him a major source of theoretical inspiration, the intention is to defend Gramsci against the charge that he could not have had a political understanding of the world politics that we currently live under and to suggest that it would appear, to the contrary, that he could actually have had one, and more of one than he did. What appears to be the case is that his theorization of international relations was underdeveloped, especially for a Marxist theorist of his period, an error on his part that possibly led to various strategic miscalculations, possibly even to his own arrest and imprisonment.

Let us conclude this section with a brief illustration of what Gramsci's Marxism might offer to a rethinking of Marxism today. To do so let us return once again to the subject of business decision making, as it will allow us to see at once how a wider materialist approach changes Marxism from what it is at present. Let us locate the discussion in a hypothetical country of the advanced capitalist world.

In this country, we might assume that businessmen as well as politicians depend on persuasion as well as coercion. Where politicians need to project a certain image of themselves to get elected, businessmen need to create and maintain a certain image of their products to stay in business. The media work to maintain the subject population as a consumer by entertaining it, informing it, and selling these two forms of commodities to it. To perform its function, the media need stars, which in turn makes them dependent on organized sports and Hollywood to generate stars that they can then hype. It is the hyping of stars that creates and maintains the audience that becomes the voter and the consumer. What is understood by this process is that markets do not exist on their own; they are made inside states a piece at a time by the creation of these consumers. This would not happen if people were not being conditioned in a certain way, by the media, the religious institutions, and the educational system. No modern hegemony could function without such institutions, nor could capitalism as an economic system. Coercion alone, by way of contrast, seems to work, but only for very short periods of time. No hegemony can survive for long simply on coercion, even a dictatorship. It is on this basis that one could make a claim for the autonomy of politics and for a need to profoundly rethink historical materialism.

Most business school professors, most historians, and certainly most Marxist historians would have a very different set of opinions about such matters. Business school professors, for example, teach business decision making as an essential part of their pedagogy. In their work at least, market sovereignty or capital logic is believed to underlie decisions taken by business executives, business executives fearing the wrath of investors if the rate of return on the stock falls as the result of their following any other approach. Although business decision making no doubt prevails on occasion, a closer look suggests other factors would almost necessarily have to be involved as well, including the ones mentioned above. Of course, these factors too would be acknowledged, but the point here is how they would be acknowledged. What one expects is that any monographic work from a business school would doubtless present a multicausal form of analysis. What the author would conventionally do would be to include a chapter called "The Business Setting" or "The Business Environment." This title would reveal the methodological premises quite clearly. On the one hand, there is business decision making, and then there is the environment or setting.

But consider the following everyday occurrence and how misleading such an approach to analysis might potentially be. Faced with a possible shortfall, a manager would sell subsidiaries, lay off workers, and move production offshore. Although the financial page would improve, the business would have lost control over production and subsidiary linkages. One could argue that the manager in this example was not necessarily following something called business decision-making but may well have been operating from other motivations, perhaps simply a fear of losing his job. Moreover, in the process, he by himself or in conjunction with others had made a series of political choices. The sudden job loss that would result from his decision might affect the careers of a number of incumbents in public office. Risking such consequences amounts to a political choice. The manager might then begin a marketing campaign to improve the company's sales position. Certain countries would be targeted, and these countries would be the ones where the United States had a strong political relationship. Some other country might have a potentially larger market for a given product, but it would be overlooked for political reasons. In effect, a fairly complicated and multidimensional series of events is taking place, all of which will be attributed—and in my view misleadingly so—to something called business decision making.

For the Gramscian tradition within political economy with its wider materialism, what has been termed business decision-making enters into the concerns of management but does so along with other concerns. Among these other concerns, one would expect a concern with social control or security or maintaining the existing social hierarchy, that is, in effect protecting one's position and property—in other words, power.

The issue for CEOs and rulers is not just one of upholding capital logic but of balancing these different types of concerns. How this balancing act plays out will depend on the way the class struggle evolves. Here Gramsci provides some additional insights. When the issue of social control is uppermost, as one finds was the case in Fascist Italy, the larger, more regulatory state with its multiple non-market-oriented concerns is often the more effective way to rule. It can serve to rally the country and to create solidarity. Under these conditions, factory or productive capitalism is often useful. When social control ceases to be the priority of the moment, then nothing beats a return to the minimal state and finance capitalism for profit making. There is much more profit to be made investing speculatively around the world than in building more factories at home. Thus, depending on political conditions—meaning the level of counterhegemonic struggle— sometimes one finds a dominance of finance capitalism and the minimalist state, and sometimes one finds nation-centered, production-centered capitalism with the large state. The result so far in a Rise of the Rich formulation is that the actual movement of contemporary history looks like a spiral, that is, a slowly lengthening oscillation back and forth between these two forms, the lengthening oscillation a function of the development of multilateralism.

A way to understand the difference between Marxism and liberalism arises at this point quite clearly if one considers the position each of these worldviews ascribes to the middle classes. For liberalism, the progress of modern history was synonymous with the rise of the middle class. With New Liberalism there has been some retreat from this view, but it is still present. For political economy in a Gramscian mirror, different eras are marked by a policy aimed at either building up or diminishing the power of the middle classes, depending on conditions. At one moment the middle classes may serve as a guarantor of some level of security for capitalism;

at another they may serve as something of a constraint on its development. Sooner or later this constraint would have to be removed, especially if a state wanted to return to finance capitalism. Yet as past history also suggests, if one weakened the middle classes too much, it would be easy to sink into domestic chaos. Pandemic diseases could spread where food supplies had not been inspected, anarchist terrorists could assassinate people when too few elements in society were included in politics, and problems of immigration, child labor, and narcotics addiction could grow when there was no one to deal with them. When such calamities begin to mount up, the dominant elements, keen as they may have been about maximizing profit, would begin to fear revolution. At that point, they would finally stop denying there were problems that had to be dealt with and would turn to the middle classes and the upper working classes to restore calm. However, it may also be noted that years of social crisis might go by before this historic turn would come to pass. But finally it would come to pass, coming more as Fascism, sometimes more as socialism depending on the prevailing political alliances.

． ． ．

IN SUMMARY, this chapter postulates that there is a crisis in economic theory in both liberalism and Marxism and that this crisis affects how world history is written. In recent years, New Liberalism has arisen to remedy the problems of the old liberalism. For New Liberals to study history, however, they virtually had to jettison any theoretical concern with the human past if they were to retain their preoccupation with the present. Where Hegel found a development over time of the human spirit, today his heirs seek merely to catalog the older civilizations and trade routes. Where Hegel's philosophy in the past lent itself to rather complicated forms of idealism and materialism, today's New Liberalism and its historians reject that complexity and extol the virtues of a fairly unitary model of globalization.

The next chapter completes the discussion begun here on history and the crisis in theory. There we will look at the contemporary theorization of politics, according to New Liberalism and Marxism, and then consider its impact on the writing of world history.

MODERN WORLD POLITICAL
HISTORY BETWEEN LIBERALISM
AND POLITICAL ECONOMY

WHEREAS IN THE PREVIOUS CHAPTER we concentrated on economics and history, in this chapter we will focus on politics and history. What we find are more examples of how New Liberalism is attempting to prop up Hegel. New Liberals appear to recognize that to do so at this point requires even more sacrifices on their part. For example, to retain the traditional West–Third World distinction found in Hegel, New Liberalism appears to be willing at this point to abandon a number of its traditional positions. This we will also find is the case in contemporary Marxism, contemporary Marxism often following the lead of liberalism, occasionally making small critical interventions. I will conclude this chapter by illustrating how the use of the Rise of the Rich provides an alternative approach to politics.

To introduce New Liberalism's politics, commonly called New Politics, I am choosing three of its concepts, these being the ones that play a demonstrable role in the conceptualization of world history. The first of these concepts is that of the Risk Society. Risk Society is a characterization of the modern West. The second of these is Fourth World New Social Movement; this in effect is a description of Third World political struggle. And the third of these is the Fallacy of Westphalianism, which is how New Politics explains the importance of the concept of empire over that of the nation-state. These three concepts are very much interrelated.

Risk Society is one of the distinctive categories of New Liberalism today. It is not one that is found in the work of earlier writers in the liberal tradition. Risk exists as a part of the earlier liberal scholarship, but it is not something that defines the society. There were always adventurers and individuals who took risks, but they were on the whole outside of society. The society itself was characterized on some other basis. Over the past generation, there has been a change. Risk Society has become central to how New Politics characterizes what is new and modern about Western society.

If New Politics depicts the West as a risk-taking society, how does it characterize the Third World or underdeveloped world? Here one encounters the term *Fourth World* and the term *New Social Movement,* terms unknown to earlier liberalism. What one now finds is a virtual abandonment of such concepts as Third World or underdevelopment, terms that had been the mainstay of liberal theory for the preceding half-century. To a degree, of course, realities have changed. One could argue that underdevelopment is not the key that it once was because development is not the key that it once was. Today, some would claim, one may find poverty, but one may also find rapid development and new wealth thanks to global capitalism; thus, it no longer makes sense to keep using the term *Third World* in the sense of economically behind à la the older liberalism. Some writers who want to emphasize the dated nature of the term *Third World* even use the phrase the "end of the Third World." If one wants to understand these countries correctly, one needs to look at them as the opposite of risk society, and here one finds what appears to be a growing consensus. For New Liberals, this new consensus appears to be that one needs to look at these countries more in terms of culture and identity than in terms of history. To introduce this development in New Liberal thought, a logical category would be Fourth World New Social Movements. The use of the term *Fourth World* allows one to bypass the term *Third World.* It also thereby allows one to establish an alternative epistemological basis for the analysis of that part of the world. According to New Politics, the Third World nation-state is a Western imposition. Its failure on an economic and political level is proof of its unsuitability. Success for these countries would require their working from what for them would be more authentic models. Authenticity in all probability would not be found by their emulating Western political models, but it would come from the local culture, hence the use of the category Fourth World. According to the New Politics, Marxists and old liberals misconstrue the nature of these countries by using Western categories to describe them. They thus misunderstand the causes of the economic and political problems that these countries frequently experience.

The term *New Social Movement* is also an important category in New Liberal thought.[1] It is one currently used in a variety of ways—for example, to characterize youth movements, cults, religious movements, various political movements, and the like. When one finds the category of New Social Movements connected to the category of the Fourth World, it is clear that what is intended is a characterization of a movement understood to be based on cultural identity, which is different from an approach that would be used in a traditional history of the movement or of the country in which the movement exists. Here there has been some interesting research done in recent times. One of the better-known examples of this type of New Liberal research is the subaltern studies from India. The struggles of subaltern peoples in India we learn are cultural struggles; they are therefore not the same as the anticolonial or socialist struggles of other groups.

The example chosen for discussion in this chapter however is even better known. It is the one currently most written about by New Liberals themselves, the Zapatista movement in Southern Mexico. The Zapatista, New Liberals find, are essentially animated by issues of their traditional Mayan identity, not by modern grievances. To highlight the difference between New Liberal politics and the Rise of the Rich, this account is followed by one portraying the Zapatista as a part of Mexico and Mexican history. In this account, their Mayan identity is a very subordinate part of the analysis, the larger issue being whether the South of Mexico is better portrayed in terms of internal colonialism or in terms of Mexico's "Southern Question."[2]

RISK SOCIETY

Today one finds that "New Liberal politics" has put the traditional liberalism of positivism, narrative, and progress on the defensive by introducing an alternative set of terms such as *globalization, Risk Society,* and *New Social Movements.* To study the West, "Risk Society" has become the concept of choice. German theorist Ulrich Beck is a leading writer on the subject of Risk Society. Beck is the author of a number of books and, in addition, is an important figure in the New Europe of the Common Market as well. As a writer, Beck is well known for distinguishing the New Liberalism from the old, an important part of the New Liberalism being its openness to what is spontaneous and risk taking.

The Risk Society, according to Beck, is the "world of new opportunities." This world began with the collapse of the Soviet Union. Although one still finds in the years after 1989 a level of formal or state-centered politics, that pattern is contested increasingly in Beck's view by subsystems, or New Politics. Interest groups at this point became more organized and more influential. Politics could thus be formal or rule directed or, alternatively, new, meaning rule altering. Small traditional struggles tended to be characterized by the former, but larger issues such as shifting to a global organizational level tended to be a part of the latter. Beck goes on to characterize the New Politics as beyond Left and Right, arguing that it is not obvious how to use such terms when addressing many real-world issues, such as developments in today's Russia. The new opportunities, Beck finds, reward those individuals who take risks and believe in an individual's capacities.[3] Risk taking thus becomes Beck's point about the nature of the Western world after 1989.

Much of contemporary liberal politics—here to continue with Beck's idea of a watershed ushering in the world of new opportunities—dwells on this theme of the "transformation of modernity" or "transformation of sovereignty," the one allowing for the other. Here a bit more background may be in order. The traditional liberal view of sovereignty was one based on the idea that the state emerged, gaining sovereignty apart from the ruler, this gradually becoming solidified in the Peace of Westphalia in 1648. Regardless of the accuracy of this description of the development of state power, and we will return to this matter shortly, Beck's real concern is to show that the reverse process, the process of the limiting of state power, was clearly in evidence by the late 1940s. At that point, most states bound themselves to covenants against genocide as well as to covenants respecting human rights. This commitment on the part of their leaders was a natural reflex from the horrors of World War II. A more formal level of derogation of state power began in 1950. In that year in the Treaty of Paris, European integration can be said to have begun. From that point onward there was a steady growth of privileging of the European Union and, in his view, a deprivileging of the state. It is from that generic background that transnationalism took off. Points commonly mentioned in that discussion that also enter into the discussion of Risk Society include the rise of a transnational network of legal relations, legal personhood extending even to stateless people, a global human rights culture, and so on.[4] Although these points represent important insights, still one might wonder about how this theory would be applied on any expanded basis at least for that period in time. Only a few states in the core of the world market ever enjoyed the kind of sovereignty that could then allow for one to speak meaningfully of devolution. Most countries, especially the ones that were colonies and even many that were not, suffered numerous involuntary infractions of their sovereignty. Perhaps as a consequence, the New Politics confines the discussion to where sovereignty is thought to have once existed but later one can observe it to be in decline. The experience with the devolution of sovereignty of other countries around the world is perhaps simply assumed to be less relevant to the "transformation of modernity."

Even accepting an entirely Europe-centered discussion of the decline of national sovereignty, one might still ask, as we did in Chapter 1, what exactly is meant by decline? The state, one learns, is weaker today than it was a generation or so ago. There are people today with multiple passports and extended families living in different countries, people who form diasporic solidarities. Corporations move in and out of countries without sharing vital economic information bearing on those countries (for example, information about oil resources). Further, certain media in a country may not be regulated by the government. All these developments are certainly occurring, and they require some interpretation. However, the interpretation need not be that the state today is weaker than in the past, even if it is showing some signs of crisis. Another possibility is that over the past generation, the state chose to pull back and to function more minimally, doing so from strength and not from weakness.

In fact, it might be really quite plausible to hypothesize that the state has gradually grown stronger as the century has progressed, not weaker. A century ago not only was there no Interpol, but what information the state possessed about its citizens was not available to every clerk on every border through a computer, as it is today. A century ago there was no federal income tax, so an individual's wealth was not something that the government could easily ascertain. A century ago, the whole question of opposition was different. At that time, the amount of weaponry that states had in relation to their people was much less, so armed popular uprisings were a potential threat. In the case of the United States, for example, the FBI did not yet exist. Imprisonment, when it occurred, tended to be more local and was on the whole less common. Today, by way of contrast, many people are held in prison, and there is a considerable coordination of the prison system on the federal level. In short, it would not be hard to build a case for the idea of the growth of state power.[5]

For contemporary liberalism, however, given what it assumes about the weakness of the state, a logical place to look for recent evidence of power would be the subnational level. If the state is weaker, it is assumed this level would become stronger. Not surprisingly, much New Liberal scholarship takes up subjects such as citizen participation, human rights, issues affecting civil society, nongovernmental organizations, and grassroots movements. Certain subjects, such as freedom of the person and freedom of sexual orientation, today command particularly wide attention.[6]

As these events imply, liberalism takes, as it always has, a reformist approach to politics. Reformism today means that sovereigns are being tamed, that we are on the threshold of an era of new democracies, that new possibilities are before us but the further development of civil society will demand yet greater accountability and transparency from its rulers. In some ways, these phenomena are occurring. There certainly is an increase in the number of countries in which there is some reference to the idea of democracy. One also finds, however, an increase in the size and number of new subnational movements of a sort that are utterly incompatible with the maintenance of civil society or rule by law or other institutions we associate with democracy. Such movements generally do not receive much attention in liberal political thought. The ones that have a more positive orientation are the ones that receive the attention. In Europe or the United States, those groups with a more positive orientation are the ones commonly considered to be New Social Movements, unlike narco-terrorists, mafias, and cult movements.[7] This discrepancy seems worth mentioning, as it points to epistemological problems: a category is created, but potential examples that would fit the category cannot be accepted without the category being corrupted.

THE ZAPATISTA MOVEMENT AS AN EXAMPLE
OF A FOURTH WORLD NEW SOCIAL MOVEMENT

The preeminent example of a Fourth World NSM for many New Liberal political writers is the Zapatista movement in Mexico. The Zapatista are represented as a symbol of an archaic form of progressivism and the Mexican state that opposes them as a symbol of failed modernity. At the same time, their exotic and non-Western profile serves to clarify what for a Western liberal is self and other.

How does one explain the success of the Zapatista? For the older liberalism, wealth and technological superiority are decisive factors in history. When for some reason they do not yield predictable outcomes, this result is a quandary. How is it that a small group of lightly armed Indian peasants largely in the one province of Chiapas have been able to force a fairly modern country into a state of emergency by absorbing the energies of its army? Here once again New Liberalism comes to the rescue. A New Liberal explanation might run as follows. The new more democratic regimes differ from the authoritarian regimes of earlier times. Arising out of globalism, these new regimes respect human rights and no longer oppress their citizenries as their predecessors did, the reason being that globalism has spread democratic values, the local hegemonic discourse in this case in Mexico accepting the international liberalism of globalism.[8] It is this new democratic ethos that protects even Fourth World people such as the Zapatista and allows them to function.

A related strand of New Liberal analysis, one that bears on the subject of the Zapatista as well, emphasizes the Information Revolution brought by the computer, the Information Revolution being what constitutes the other watershed of our times along with the breakdown of the Soviet Union. The Internet in this line of analysis facilitates a revolutionary distribution of news and other knowledge, which in itself weakens the state, the state in earlier times having had a capacity to limit what citizens had access to by being able to monopolize the sources of knowledge.

It is not an insignificant detail that the Zapatista have a support network connected worldwide by the Internet ready to report the misdeeds of the Mexican government. And no doubt the existence of this rapid reportage has on occasion embarrassed the Mexican government into showing some restraint, given the country's dependence on international investment. It should also be noted that some of the most passionate statements about the emancipatory role of the computer have as their main example the Zapatista movement and its global Internet support cast.

The problem for the historian is how to weigh different factors potentially affecting the behavior of the Mexican government toward the Zapatista. Without gainsaying the significance of the international contribution to the Zapatista struggle or the role that technology may play in it, a Marxist historian nonetheless might choose to privilege what he or she takes to be the main internal trends in Mexico. He or she might well observe that the Mexican political and economic system underwent major changes in the 1990s and early 2000s. Not only did these changes affect the fortunes of the ruling party, the PRI, but they affected those of the official trade union movements affiliated to the PRI as well. The membership in the latter dropped; at the same time, there was a sudden growth of nonofficial unions. Often, these unions were much more militant and much more pro-Zapatista than were the official movements.

According to one account from that period, the Chiapas uprising energized the workers in the nonofficial unions. As a result, these unions made a large-scale mobilization in Mexico City, on January 7, 1994, distracting the army and its "Iron Circle" in Chiapas. On January 12, 1994, students joined the trade unionists in a huge march from the Monument of the Revolution to the Zocalo, demanding an end to the aggression against the Zapatista. Over the next twelve days, the protest spread to electrical workers, teachers, and autoworkers. Over the next year, the Zapatista tried to capitalize on this support, holding three major meetings. This initiative, however, failed. Given the differences among the groups involved, no real alliance came about, and the state felt emboldened enough to go back on the terms of the San Andreas Peace Accords and give free rein to the landlords' thugs and militias. This betrayal in turn produced another set of demonstrations in 1998.[9] Looking at this dynamic a bit more closely, one wonders where did the recent generation of Mexican workers in these nonofficial unions come from? Presumably, they came from all parts of the country, but given the great extrusion out of the South of poor workers, one might surmise that many southern-originated people are now living and working in the North and that the Southern Question, here to use a "classical" Gramscian formulation, is now partly existing on the streets of Mexico City in these unions.[10]

Do the Zapatista really represent a strong example of an NSM? Let us consider what the New Liberals have been claiming. For the New Liberals, the story of the Zapatista is one of a subalternized people awakened and led by an urban intellectual, Sub-Commandante Marcos. The Zapatista movement's Indianness makes it clear it is identity based, the fact that it arose at the time of the North American Free Trade Agreement (NAFTA) gives it the kind of link to globalism that NSMs often have, and finally the Zapatista movement fits into the model of global and local. It has supporters around the world, these supporters linked together through the Internet, but it is located essentially in a localized periphery, both in the sense of the periphery of the world market and even of the periphery of Mexico. It is only in a derivative sense Mexican in this reading.

Neoliberalism—for example, the "Neo-Gramscian" trend—then claims that the Zapatista are subalterns as well, that is, their movement is from outside of history, a movement held together by its primordial culture.[11] If this reading is accurate, then much else follows. For example, their members would not be able to speak for themselves. The function of the (outside) intellectual involved in the Zapatista struggle would become one of speaking for them—even "translating" for them, perhaps even mediating for them.

Stephen Gill, an influential writer in international relations and a leading Neo-Gramscian, has claimed in some of his recent writings that movements demanding human rights, such as the Zapatista, make sense because the atmosphere of globalism (thanks to the United States) is so suffused today with democracy that it inspires others to assert themselves.[12] According to Gill, the United States, though in a certain sense an imperialist country, is not simply another traditional hegemon but something altogether new, a great power creating a system based on worldwide consent. Gill likens the rise of the American neoliberal hegemony of the 1970s to the birth of a new mode of production. Gramsci, he recalls, wrote about an old order dying and "a new one struggling to be born." Like Gramsci in the 1920s, the Neo-Gramscian IPE (international political economy) writers today see themselves participating in another era of great change, Gramsci's career serving as a kind of model for today's liberals.

For Gill, what transpired in the half century after Gramsci's death was a disaffection of the masses, especially in the years of the Great Depression, and a turn on the part of the states toward coercion and Fascism. Contrast this with the one in which we live today, where world hegemony is based in the United States, radiating in many directions through a shared belief in rule by law, democratic values, and the market, somewhat analogous to Gramsci's "new mode of production." Gill, however, unlike Gramsci, moves the discussion of politics beyond the level of the nation-state to the level of the empire. There are nation-states and then there is a democratic overlay of shared values beyond any one nation-state, one that could be termed the empire of democracy. Another important difference between the two is that for Gill, politics is top-down. Class conflict and the struggles of peoples oppressed by democracy are not important given where history is moving.

Adam David Morton, another writer of note in the IR/IPE tradition, follows rather similar lines to Gill but reaches slightly different conclusions. Morton dates the emergence of this Gramscian-inspired New Liberal IPE analysis back to the 1980s, to the days of the early antiglobalization movement. The main IPE writers assume, according to Morton, that

> globalization, in addition to a shift from Keynesianism to neo-liberalism at the ideological level, can be defined as the transnationalization of production and finance. A neo-Gramscian analysis of it would likely lead one to conclude that such a large change in the structure of production would lead to the emergence of new collective actors, i.e. transnational social forces of capital and labor. Within the EU, for example, transnational capital promotes a compromise of "embedded neo-liberalism." It (the EU)

is pre-dominantly based on neo-liberalism, but it also includes mercantilist aspects to attract capital fractions, which concentrate on the European
market and which would prefer protection against global competition.[13]

In discussing the potential role that subaltern New Social Movements
might play in the globalized world, Morton notes in the same context that
for IPE analysis, "a Neo-Gramscian perspective might analyze empirically
how certain social forces have attempted to construct hegemonic projects
through neo-liberal globalization and how these have been contested by
subaltern classes. This is obviously a fairly broad subject, one encompass-
ing how the interests of transnational capital, stemming from changes in
the social relations of production, have been internalized within particular
forms of the state to thus configure state–civil society relations and cir-
cumscribe the activities of subaltern groups." Such a framework, according
to Morton, "could then also lead one to consider associated questions of
resistance. For example, how changing forms and relations of production
embodied by neo-liberal globalization lead to a recomposition of state-civil
relations generating new structures of exploitation, forms of class consciousness, modes of resistance and class struggle." Horizontal contradictions
among elites in Western power centers create ripple effects that subaltern
populations such as the Zapatista get caught up in and react to.

THE ZAPATISTA AND THE RISE OF THE RICH

In some ways, despite their use of New Liberal vocabulary, Gill and Morton are not too far from the political economy–type conclusions of the sort
hypothesized here. The difference is, as has been noted, one of epistemology. Epistemology drives assumptions, questions, and ways of inquiring.
Here the differences sharpen.

Starting from the Rise of the Rich, one might think, for example, that
it really is not necessary to try to find some ironclad connection linking
the rise of the Zapatista to the passage of NAFTA, as most NSM analysts
insist on doing. The Zapatista might be more easily understood as a part of
the long-term crisis around the land question, and NAFTA for them was a
coincidence. Indeed, when one looks more closely, the connection between

the Zapatista and NAFTA does not seem terribly certain. Although the passage of NAFTA led directly to the Zapatista movement in a temporal sense, the deeper causality behind the movement—here just to stay even on the level of transnational capital—might well lead one to place more weight on the decisions in the world coffee industry, decisions that were having more of an effect in Chiapas than was NAFTA per se. Coffee prices had been declining worldwide over a number of years, and this decline was being used as leverage against the local population in Chiapas by the plantation owners and behind them the cartel owners. This tactic seems to have spurred the uprising. NAFTA, initially at least, had more impact, here by way of contrast, on the labor market of the North of Mexico. Oil exploration in eastern Chiapas might also have been a factor. It too had no precise relation to NAFTA, but it did relate to the land question in Chiapas. Herein may lie a problem for global analysis: the dynamics of globalism may or may not be very useful in explaining what is happening "locally" unless it can incorporate other factors into its analysis.

Still, it is unwarranted to dismiss NSM analysis, as many liberal and Marxist writers do, as being entirely unhistorical. A certain reading of modern history by writers in the IPE tradition in fact bolsters its interpretation. This is true on the level of its general analysis of history as well as on the level of its more specific analysis of the Zapatista. Neoliberalism, Gill wrote, began in the Third World with the Pinochet Coup in 1973 in Chile. What makes this event a watershed has to do with the new role of the Third World army at that point. In the late nineteenth century, when countries such as India and Egypt were being changed to free-market economies by imperialism, their armies were weak but nationalistically inclined and therefore had to be neutralized. A century later, the army in the case of Chile was quite strong, but it was open to the highest bidder. Following 1973 one could generalize this last point and claim that the army as an institution in the Third World served the highest bidder. Gill's point of entrance here, it might be noted, allows him to assert the newness of globalism.

It follows that the United States in 1973 could not have played the same role that Britain did in the nineteenth century. Both countries exerted their power through multilateral relations; the United States, however, had a spiritual power that England did not have. No doubt this is Gill's major point. Democratic ideology ties many people to the philosophy of the United States, giving its acts added legitimacy. Although this point may be true, there is left unexplored the possibility that the British Empire, notable for its long life, may also have enjoyed such prestige as well.

IPE, like other contemporary forms of liberalism, is thus not necessarily proimperialist; its practitioners simply try to explain American imperialism as they see it. Thus, Gill, despite his attraction to American policy, does not see the New World Order as something inherently harmonious. He suggests there are major distributional issues, even contradictions. For example, there is a contradiction in New Liberal logic between the promise of an expanding pie and the reality of a declining ecology out of which this pie is to be renewed and expanded. In recent times this contradiction manifests itself as a conflict between the American and the Third Way capitalism of Japan and Germany. Then there is the contradiction between democracy and big capitalism as manifested in the anti–World Trade Organization protests. One contradiction not emphasized by Gill, however, is class conflict.

Is the Zapatista movement more a New Social Movement or more a part of the historic Southern Question of Mexico? This issue is the paradigm question in its absolutely sharpest form. For the Rise of the Rich, a globalist analysis of the Zapatista may well be a coherent one but not one that allows history to play any pronounced role, here to allude to the problem of epistemological narrowness. *Internal colonialism* is Morton's term, but like *subalternity,* it still begs the question of class struggle in history. What is one to make of the long-term political struggle against the oppression of the southern part of the country on the part of a peasantry trying to hold on to its land, what of the long-term use of the Indian population from that region by capitalists in the North of the country in harvest seasons, and finally what of the long-term concentration of modern-style institutions in the North of the country? None of these things finds a place in a New Social Movement type of analysis, even one cast in terms of internal colonialism. In becoming a New Social Movement, today's Zapatista—to repeat a point made earlier—lose their link even with Emiliano Zapata, their namesake, a peasant leader of the Mexican Revolution. What they become is, on the on the one hand, a part of the present and, on the other, a part of the timeless past, but not of the historical past. If Chiapas is understood to be a victim of internal colonialism, this would have still other meanings. It would mean, for one thing, that the plantation owners had no role in the Mexican political system; they exist simply to take orders from Mexico City. This is definitely not the case.

THE ZAPATISTA AND GRAMSCI IN THE "RED YEARS":
A COMPARISON FOLLOWING THE RISE
OF THE RICH METHODOLOGY

The Rise of the Rich as a methodology relies on being able to find parallels and repetitions. The interpretation of some particular country or historical event loses its persuasiveness if it appears to be unique or different from all others. If the Zapatista movement was looked at in terms of possible comparisons, one possibility would no doubt be the Mexican Revolution, another the "Red Years" in Turin of the early 1920s when Gramsci tried to unite the northern worker with the southern peasant. The events of Turin, like the circumstances of the Mexican Revolution, were part of what scholars call "interrupted revolutions." It is not inconceivable that what is going on in Mexico today around Marcos and Obrador may fall into that category.

What Gramsci managed to do was politicize a small number of workers in Turin, have them control the workplace, and reach out to the migrant laborers in the fields of the Piedmont. While this was still in process, it brought a hysterical reaction from the Italian liberals. The liberals abandoned their belief in rule by law in order to protect their property. Soon they voted in the Fascists, and the Fascists ushered in repression and the destruction of the Left for the next twenty years. Gramsci's strategy, which was in practice a disaster, in theory had not only worked but had revolutionized the world's understanding of politics. In fact, something new had been added to the theory of revolution. Revolution was no longer simply seizing the state, as Lenin had postulated in regards to 1917; it was now a matter of taking it apart and remaking it in order for the revolution to be the revolution one wanted. In hindsight, one might conclude, however, for all Gramsci's theoretical brilliance, his tactical choice of where to begin resisting the Italian state, given the power differential between the Left and the state, was a very poor one.

What Sub-Commandante Marcos, the Zapatista leader, did was begin his campaign in the South. There the weight of numbers, the filter of culture, the remoteness of the region, and the long-term hatred of the state felt by everyone in the region worked for him. In the 1996 demonstration in Puebla, a city in south-central Mexico, he reached out to northern labor; in the 2001 march on Mexico City, he reached out to the Mexican people as a whole. The results so far have been amazing: the fall of the PRI and the dependence of President Fox and now President Calderon on foreign backing.

What will be the outcome in Mexico? The result is of course unknowable, but the way the issue is framed on the level of scholarship certainly leads in quite different directions. Will the success or failure of the Zapatista movement hang on the global support movement through the Internet? Alternatively, will the success or failure of the movement rest on the choices made by the Mexican working class? Will the working class choose to make a deep alliance with the Zapatista this time, or will they buy their own peace, as they did in the Ayala Plan during the Mexican Revolution? To paraphrase the Mexican writer Adolfo Gilly, the revolution could once again be "interrupted." Seize the opportunity now, or watch the Zapatista fragment over issues such as land registration and the hegemony continue as before. Such are the ways the two paradigms diverge.

Since early in the twentieth century, Morton states, the Chiapas region has been inserted in the market, and since that time it has produced a large quantity of crops relative to its size and population.[14] It is a small region that has been producing a greater and greater percentage of Mexico's gross domestic product; thus, one could look at Chiapas in terms of internal colonialism. Colonies are notoriously exploited. So are internal colonies. The term *internal colony* added to the idea of an NSM in this case has the advantage of fitting a particular province of a specific ethnic makeup into a globalist analysis, freeing it from getting bogged down in a discussion of class, region, and hegemony. And this was doubtless the intent.

Ethnicity indeed plays a role in an analysis of the Zapatista movement, as we will now see by following Morton's argument in more detail.[15] Let us do so now, turning to one of his main sources, *Mexico Profundo: Reclaiming a Civilization,* an influential book on the Meso-American identity of modern Mexico, written by the late Guillermo Bonfil Batalla. According to someone following Bonfil Batalla's approach, the Zapatista leadership has tapped into the *indigenismo* sentiment, or *Mexico Profundo*. In so doing, the leadership has affirmed what the state has been hiding for years: the existence of a Mayan substrate underlying modern Mexico. Marcos's appeal comes from this recourse to authenticity. It is not, Morton claims, echoing Bonfil Batalla, that Marcos listens to what the people want, but he responds to what the people are. Something, however, is missing here. What neither Bonfil Batalla nor Morton mention is that an important part of what upholds the idea of the Zapatista as an identity movement as well as the prestige of *Mexico Profundo* is related to the need of the Mexican state to have the Zapatista portrayed that way, the need on the part of the state to isolate the Zapatista from other Mexicans, Bonfil Batalla performing this function as a state intellectual, even posthumously.

This brings up another aspect of the paradigm conflict. Is the identity of the Zapatista, whose description we are familiar with, a product of state cultural strategy, or is it actually what these people are? Here there is a sharp distinction to be drawn. From a political economy perspective, all ruling classes aspire to cultural hegemony; there is nothing special about Mexico in this regard. Scholars caught up in hegemonic projects produce ethnographic images of the sort desired, and these works are valorized. It is something of a leap to then claim, as some New Liberal writers have, that such images actually convey what people really are. If one adopts such a view, there would be no social history, as no government wants a subject people to claim to have history. If the Mexican state in effect can erase the history of a century and a quarter of peasant struggle against the large estates of the South, then not only does it erase a considerable piece of social history, but it also delegitimates those individuals who want to use this history to put forward their claims today. It erases or delegitimates as well the fact of choices made or not made by the working class in the Mexican North to support or not support the Zapatista at different times. Though no doubt such erasure is what the government would like to achieve, there is something paradoxical in the New Liberals being generally sympathetic to the Zapatista but writing their history from a government point of view.

Even if there has been an ethnic dimension or an identity dimension in the Zapatista struggle, were historians to base their analysis on it, they would be confusing the use of a cultural strategy in the struggle with the struggle itself. Cultural identity politics anyplace else, if this is what one found, would be recognized as a strategy, not as an explanation for why a struggle is taking place. Why cannot New Liberals see it that way here? Does anyone believe that no Zapatista can speak, they are all subalterns, or that all Zapatista speak only Indian languages, not Spanish, or that there is anything all that unique about their struggle compared to the rest of the struggles going on in the Afro-Asian countryside? Clearly, this direction is where New Liberalism takes us, elucidated however paradoxically by frequent references to the writings of Antonio Gramsci.

What, then, would a political economy analysis look like in this case? A political economy writer would probably begin by assuming that an analysis of the Zapatista movement requires a look at the Mexican state, its attempt to control its people and the resistance of the people that this attempt engenders. The outside world, globalization, and the Internet would be present but all rather secondary. This assumption could be put aside if proved wrong, but for now it is well supported by previous work on Mexico and on other countries.

In such an analysis, Bonfil Batalla's book would obviously have a place. The organization of culture in Mexico, one could hypothesize, exists as it does elsewhere so as to incorporate a range of views that form the terrain of acceptable discourse. The existence of such a terrain would allow the state to define other discourse as unacceptable and therefore as excludable. It would not be surprising, therefore, to find that discourse about Indians and about race in Mexico more generally would have an official Right and an official Left as well as a center and other positions that would doubtless be less well received.

Mainstream Mexican social science would be part of that organization of culture, its interpretations of Indian culture in modern Mexico a part of that official culture. The two most common interpretations of Indian culture found in that mainstream social science are the liberal one (that Indians are a residual category, their last remnants clinging to their identity) and the political economy one (that Indians today are not so much a residual category as they are a group newly constructed each century by the reproduction of the logic of the system, being an Indian becoming a role among others). *Mexico Profundo* is part of the liberal tradition seeing Indianness as a given and not as a construct. If the book differs from other liberal books, it is in giving more weight to Indianness than do other books. From the perspective of political economy *Mexico Profundo* naturally is ahistorical; it interprets race in an essentializing way, missing the key point that race itself is simply part of a larger set of historically contingent and interrelated constructions.[16]

Bonfil Batalla, who might be taken to be on the official Right, at least since the rise of New Liberalism, represents a position that made an unexpected comeback from the fringe of Mexican social theory. Who would have thought this type of nineteenth-century racial ideology had the slightest chance of returning to a position in the mainstream? From the period of the Mexican Revolution until a few years ago, one would not have guessed that it was at all likely. Since the period of the Mexican Revolution, for most mainstream scholars the idea of Indians as a distinct racial group had been one that was rejected in favor of the theory of *Mestiaje*. And though *Mestiaje*, the idea of the Mexican people as a mixture of European and Indian, is still today the dominant trend, there now appear to be elements in the state anxious to downplay the idea of mixture, as it carries with it the idea of an expanded Mexican citizenry and by extension the idea of expanded social entitlements.

In *Mexico Profundo*, Bonfil Batalla looked at what he termed the phenomenon of *indigenismo* and characterized it in a nineteenth-century way as a battle of racial survival, a battle of two enemies, the Indian and the Westerner. In a sense it was a variant of *Criollism*. Where the *Criollistas* at one time were concerned with the preservation of "European" blood in Mexico, *Mexico Profundo* created a space for a concern with Indianness. And while one might agree with Bonfil Batalla that in Mexican history there were some conflicts that ran along such lines—for instance, the Caste Wars—the larger picture as regards race and politics, most would insist, and correctly so, was that of *Mestiaje,* or a mixing of racial backgrounds, not of race wars. For Bonfil Batalla, it was otherwise; ethnicity and culture were racially fixed. *Mestiaje* was a socialist myth. Following the paradigm of *Mexico Profundo* the sudden rise of an oppositional movement such as the Zapatista could now be looked at by the state not as an oppositional movement, which is what it is, but as a New Social Movement, one arising out of a timeless subaltern culture.

Cultural hegemony—here to continue the presentation of political economy—not only accommodates a spectrum of views but also reinforces one central position. As the Mexican regime moved to the right, this spectrum also moved to the right. By the 1970s, though one might note signs of a challenge to the position of *Mestiaje* in the idea of the Indian as rural and southern, this seemed very imprecise. The problem with such a view from any commonsense perspective, theoretical issues aside, was that it could scarcely account for the fact of the permanent migration of large numbers of Indians to cities such as Mexico City.

Indeed, as early as World War II, a commonsense view of Mexico City would note the Indian Question. It was apparent to anyone walking along the streets. With the rise of New Liberalism, however, came a generation of politicians and scholars who set out to ignore that fact and to portray the city on a basis closer to their perceptions. From that point scholarship, both Mexican and Western, began to claim that the city was a center of globalized modernity and thus by extension of non-Indianness and of "non-Southness." The several million Indians along with the others who happened to live on the city streets were as a result an anomaly, if not an outright contradiction. *Mexico Profundo* fitted with this new scholarship and was thus not surprisingly rediscovered in that context.[17]

Whereas Mexico City may be considered a primate city and a global city, as the foregoing suggests, this fact does not reveal the actual role the city plays in Mexican politics. Since World War II at least, Mexico City has increasingly been part of the Southern Question as a result of internal migration. Looked at in a classical Gramscian mirror, Mexico City, like Rome, São Paolo, or Cairo or other such major cities, appears bifurcated in a complex way along North-South lines. Less a discrete entity standing against the countryside around it, what it appears to be is a great sprawl of humanity, an arena of conflict in which the nation as a whole is present in a condensed form, regionalism brought to the city by the migrants, some of whom are southern. Following this line of interpretation, urban studies, in order to fulfill the requirements of a political economy analysis, would need to be drawn from a field such as political geography. Although there are barrios and other official divisions in the city, overriding this layout is a political geography of North-South, a reality revealed somewhat along class lines, somewhat along cultural lines, as well as occupational and linguistic lines. Northerners enter the city for education and white-collar jobs. Southerners migrate, becoming construction workers, street peddlers, or maids in the city. As a result, over time the institutions of the city—the school, government ministries, the police, armed forces, and media—have come to serve as a meeting ground for these two regions, functioning in a way like the borderland provinces dividing the North and South in the country as a whole. In the years since the 1970s, the population of Mexico City has mushroomed, with poor migrant southerners making up a greater and greater percentage. This point raises all the more urgently questions about the adequacy of the model of Mexico City as a "primate" or a "global city," as one finds in the dominant paradigm.

Another point enters the discussion here as well. Mexico City has absorbed most of the resources of the country in the past few generations. This fact has been sometimes politically a source of pride and sometimes a liability to the ruling class. State intellectuals have tried to naturalize this fact, suggesting that Mexico City is the "center" and the seat of high culture, whereas the countryside is the "periphery," a region typified by its popular culture, that these circumstances are simply matters of fate, that they are thus beyond judgment and so someone objecting to the distribution of rewards has no case. At the same time, it is pointed out that different parts of the so-called periphery are not all of a piece. Some parts are from one point of view or another on a higher level than are others. In fact, the periphery is filled with pockets of growth and "modernization" as well as of stagnation and backwardness. However, as noted, an inventory of the areas characterized in the hegemonic discourse as pockets of growth and progress would be composed of areas largely in the North. And, not surprisingly, according to the same hegemonic discourse, it is such areas with their "greater cultural strivings" that most deserve the help and benefits given out by the state. Such areas are the more energetic, more hopeful. The South, on the other hand, perhaps because of benign neglect in the past, has suffered whole populations to be uprooted for lack of work, masses of people forced as a result to make their living through seasonal migration. It is the South, such observers would note, that has needed the presence of the army and the police the most, the reason cultural as much as anything else. Indian culture has violent features. In the South one finds rampant vendettas and feuds that must be controlled. If the South lags behind, it is the fault not of the state but rather of the southern culture; if the soil in the South is worn out, again it is no one's fault in particular.[18]

The fact or at least the likelihood that Mexico has a Southern Question is not an easy or painless insight to come to, even for someone in the political economy tradition. It is in fact controversial. It goes against the way academic knowledge has been developed and organized, not just the discourse on race but all academic knowledge. For example, anthropologists and historians have long divided the study of twentieth-century Mexico in a particular way: the South was for anthropologists, the North for historians. This division has meant in effect that most events considered historical are found in the North, whereas the South appears simply as a part of culture. This view prevailed in some sense long before the writing of *Mexico Profundo* or the rise of the Zapatista, and it remains today.

The field of geography contributes to this tableau as well.[19] When one looks at the approach used by a number of well-known geographers of Mexico, one finds that the study of the region is often the same thing as the study of the province. Of course, there are good technical reasons to proceed this way. Researchers clearly benefit from making use of the provincial archives located in the capital cities of the various provinces. At the same time, there are contexts in which provincial studies in geography serve to obscure the actual politics. For example, in the study of a province such as Veracruz, the geographer encounters two very different dynamics: the Indian peasant growing coffee (fitting with the South) and the modern oil industry of PEMEX and of its union (tied to the North). This dissimilarity does not invalidate Veracruz studies as a unit of analysis, but it points toward something that is lacking, from a political economy point of view: a national political geography, a field that would relate region and nation, crosscutting the existing provinces where necessary, a field overcoming the divisions existing between geography and political economy, anthropology and political economy, urban studies and political economy, and so forth, here to recall the discussion about Mexico City.

What a national political geography might show is not just the existence of a "North" and a "South" but the existence of "contested" states as well. If, for example, in Veracruz one finds the juxtaposition of different social formations located in different parts of the same province, in a province such as Morelos one finds a protracted struggle over which of the two different formations will prevail and will then define the province. Struggle seems to go on for generations. A national political geography would make such provinces as Morelos, that is, contested provinces, stand out. They would become important because it would become apparent that they serve as the borders of North and South. One could surmise that if the struggle in these areas was to continue and the provincial hegemony was to remain weak as a result, another Zapata in Morelos or another Lucio Cabanas in Guerrero could be born and develop, the borderlands still being potentially the cradle of the leadership of counterhegemony.

Having looked at New Liberal Politics as it applies to the West and to the Third World in contemporary history, one might now ask how does New Liberal Politics deal with the history of the early modern period? This topic leads us to look at recent works in IR, as they have become important to the development of the New Politics paradigm in such areas.

NEW POLITICS, IR, AND THE CRITIQUE OF WESTPHALIANISM

In the previous chapter, it was noted that New Liberals periodize world history around trade routes, contacts, and civilizations. Earlier in this chapter this point led to some brief comments about the New Liberal critique of Westphalianism. What is meant by the critique of Westphalianism? As will now be shown, this subject is in fact large, much larger than is suggested by the use of the term *critique*. It is, in fact, the key to understanding the New Liberal view of early modern history.

In a recent article two professors of international relations, John M. Hobson and J. C. Sharman, make a closely argued critique of the idea of the 1648 watershed of "Westphalian sovereignty" and relatedly of the link between contemporary political history and the nation-state in favor of an approach assuming a more long-term buildup to the contemporary world, one marked by more of an emphasis on empires and, in the process, calling into question the long-term assumption that one finds either nation-state sovereignty or anarchy.[20] This new line of thought clearly speaks for a growing constituency of scholars, among them world historians as well as others influenced by New Liberalism.

Hobson and Sharman argue that the nation-state sovereignty versus anarchy distinction explains very little about actual political order in history; rather, what should be considered as being potentially more fruitful is the study of imperial hierarchies. In other words, one needs to get beyond the nation-state in terms of how one understands early modern and indeed modern history, the focus on the nation-state obscuring for scholars the fact that since the seventeenth century much of mankind has lived in empires rather than states and that the existence of these empires, if anything, tended to block the spread of the nation-state-type sovereignty. The authors put forward as evidence for this last point information about the variants of European colonial protectorates, condominiums, and Chartered Companies, which they characterize as "half-way sovereign arrangements" within an imperial context.

Political economy and especially the Rise of the Rich would take the opposite view. Before the nineteenth century, international class interests sometimes dictated arrangements other than national sovereignty. If there was no pressure to uphold nation-state interests from within a given country, the ruler would be free to go along with these other arrangements if he wanted to. As a result, if rulers were not pushed into seeking independence, states might remain imperial provinces or colonies for centuries unless and until they were driven by popular pressures to assert a national-type sovereignty. As the next chapter will show, mercantilist regimes, or at least their rulers, could often thrive in an imperial context. As capitalism developed, however, and as the system of national markets became more prevalent, this situation changed, the nation-state becoming the more conventional political unit. The question New Liberals ask, however, is why one should write history predicated on the idea of national sovereignty when national sovereignty did not yet exist. This position is, however, a bit extreme. Given the power possessed by people, a country, even one that may have been in a disassembled form such as a colony or an imperial province, would still be an entity defined by its hegemony and counterhegemony, regardless of whether the country's sovereignty was acknowledged on a piece of paper; this situation existed as far back as early modern history. Thus, it is not unreasonable to start with the expectation that the national roots of modern countries emerged in this period and require study. Here the elitism of liberalism, if not its Eurocentrism, is an obstacle.

ORTHODOX MARXISM: ITS POLITICS AND HISTORY, ITS VIEWS ON EMPIRES AND ON GRAMSCIAN INTERPRETATIONS, ITS CONTRIBUTION TO THE CRISIS OF SOCIAL THEORY

As noted in the preceding chapter, some of the most useful work of contemporary Marxism takes the form of critique writing, and a good deal of that critique bears on the liberal defense of the contemporary status quo. To illustrate this point, in this section I will survey a recent book by a well-established author debunking the New Liberal idea of history as empire history. I will then look at this same book in terms of where it suggests contemporary Marxism is in relationship to the longer history of Marxism. If at first the book seemed simply like a useful work of critique, now it seems like a book fairly close to the old narrow orthodoxy. This becomes especially apparent when one looks closely at the author's use of Marx. The relevant Marx, we discover, is the Marx of *Capital,* the work of the "mature" Marx and the main work of "classical Marxism." Marx's political career and his political writings that had come earlier are not only irrelevant to this mature or classical Marx but somehow seen to be incompatible with it. Here, obviously, is a crisis. Marxism today can absorb only a small part of what Marx wrote. Frustrated with this state of affairs, we will then turn to consider the prospects for renovation in Marxist thought, turning to the writings of Antonio Gramsci.

Marxism and the Critique of Empire History

Empire of Capital is a recent work by the well-known American Marxist Ellen Meiksins Wood. Wood says she wrote the book to address the growing tendency in New Liberal thought to make empires eternal and natural or essential to the West or to capitalism, thereby diminishing the rather unprecedented features of the present-day American imperial venture. Wood argues that the only systematic way to study empires is in terms of the mode of production of the period in which the empire played an important role. Superficial similarities between the Roman Empire and the British Empire are just that and nothing more. This reliance on superficial similarities is the wrong way to proceed. It legitimates imperialism as something natural and timeless. Much of the book is spent working through these points, the subject having obvious relevance to the field of world history.

To establish the historicity of empires and their dependence on the prevailing mode of production, Wood not surprisingly takes up the issue of the transition from feudalism to capitalism. She proceeds to show that feudal empires differed from capitalist ones. They were on different sides of a watershed. She argues that the transition to capitalism was characterized by an enormous rupture in history, marked by the emancipation of economic forces from extraeconomic forces.[21] An imperialist of the one sort might be a crusader, whereas an imperialist of the other could be a pioneer businessman. Clearly, the two are different, although how categorical the difference of course might not always be that clear. Overall, however, Wood's book should be rated as a well-thought-out engagement with New Liberal politics.

Turning now from this set of observations about *Empire of Capital* to the issue of the location of this book within Marxism, questions suddenly arise. Given that Wood's book is a study of history, what one might have expected to find would have been some reference to Marx's political and historical writings; what one in fact finds are references to *Capital*. But why should anyone represent Marx's theory of history simply from *Capital*, as Wood does (and as in fact many other contemporary Marxists do)? *Capital* contains an account of history as it relates to capitalism, but it is not a history book. Doing so implies separating what Marx did and wrote into various rather rigid time frames. When Marx arrived in England and sat down to write *Capital* he never repudiated his past work on history, politics, philosophy, and other fields, works that he had written while he was still on the Continent before 1848. To rely solely on *Capital*, therefore, without reference to his past writings or his future writings, which appears to be what Wood is doing, is a modern political choice, not a choice that Marx himself made. However, useful or not this choice may be in terms of the subject at hand or even in understanding Marx—and this is a matter of perspective—it has clearly left many Marxists unprepared for the actual course of events taking place around them. For example, those individuals who relied simply on *Capital* were shocked by the location of the Russian Revolution on the periphery where capitalism was weak; they had expected the revolution to be in the advanced industrial countries, as those nations were where the working class was supposed to be strong and where therefore socialism was supposed to emerge. The idea of a revolution coming at what Lenin called the "weak link of capitalism" not only was then a surprise, but it appeared to call into question the prevailing interpretation of the meaning of the political struggle that had gone on in Western Europe in all the preceding years. In more recent times, those individuals who have relied simply on *Capital* have been surprised by the deindustrialization of the core and the reformulation of the proletariat in erstwhile Third World countries as a result of the internationalization of the economy. Finally, those individuals who relied simply on *Capital* were shocked that the reserve industrial army of extra workers continued to grow at such a rate. How could one explain the fact that such large numbers of people have been uprooted, especially in the Third World, and have swarmed into the cities, casual labor dwarfing the official working class, making a mockery of the older idea of a reserve industrial army existing in tandem with the official working class. Thus, we find in current usage terms such as *casualization* or the *end of the working class*, terms as much a part of the liberal tradition as of Marxism, terms that certainly do not jibe very well with *Capital*.

This point leads to still other questions. Under contemporary conditions, is the organized working class still the vanguard of the proletariat, or is it simply a group of people no longer the vanguard of anything who are nervously holding on to their status? Contemporary Marxist historians such as Leften Stavrianos and Eric Hobsbawm, among others and certainly not just Wood alone, have had difficulties with these issues.[22] Philosophers

such as Louis Althusser, who defended the 1848 rupture approach to reading Marx, have not successfully addressed these issues either.[23]

Marxism, as this discussion implies, has grown rather narrow. The very
limited use of Marx's own writings is symptomatic of this narrowness. In
short, Marxists have not been able to keep up with Marx, much less their
own world. Beginning in the 1970s there was the problem of how to bury
Stalin and the Russian Revolution, and to free Marxism from the Soviet
Union. Following the capital flight of the 1970s, Marxists began to face a
different set of crises. From this point, it was obvious that the oppressed
classes were much more fragmented than they had been before. As a result,
the issue of their diversity as opposed to their commonalty began to stand
out. What was wanted, especially by many in the younger generation in
Europe and the United States, was a materialism that addressed diversity,
one that would therefore be clear in materialist terms about race, gender,
age, and so on. Marxists failed to provide it. The writer who came the closest to fulfilling the demands of the age was the leftish French philosopher
Michel Foucault. In the 1980s his works were much more influential than
were the studies of the more orthodox writers of the Left. Governmentality,
his master concept, which was so all-embracing it in effect lacked a dynamic
of change, fitted with its times, resonating with the feelings of despair of
the new generation that was emerging in the actual year of 1984.[24] To that
generation, the historical process did not seem so important, as the future
did not seem to be leading anywhere. What Foucault offered was more
credible than what the prevailing political economy did, and perhaps it was
even more materialist. Progressive struggle could come from anywhere and
be either larger or small. This notion was very liberating for many who
dreaded waiting for a trade union bureaucracy or a political party or some
other such large organization to embrace their issue.

Finally, if Western Marxism had grown rigid, what then of Third World
Marxism? Third World Marxism has always been an important force in
its own right; on occasion it has influenced Western Marxism and Western ideas of world history. How has Third World Marxism fared in recent
times? Did Third World Marxism escape the problem of the narrowness that
befell Western Marxism? The answer seems to be no. Third World Marxism as represented in this period by the Egyptian economist Samir Amin,

among others, argues that accumulation in the sense of unequal trade or even plunder underlay the prosperity of the core in relation to the periphery. And here Amin means the core and only the core. This position led to debates over primitive accumulation. Most Marxists continued to dispute the importance of accumulation to modern capitalism, viewing accumulation as "primitive accumulation," that is, as something that had ended with the abolition of the slave trade following the Industrial Revolution. Western Marxists in particular disputed Amin's claim about unequal exchange: that the Third World worker is exploited by virtue of his being paid less than the Western worker. They argue that the Western worker by virtue of his use of advanced technology is worth more to his employer because technology made this worker more productive and thus he deserves to be paid more than a Third World worker, that pay differential has a logic rooted not in theft but in productivity. However, as history has shown, they lived to regret this argument. The internationalization of the economy resulted in the replication of comparable forms of production in a number of different countries, some of which were in the Third World. The question thus remained: why not equal pay for equal work? At that point dominant strands in Western Marxism began to adopt the liberal view of the "end of the Third World," against the theoretical and empirical arguments of Third World Marxism that the periphery lived on, as evidenced by the wage structure and continuing imperialism of the West. In rejecting these rather essential points, Western Marxism drew ever closer to liberalism and ever more narrow; Third World Marxism remained, in an objective sense, Eurocentric.

Problems in Western Marxism—to return now to an earlier point—had been building over a long period of time. As early as the 1870s, Western Marxists had become aware that the colonial working class was competing with the Western working class. At that point, tied as they were to the European trade union movement, Western Marxists found it strategic to drop the labor theory of value. They began to express doubt that one could compare the value of cotton produced in Egypt with the value of cotton produced in a Western country. In hindsight, what became apparent was that by dropping the labor theory of value, for all intents and purposes Marxism had to give up the dialectic. Thereafter, although the dialectic was sometimes invoked on the occasion of a strike by some trade union,

Marxism as a whole had become nearly as positivist as liberalism. This is where matters stood in a theoretical sense from World War I onward. Even in the heyday of the Non-Aligned Movement, Third World Marxists were not up to the challenge of reintroducing the original concepts to revive the tradition. They too had their ties to trade unions. They too preferred the dialectic be confined to strike history. They too in effect accepted positivism.

Gramsci in a Contemporary Marxist Mirror

This leads to the question, what happened to the attempts of those individuals and groups that did try to renovate Marxism? To look into this question, one might do well to consider the fate of Gramsci in Fourth International thought. In Fourth International thought, as is well known, Gramsci was ignored for many years altogether and then picked up rather casually after World War II and read with an eye to existing orthodoxies.[25]

Representing New Left Marxism of the 1970s, Perry Anderson, the editor of the *New Left Review,* claimed that despite his precocious insights about Fordism, Gramsci's utility was essentially limited to his period and that his writing looked at on a theoretical level was filled with contradictions. A decade later Stuart Hall, a figure who was less part of the orthodoxy than was Perry Anderson, found otherwise. Hall's early works on Thatcher's Britain thus served to popularize a somewhat wider range of Gramsci's key concepts, from hegemony, to common sense, to national-popular. Hall and more pointedly the American Gramsci specialist Carl Boggs have both noted the rather considerable irony of Marxism arising as a political movement, allowing thereafter for little or no politics in its theorization, Gramsci excepted.[26] To add to the irony, a survey of what has been written about Gramsci in English in recent years would suggest that a good deal of it was written on the assumption that Gramsci was useful for New Liberalism. It even appears in many cases to have been written by New Liberals, as this chapter has already shown.

Looking back, it would appear that Gramsci entered into Marxist theory, broke with the prevailing positivism and Eurocentrism as Marx himself had done, but then found himself marginalized for doing so by

"Marxists" who were still in fact Hegelians.[27] Seventy-five years later, it is as if Gramsci's prison experience has yet to end. One might recall here Marx's famous quip that he was not a Marxist. This would apply to Gramsci; he was not a Gramscian.

It is perhaps therefore not surprising to find that much of the commentary on Gramsci today assumes that his analysis of hegemony was the same as the analysis of the superstructure. For this reason commentators refer to Gramsci as the theorist of the superstructure or as a political Marxist. This characterization, however, is imprecise on a number of accounts. It is imprecise because of his theorization of modern capitalism, which gets left out. It is imprecise as well because in fact Gramsci stands out as the only Marxist theorist who overcame the dichotomy, which is implied in base-superstructure analysis, and thus he is not at all a theorist of the superstructure. Finally, it is imprecise because it really tells us more about the denial of the role of politics in standard Marxism than anything about Gramsci.

In sum, if Marxists had read Gramsci more on his own terms and less in terms of Soviet ideas about orthodoxy, accepting the fact that some aspects of his theory remain undeveloped, one could see how Marxism might have kept developing. After all, we still live in nation-states. The question of how the nation-states work and how they cooperate with each other still remains to be clarified. Marxists are remiss in not pursuing this line of inquiry.[28]

An example or two would help make this point clear. Let us take up the issue of the form of hegemony of the nation-state as a factor in geopolitics and world history, doing so by focusing on how different forms of hegemony legitimate their international alliances. Here one begins to see a part of what could be a reformulation of Marxism in the works. What sort of hegemony-based legitimation underlies the strongest and longest-running alliance among states in the modern world? If one knew that one could begin to sort out the question of power within the Rich, one would be a bit closer to understanding what is meant by multilateralism and much else. This question is at least two questions—first, what is the strongest such alliance, and, second, why is it so strong and so long-lasting? Concerning the first, one is more than likely to conclude that it is the alliance uniting the bourgeois democracies, in other words, it is an alliance involving the United States and the UK, among some half-dozen other countries. Several bodies of evidence suggest this may be the case; many researchers—albeit perhaps not Marxists—might take it at this point almost for granted. Anglo-Americanism, for example, is a theme that has long found acceptance among researchers in fields such as U.S. history and British history, and not accidentally so, for, indeed, it often seems to be the case that if a politician in the United States or the UK or for that matter in any other democracy wants a war, all he needs to do is proclaim the need for it, as he can assume there will be an alliance to support it once it gets going. It would suffice if he alluded to the notion that his fellow citizens plus a few others are "Westerners" or Chosen People, while the rest of the world's people are not. Is it not the case that the rest of the world lives in dictatorships? Do people in such countries as Iraq or Syria, for example, respect freedom or the value of human life? Is it not the case that one must fight for one's values or risk their loss? Is not the only thing we have to fear, fear itself? This rhetorical appeal usually suffices. People in this handful of countries seem to spontaneously rally "to make the world safe for democracy." Given that one is appealing to their identity and not simply their material interests, a "threat" to one is perceived to be a threat to all, the dimension of class collusion, if there is such a thing, rendered invisible. Democracy, it would seem, is thus the ideal war-based economy; perhaps this explains its strength.

The reader may at this point be wondering, what is it that has been presented? Clearly, this is not a line of thought typical of today's political economy. Today's political economy, like today's liberalism, is either "high theory" or empiricism. By way of contrast, what was just presented was an example of middle-level inferential reasoning. There is a great deal of evidence that would support those propositions, but ultimately such evidence would never pass muster from a classical empiricist perspective nor from a high theorist's perspective. The point being introduced here is the following: a wider materialism would welcome this kind of middle-level historical sociology; a narrower one probably would not. Point number two: the reformulation of Marxism depends on a wider materialism.[29]

Let us expand this discussion with another example. Let us proceed now to consider the "Russian Road" or "state-centered" form of hegemony and how it fits into the Rise of the Rich. In doing so, let us use Western or American thought on the subject as a familiar shortcut. Western thought, as is well known, typically regards the Russian Road hegemony system of rule as totalitarian and thus evil. It thus takes little effort for an American politician to remind his constituency that if the state assumes the responsibility for an individual, then the individual can never develop as a moral and free person, and that this will have permanent political if not theological consequences. Statism is therefore something to be resisted as evil and not appeased. Examples of this evil are to be found in what befell innocent Chechnya at the hands of totalitarian Russia and innocent Kuwait at the hands of totalitarian Iraq. Other examples where politicians mobilized such sentiment could be drawn from the conflicts between the United States and Japan, the United States and Russia, the United States and Iran, and the United States and Nicaragua. And it should also be remembered that Russian Road–regime politicians there and elsewhere could also evoke popular reactions to the "threat" posed by the West and use such sentiments for their purposes, and this they have been doing.

Tribal-ethnic states, looked at from the perspective of democracies, are, by way of contrast, "primitive," meaning they are not science centered. Although primitivism may have a place in art, in politics and economy it has a somewhat negative connotation in the democratic imaginary. It tends to mean nonstate, therefore nonpeople. Tribal-ethnic states are thus imagined to be barely states, always on the verge of collapsing into nothing. The West Bank Palestinians come to mind as a contemporary example. What if an American politician wanted to control the resources of such a country? Could he not term what he was undertaking a matter of foreign aid or a matter of introducing civilization, given the prevailing assumptions?

Moreover, given the power of the democratic bloc in the modern world, the rulers of tribal-ethnic states, for their part, frequently benefit from a hegemonic form making them appear to be primitive and weak and in need of foreign aid. At the very least, it helps them disguise their own class interests, as primitivism and weakness do not convey the idea of responsibility for what is actually transpiring. Consequently, it is not surprising to find that the most common way a tribal-ethnic state enters international politics is when its ruling class selects a great power and grants it unlimited access to its labor market and to its raw minerals in return for the protection and enrichment of this class. The claim that will be made is that the weak and primitive need protectors and guides. The emphasis in the local media in such a country, however, is not on this interclass agreement but on the relations between the two rulers or among powerful individuals. It is personalized. In the case of powerful tribal-ethnic states, the terms of the agreement give some space for local imperialism, such as in the Saudi-U.S. or Taiwan-U.S. relationship. In the first case, this relationship gives some space for Wahhabi imperialism throughout the Middle East alongside that of American imperialism. Given the power of a country such as Saudi Arabia, when Americans live there, they live together as a tribe in their designated area, thereby conforming to the local hegemonic logic. Elsewhere, this would not be the case. Sometimes the mere participation of tribal-ethnic states in alliances with great powers is enough to trigger crises and even wars. If a tribal-ethnic state grows weak, and its ruling-class coalition starts to splinter, different segments of the coalition, each seeking to assert their own power, might make overtures to different great powers, giving the impression that the country is going to be in their sphere of influence. At this point, there could be a crisis. One could cite examples of such crises in the Balkans, the Congo, Vietnam, and Korea, where collisions or near collisions among the great powers sometimes even led to war. Sometimes, here to continue with the discussion of international relations, tribal-ethnic states eschew alliances with any one great power and enter the international arena by proclaiming their neutrality, as in the case of Switzerland and Finland. Lebanon tried this tactic for a while as well.

Democracies tend to regard "Italian Road" states, countries such as Italy, Mexico, and Egypt, as corrupt. The rulers of these countries find that they can use this characterization to their advantage. They can present themselves as good bargainers, and there is clearly some benefit in being a good bargainer. Russian Road states and tribal-ethnic states do not have this advantage. Italian Road relations to the bourgeois democracies are ambivalent, including both attraction and defensiveness. Not uncommonly, Italian Road politicians portray their countries as democratic but threatened by American imperialism. This depiction serves domestically to unite the society. It is therefore an adroit move. Even if these countries are often criticized, they are generally successful in their dealings, receiving large numbers of Western tourists and considerable business investment. It is adroit as well because democracies need to project the idea of corruption so they can benefit by fulfilling the other countries' needs.

• • •

SO FAR I have argued that a narrowness has crept into social thought, creating a crisis situation. In world history this crisis manifests itself in the continuing retention by historians of the Rise of the West paradigm. In these first two chapters I have tried to introduce the attempts made in recent years to salvage this paradigm, and to this end looked at several well-known experiments. What I found was that in the case of New Liberalism, the attempt to salvage the Rise of the West actually came at the expense of the field of history. As we have seen, New Liberalism today has reduced what it considers to be important about history to the history of the past twenty years. The fact that Marxism has simply been following the lead of liberalism is more evidence of the narrowness of social thought and crisis. The only hope for either tradition is a new beginning. The only hope for Marxism is that it find its way back to a wider materialism. To do so it needs to leave high theory and empiricism to liberalism and find its way through middle-level analysis.

Although doubtless few world historians today would endorse the paradigm of the Rise of the West unreservedly for the reasons already alluded to, it would not follow that most would actively pursue some alternative to it or if they did that they would choose the Rise of the Rich. The case that they should remains to be made. We now turn to a discussion of early modern history using this new framework.

THE RISE OF THE RICH IN EARLY
MODERN TIMES, 1550–1850

IN THIS CHAPTER we survey early modern history in terms of the Rise of the Rich. My main concern here is determining what went wrong heretofore with the main concepts upon which the analysis of this period has been based, resulting in the narrow Eurocentric approach that now prevails on up through the writings of the New Liberals on empire. To this end, I consider two major concepts: accumulation and proletarianization.

Accumulation plays a critical role in how capitalism was defined in early modern history; proletarianization remains part of the definition until today. Exactly what accumulation includes and exactly how important it is or was and for how long have always remained questions without clear answers. Because of these ambiguities, many historians shun the concept. Here what is assumed is that such concepts can be adapted and can and must be continuously brought up to date. In adapting accumulation to present needs, my aim is not to challenge the received meaning but to see if greater clarity can be achieved by adding meanings to it, thus making it more comprehensive. What we have known for a long time is that accumulation has usefully been associated with slavery and with the theft of mineral wealth. What has been less apparent but ultimately turns out to have been very important as well is that accumulation has always been tied up with political and sociological considerations and not simply with economic ones. As I will show, accumulation gave rise to a particular sociological type, one that is termed here *New Men*. The New Men are an important component of the Rise of the Rich, or at least they aspire to be. They are a group of people across the planet more attuned to the laws of the market and less so to the traditional laws and morality of nation-states. Many were, not surprisingly, considered outlaws in one place or another.

The rise of the New Men in this period had a number of consequences. In politics and diplomacy, their rise led to a new form of relations among dominant elements from around the world, bilateral relations. These new bilateral relations formalized fairly explicitly what each party wanted and in the process built trust between states. Some of these early agreements were written and survive. (I conclude the chapter by giving some examples drawn from several of them.) From reading these documents, one can see not just the new individualism of the age of capitalism and the whims of particular rulers but also the constraints imposed by the respective logics of hegemony out of which the parties were operating.

Proletarianization is another major concept used to characterize the rise of capitalism, especially in countries such as Britain. It too turns out on closer inspection to be one in need of expansion. Whereas proletarianization is an integral part of economic history, it also turns out to have a place in politics. Political considerations in Britain induced a landed class to allow for this proletarianization and to allow for factory development. Proletarianization, like accumulation and like a number of other key concepts, failed to develop in the past, the reason being the Rise of the West paradigm. The existing definitions of these concepts fit the needs of the paradigm; further development would be disruptive.

In the second half of the chapter I take up several other concepts commonly associated with the study of early modern history. Here the problem appears to be less in how they are defined than in how they are applied. What stands out is how the Rise of the West paradigm has limited their application. Such concepts include mercantilism, the Crisis of the Seventeenth Century, the Bourgeois Revolution, the Industrial Revolution, and the birth of the Fourth World.

ACCUMULATION AS A PART OF MODERN WORLD HISTORY

The concept of accumulation is a traditional category in economic history used to characterize plunder, slavery, and unequal exchange and the wealth gained therefrom. In a somewhat expanded interpretation of this concept, we find that it does not simply refer to this wealth or these activities, but that in addition it refers to a range of other phenomena, some of which are economic, some political, and some sociological. In traditional usage, the term *accumulation,* one might also note, is fairly Eurocentric. The fruits of slave labor and New World gold and silver are European ones. By characterizing accumulation as primitive accumulation, it fits with a particular understanding of early modern history, one in which illegal gain is recognized as something that was indispensable to the development of early capitalism in the West. This leads us back once again to the question, why was it called primitive accumulation? Seemingly, accumulation has always been called primitive accumulation because Marxists believe that accumulation played a role only until the Industrial Revolution of the eighteenth century, at which point it ceased to be important. In this double sense of its illegality and its temporal position, it is thus debatably at least primitive.

Still, accumulation, one might suppose, implies the existence of historical actors. Who was it that was most conspicuously involved in the process of accumulation? The answer appears to be that those people most conspicuously involved were an aspiring but often ignored part of the Rich, a diverse group of individuals who were out for fame and fortune, realized that the market could offer them new opportunities, and were prepared to cooperate if it was to their advantage in pursuing their interests. Some came from the established structures, some from outside them, seizing the opportunity of the latter's disarray. I am calling this group the New Men. The New Men, I find, played—and still play—a large yet often neglected role in the history of capitalism, often doing so outside of Europe, although this location is not the main explanation for their neglect; rather, they have been neglected because accumulation itself has not been considered very important and was certainly not thought to have involved politics, which in the case of these individuals it frequently did.

This, needless to say, is contentious territory. And this is especially the case for someone extending the use of the term past the abolition of slavery. How many historians perceive accumulation to be embedded in the daily functioning of the world market today? Why would one? If one assumes that price tends to equal value, as most historians do, one would not tend to look at a commercial transaction as a political event much less one with illegal dimensions. Sales are simply sales. The gross national product measures their quantity, and the Third World is insignificant in world gross national product. Even to the extent that capitalism may once have benefited from accumulation from the Third World, it was never a matter of importance compared to the legal profit made from trade. These thoughts are standard assumptions; they even creep into Marxism.

Yet one might suspect that in an era of colonialism or neocolonialism, First World–Third World commodity transactions would scarcely ever conform to market forces. Colonial realities would get in the way. So would politics. Trade relations would almost necessarily include some element of primitive accumulation or politics or both. But could these factors really have such weight in the market as to oblige a revision on the level of paradigm? The answer for a historian ought to be in the affirmative. In a situation of inequality between buyer and seller, one in which it would be to the advantage of the seller to accentuate the factor of his weakness vis-à-vis the buyer and not resist the terms offered, it would. The seller might even seek a low price for his commodity as a way to leverage his workers into great subservience while currying favor with the buyer. An example presented earlier was the politics of coffee pricing in Chiapas, Mexico. The landlords have been trying to undermine the Zapatista by ensuring a low market price for the coffee they pick. This low market price reflects not actual world market prices but the political side of accumulation.

To analyze accumulation, then, looking back to early modern history in these wider terms, we may assume that it was the New Men who were crucial to the accumulation process, in a number of ways. Some of these New Men facilitated the transition of a country from one empire to another—for example, by jumping from serving the rulers of tributary empires, as in Southeast Asia, to working as agents of Western companies that had arrived on the scene. Others worked as proxies for the Chinese or Japanese state as the modern world market developed, and still others emerged from nonmarketized regions such as Africa, visiting Europe and acquiring what they wanted without opening up their countries. Others were involved in schemes involving the playing of the powers in the core against each other in order to break one or another country out of the periphery so it could develop.[1] Many were outlaws.

Although most rulers and most powerful individuals were probably only somewhat involved in the world market and doubtless many eschewed it altogether, those who entered it enthusiastically, taken as a group, brought about enduring historical changes. They introduced innovations on the level of the state and on the level of international relations. They found ways to solidify political and economic relations among dominant elements around the world, weaving their way past the constraints posed by civilizational boundaries, hegemonic logic, and class struggle to create a patchwork of bilateral relations. As these events occurred, more and more individuals and small groups found ways to impose the market on subject populations in return for various rewards, latecomers naturally picking up the crumbs that were left.

In trying to locate the New Men, one could assume that many would have come out of the existing world market, the one centered in the Indian Ocean. In a region where many people already had international commercial experience, a situation of changing world hegemonies would have given this group new opportunities. In the sixteenth and seventeenth centuries, island Southeast Asian history provides an obvious place to look for the New Men. This region was at that point the center of world trade. Trade, production, and urbanization had been steadily growing and doing so on a relatively large scale. This growth made it very wealthy, but as it turned out it also made it very vulnerable. The vulnerability appeared with the arrival of the Dutch. More than "a kind of crisis of the seventeenth century," this event made the region's capitalist sector redundant and marked a kind of permanent destruction of that most lucrative part of the economy. The elite survived by jumping ship.[2] Thereafter, one begins to record Southeast Asian contributions to the world market via the Dutch.

What happened in Southeast Asia has been a vexatious question for many historians. Why did the region decline so quickly? And if it did decline so quickly, how can this fact be explained apart from the older theory of the episodic nature of merchant capital? I suspect such concerns have had some influence on the direction scholarship has gone. In presenting the "big picture" of Asia in world history, some have gone so far as to drop Southeast Asia at the arrival of the Dutch and concentrate on East Asia. And there are reasons for doing so. Following the collapse of Southeast Asia, East Asia became the new center of the world economy. During the seventeenth and eighteenth centuries, East Asia managed to escape being reduced to the status of a periphery,[3] thanks to the New Men functioning in the region's commercial entrepôts but doing so less in the service of European interests than was the case in Java.[4]

One historian who has been leading the way in explaining the role of the Asian commercial structure in world history, John E. Wills, argues that given the many unknowns about world history and about accumulation, one ignores the "history of maritime Asia" at one's peril. The "long drift to European hegemony in Asian waters seems less over-determined, less a foregone conclusion, much more multi-causal and contingent, and a much more challenging and rewarding area of study" today than it was in the 1960s and 1970s. The implied comparison that Wills is making is between the New Liberal historiography emphasizing trade routes and the world-systems analysis of that earlier period that made almost everything periphery and everything on the periphery unimportant. Wills's point is also a historiographical one in another sense as well. What he finds is that as scholarly knowledge about Asia developed, writing went from externalist and Eurocentric accounts to ones rooted more in internal analysis and indigenization. Wills's observation is well taken. The question at this point becomes, how does one go beyond indigenization?[5] If one stops with indigenization, one runs the risk of falling into a kind of polycentric nominalism, or in other words one risks losing a consideration of the larger narrative of power. Commercial centers exist, so one simply catalogs them. Wills's solution to the problem is what he calls "interactive emergence," which is not too far from the idea of the New Men solution proposed here.

For our purposes, the phrase *interactive emergence* used to characterize the development of maritime Asia is one that might have even wider applicability. It might in fact be used as a way to characterize not only the Euro-Asian development of concern but also the Euro-African development and perhaps others as well. In the case of Africa, according to the Africanist John K. Thornton, a historian who argues along parallel lines, a good deal of scholarly work exists that might support this approach. However, as we shall see, general historians have not chosen to make much use of it. As a result, Africa is still commonly regarded as an isolated region in fields such as world history or world-systems analysis, though it could be looked at otherwise. What one observes by introducing the idea of interactivity, or what I would call bilateral relations forged by the New Men to be more concrete, is that much of the African leadership of the period was dealing with the market but without succumbing to it.

The African leadership of this period had the luxury to pick and choose. It was their good fortune not to have to worry even about military superiority. Military superiority was, of course, a factor in world history and has often been a factor closely linked to accumulation. In the case of tropical Africa, however, climate and disease structure protected much of the interior regions from engagement with foreigners until the nineteenth century. On the one occasion in an earlier time frame, from 1579 to 1590, when a European country (Portugal) tried to capture an African state (the Kingdom of Ndongo in Angola), it failed to do so, despite the use of more soldiers than were used to conquer Mexico or Peru.[6] As for the conventionally rather negative comments about technology and commerce in Africa by works in the dominant paradigm, they too do not appear to take cognizance of African textiles as a part of international commerce nor even for that matter African metallurgy, with recent research focusing on steel.

Indeed, as African studies now shows, the skill of African merchants is often attested to, but it too gets lost in the large body of writing in history more generally attributing a supposed lack of interest in trade to Africans owing to an economy based on use value as opposed to exchange value. More accurately understood, as Thornton has argued, it becomes apparent that Africa in the early modern period was not so disengaged from larger trends and was much less a passive victim of the world economy at large than is commonly thought.[7]

Despite such considerations, the perception of European military superiority bears on how most historians theorize accumulation, technological determinism trumping other factors. Furthermore, not only is military superiority used even to explain why the Europeans got their way and received cooperation, it is used to explain why certain countries, often enough "Islamic" ones, did not. Such countries, one learns, were doomed to lose out because their cultures stood in the way of their assimilating the "gunpowder revolution" of the sixteenth century. And although there may be examples that bear out this notion, a recent book on the history of Morocco shows an "Islamic" society integrating firearms to raise its technological level, the state trying but, however, failing to maintain a monopoly of the new weapons vis-à-vis its subjects. At the very least, the Moroccan example calls into question the use of culture or technology as the explanation for why a country might wind up on the periphery.[8] Once again, we are thus driven to return to politics and by extension to the role played by the New Men.

A consideration of a few more examples of these ambitious individuals may serve to make this clearer. One could take, for example, the Mamluk adventurers, who ruled Egypt in the eighteenth century. Although they served the Ottoman court in Istanbul (in a loose sense of the word *served*), they were clearly out for themselves as well. 'Ali Bey (al-Kabir), a leading Mamluk, tried, for example, to declare Egypt independent in the 1760s when he was ruling it. At the time he had ties to various Italians. A few years later Alfi Bey, one of the leading Egyptian Mamluks of that period, undertook a mission to London, seeking British support against his rivals. Historians find this event curious. Certainly, he was not forced to go. Alfi Bey's mission appears to have succeeded, but in fact it failed. He succeeded in getting the British and the Ottomans on his side, but his coup attempt, which he staged in 1806 with their backing, nonetheless led to a total defeat for him in such battles as Damanhur. We do not yet know enough details to know why. The results, however, are clear enough. His faction of the Mamluks in Egypt lost out, and then the Mamluks in general lost out. It was the French-backed Muhammad 'Ali Pasha who came to prevail.[9] I mention this example because at the time the southern shore of the Mediterranean was not a traditional British sphere of influence, but Alfi Bey was neither the first nor the last to try such a mission. Does this event not imply some kind of a Rise of the Rich in formation, some kind of new consciousness of what power was, where it was, even some desire to be a part of it? In Mamluk terms, the British and French had become network partners.

Coming to power was one thing, but escaping from the periphery was another; it was tried and it too bears on the issue of accumulation. A country that escapes from the periphery profoundly alters its relation to the accumulation process. Among the best-known individuals associated with an attempted escape from the periphery was Muhammad 'Ali, the ruler of

Egypt (1805–48). Muhammad 'Ali's approach was to offer high-quality cotton for the European market, a product in considerable demand, giving him a chance to make demands for industrial and military equipment that would not ordinarily have been for sale. Muhammad 'Ali has been long known to historians for this famous attempt, and correctly so, but it might also be noted that after some years of trying to industrialize, Muhammad 'Ali, pressured by Britain and the Ottoman Empire, gave up his goal of having Egypt become an industrial power or even a fully independent country. He did so despite having an undefeated army in the field, accepting in return international recognition of his family's right to rule Egypt in perpetuity. As the Rise of the Rich metaphor suggests, in a number of significant cases class ultimately trumped nation; in this case, the "escape from the periphery" was something that could be sacrificed for the sake of the gains of Muhammad 'Ali's family.

Of course, class does not always trump nation; moreover, detailed study of Muhammad 'Ali has only just begun. Thus, there is a great deal still to be learned about him and his international dealings, subjects that therefore should not be prejudged. In one recent article, the class dimension appears. In this article, the author looked at the Pasha's attempts at image construction, examining his appearance as he desired it to be for an official portrait in his later years. The portrait in question, the author finds, served to make him look very international; it did not play to some orientalizing stereotype that many other pictures of him did.[10] The author's explanation is that an oil painting was something designed for international consumption, something aimed at fellow members of the upper class in Europe and elsewhere. His choice of appearance helped to build his image among them. And although such an approach to documenting international dealings may strike some historians as a bit unusual, it fits with a good deal else that is known. It is indisputable that when the British found it in their interest to invade Egypt in 1882, they did so, they claimed, to uphold the monarchy, that is, Muhammad 'Ali's descendants. And thanks to British backing, this monarchy continued to hold on in Egypt until the 1952 Revolution. The dynasty had been accepted as a member of the club.

Another common variant of the New Men were Western businessmen adventurers who sought their fortune abroad. A number of ambitious individuals in the early years of capitalism realized there was more to be gained by going abroad than by hanging around polishing the lord's silver in their hometown. Although typically New Men started as protégés of the authorities in their country's empire, nothing seemed to stop them from jumping ship not only economically but also politically if the conditions looked promising. Although there were some Tories in the American Revolution, many others went over to the new country, here to give one example. Probably most did not go so far. They simply went to the margins of what was still legal so as to avoid too many risks. For example, after the Seven Years' War (1756–63), adventurous British businessmen entered the West Indies hoping not only to transform the still undeveloped parts of it into sugar plantations but also to benefit from governmental protection while doing so.

Two such businessmen who made their fortunes in West Indian sugar in this way were Alexander Bartlet and George Campbell. They managed to buy large tracks of land and maintain business offices in Europe and the New World in the middle of the eighteenth century.[11] It was as a result of their efforts and of others like them that the Crown decided to expand its authority to more islands and involve itself politically in a more complex way in the Caribbean by the early nineteenth century. Thus, the empire kept growing as well as the market and the local states.

The activities of these new adventurer businessmen had consequences that they themselves could scarcely have foreseen but that also fit with a Rise of the Rich type of interpretation. As the demand for slaves rose to meet the needs of sugar production in which they were of course involved, Africans from various countries began to argue for an end to slavery, slavery being, as several authors put it, an institution contradictory to British values. Two works written by Africans found an audience in Britain. Soon some Englishmen, such as the craftsman Wedgwood and the writer Wilberforce, threw in their lot with the abolitionists. And not long after as a result, British culture faced a crisis, one that in turn threatened the accumulation process.[12] The fact that Africa was producing such intellectuals in this period and that they were able to influence British public opinion suggests that the research about the dominant classes of Africa is indeed not being assimilated in general culture.

For others among the New Men, participation in accumulation took a different direction. The Japanese and Chinese governments kept their markets closed. They worked through proxies and intermediaries, giving unusual opportunities to certain Dutch and Portuguese merchant groups who became yet another variation of the New Men phenomenon. Other rulers, such as the Ottoman sultan, designated minority groups as commercial groups. By definition, such groups were not from the dominant religious community so their profit-making behavior could not be generalized to the population at large. This minority status explains why these groups were in turn vulnerable to exploitation. For the Ottomans, it came to mean the Greeks, Armenians, and Sephardic Jews but not the Muslim Turks. For the later Mughals, it came to mean the Parsis; in Southeast Asia, it meant the Chinese; in Africa, it meant the "Arabs." Once the designated commercial groups were in place, the ruler could take a more aggressive approach to the pursuit of profit making. If he required more peasants or soldiers, he could sacrifice artisans and other merchants, as whatever was needed could now be procured from abroad.[13] Other choices might then follow, among them a change in the local cultural policy. Politicians who wanted to rationalize importing European finished goods and exporting local raw goods often found it useful to have intellectuals create an "agrarian ideal" model of the society as its civilizational norm, one that had few crafts and industries and was organized on the local level in small units, such as the Russian mir or the Chinese or Indian village.[14] Oriental despotism comes to mind.

These arrangements sometimes worked, but they were never guaranteed to work smoothly. For example, in the case of the Dahomey slave trade, the ruler could not successfully designate a commercial minority. As a result, the commercial sector became open to too many people. The ruler ultimately needed to reconfigure tribal ideologies to further segment society and thereby lessen the risk of there being too many merchants and thus too much upward mobility.[15]

In sum, the rise of modern capitalism rested on finding collaborators who would participate in one form of market restructuring or another or would go out into the world and make new connections. Without such developments, there would have been no overseas market for the early capitalist to sell to and to expand into and no organized arena for plunder.[16]

The activities of these New Men, legal or otherwise, were thus a quite crucial part of the history of capitalism through their role in accumulation. This point, I believe, has rarely been given its due. Adam Smith, the famous eighteenth-century economist, was an early observer of the rise of modern capitalism. Taking what would be today a rather conventional marginal utility view, he claimed to have detected an apparently symbiotic relation among rulers, some functioning more as producers of goods, some more as producers of markets for those goods. Smith thought this relation was an expression of an iron law, a law that a rational ruler was bound to obey.[17] Choice, strategy, and strategic consumerism seem absent from his thought. He seems to have missed as well the point that Marx was later to make well known in his discussion of commodity fetishism: beneath the flow of goods, all participants were concerned with power—trade, statecraft, consumerism, restructuring, and adventurism all serving as a means to that end.[18] And Smith was not alone; few if any even until now have tried to develop what Marx meant by commodity fetishism to the point of making it a part of historical practice, another part of the reason the role played by the New Men has often been overlooked.

Yet Adam Smith had a point, even if he oversimplified it. By the eighteenth century, more and more ruling classes from around the world found it in their interest to buy new-style goods made in Western Europe as a part of their foreign policy following a course of strategic consumerism. Thus, more and more ruling classes chose to take the raw goods that they had previously turned over to local artisans to generate products that the rulers would then buy and to sell those raw goods instead to Europe and then to buy finished goods from Europe, presumably for political as opposed to purely economic reasons. European goods might be more or less expensive, but the important point was that their purchase helped secure an alliance. And this commerce was done in full knowledge that abandoning the local artisans meant beggaring them, also a political choice. In such moments, one sees how statecraft and global class loyalties intertwine and how as a result a ruling class could bring about underdevelopment within its own society. It is not "uneven development," as some Marxists have claimed; it is deliberate impoverishment. Thus, for example, in eighteenth-century Egypt, clothes, which the Beys had previously bought locally, were now sometimes bought from Europe. Looked at from the vantage point of social history, the Egyptian case being generalized, the consequences of the rise of modern capitalism were one thing for the dominant classes and quite another for society at large.[19] In countries such as Egypt, to which one might add India, that is, countries not well placed in terms of the new international economic competition, the rise of modern capitalism brought on deindustrialization, in effect an economic crisis for the urban masses, in contrast to the prosperity of the consumer class. By the early nineteenth century, Indian textile workers, like Egyptian artisans, found themselves unemployed while the rulers were living a life of luxury. The impact of the world market on Africa represents an even more extreme case of societal disruption than the repercussions in the Middle East. Following the rise of the slave trade, African society suffered significant depopulation.[20]

These trends, it must also be noted, were world trends, not simply Third World trends. Even in Britain, many of these same trends appear. Historian E. P. Thompson and others have characterized the "moral economy" protests of eighteenth-century Britain as an early form of mass resistance to the imposition of the market. The protests apparently arose in reaction to the rise of a class seemingly benefiting from accumulation to the extent that it was no longer rooted in the local tradition and its morality, a class emerging but not emerging understandably out of the dynamic of national history.

Everywhere, whatever the precise local details, the new consumer strategies worked to solidify the relations of dominant classes and to split and divide the dominated groups. And whether the ruling classes were more capitalist or more feudal, they gained in wealth through their collaboration with each other in the accumulation process. Each hundred years that went by, the ruling classes appear richer and more aware of each other and more able as a result to impose the discipline of market relations on a greater part of the globe, whether in Western Europe, Eastern Europe, or anywhere else.

More generally, we should note that there were risks involved in the careers pursued by the New Men. Apart from the risk of being killed, there was the risk of being exploited. Some rulers would alternately back their merchant sector and then exploit it as a cash cow, merchants as a result often complaining of extortions or Avanies.

For historians, all of this is familiar; however, none of it is especially important. British agriculture financed British industry through the consumption in the home market; as a result the Third World played little or no role. Doubtless there is some element of truth in this position too. British agriculture was indeed long the mainstay of the British economy, and the domestic market for industrial products came from the wealth created by British agriculture, but there is still the question as to where the early British industrialists got their credit. To enter industrial production was an expensive undertaking. According to studies of the period, credit was usually provided by the British country bank, a kind of bank that typically had important ties to foreign trade. In other words, if one reinserts credit and banking back into the industrial and agricultural revolutions, then one reinserts the contribution of the world economy back into the subject of Britain's economic growth.[21] This point, among others, calls into question the more traditional Eurocentric approach to the Industrial Revolution.

Accumulation, as the next chapter will show, carried on until our own times. It did not end in the eighteenth century, as Western Marxism has claimed. Accumulation saw the collapse of the divine right of kings in the name of democracy, then it saw democracy in its heyday, and then it saw it in crisis with the rise of the masses.[22] It is thus truly a foundational concept for the analysis of the development of capitalism.

In summary, I have provided a revisionist view of the subject of accumulation. I claim, on the one hand, that in terms of the history of capitalism, accumulation has been more important than is generally acknowledged and, on the other, that accumulation has been as much a sociological and political phenomenon as it has been an economic one, going hand in hand with the rise of the New Men, a very important subgroup within what I call the Rich. Within this framework, the moral economy protests in eighteenth-century Britain were parallel phenomena to other protests occurring at the same time globally. Still, one might wonder, if British society is taken to be broadly comparable to others, how can one understand the history of proletarianization in Britain? No other society was so capitalist nor had such a large proletariat so early in history as did the British.

PROLETARIANIZATION AS A PART OF THE HISTORY OF THE UK

Proletarianization is widely regarded in scholarship as a central feature of modern capitalism, its appearance a dividing line with precapitalism, its appearance implying a system based on wage slavery that defines capitalism and defines it as being in the West.[23] A considerable body of theory, empirical study, and inference builds on these premises, undergirding the idea of proletarianization's essentially economic character and, by way of criticism, paying scant attention to what larger political purposes it might have been serving or even where it came from, to return to the case of Britain. Highlighting these obviously nonstandard elements in the definition of proletarianization serves to make clear how rigid the orthodox views on the subject have become. I believe that a reliance on a wider, if less orthodox, view of proletarianization would be one way to get away from the problems alluded to, such as the extreme Eurocentrism the term currently embodies, while retaining its core insights about labor and a monetized economy.

To begin, let us clarify what the orthodox meaning for the term is and progress from there. Classical Marxists have long thought that it was the cash nexus that capitalism brought, which was what created the proletarian by forcing more work from him or her than any previous system would have been able to. On this basis, one could argue that capitalism was revolutionary and revolutionary in an ongoing way, because the British capitalist class could keep introducing new technology into the factory and the proletarianized worker using this new technology would become increasingly productive in the process. Increased productivity, the theory goes, meant increased wealth for the British ruling class, the increased wealth produced allowing it to break into the old markets of Asia and elsewhere. Still, if proletarianization was so profitable for British business, why was it not immediately "adopted" in other countries more than it was? One wonders as well what to do with Thompson's research on the eighteenth century and its description of actual worker consciousness.

In light of these considerations, I suggest a rethinking of the term, one turning on the particularity of British politics as much as of economics. All through early modern history and even into the nineteenth century, we find a predisposition to a romanticized image of a tranquil medieval past on the part of the ruling class, one leading it to hope for a return to the medieval caste system as a cultural system that would eliminate the political radicalism of the existing lower classes. Given this mind-set, it would seem likely that the British upper classes, that is, the peerage, would see some utility in having a more organized working class, even a very large one, as opposed to a smaller and less organized one.[24] An organized class, one could assume, is a class that could be controlled. Although these points do not altogether negate the orthodox view, they speak to the issue of political power, political power being the power to shape society, a notion that is apparently absent from the orthodox formulation.

In orthodox thought, it is as if there was a fear that to choose politics, one ignored economics. But this is by no means necessarily the case. Consider the main explanations for the birth of the British proletariat in the sixteenth century, or "why Britain was first" suggested by economist Samir Amin, geographer James Blaut, and historian Robert Brenner.[25] All of them in fact carve out a terrain that includes politics and culture. Amin looks at the mode of production that preceded the capitalist revolution. He argues that Europe, with its military style of feudalism, was far less stable than were the tributary states typical of the old Afro-Asian trade route. Highly armed, often at war, often as a result driving peasants off the land and forcing them to flee as proletarians to the so-called free cities, European lords after the year 1000 gradually brought down feudalism, presumably inadvertently. The Europe that they created in the process was highly proficient in the military arts and in conquest and more proletarianized than any other region of the world. Amin's argument fits to a degree Brenner's argument of the uniqueness of British feudalism in relation to the feudalism of continental Europe. Not all feudalisms were destined to easily make the transition to capitalism, both in Europe and beyond Europe as well. For example, Japan and Ethiopia were also feudal, but they were not as unstable as were the regimes in Western Europe and did not make the transition to capitalism in this period.[26] What Brenner ultimately shows is that British feudalism, by way of contrast, broke down the most, rapidly giving way to market relations the most completely and this point was what was decisive. One wonders why. Was it simply internecine wars? Why, then, the size of the proletariat but the weakness of proletarian consciousness as late as the eighteenth century, as noted by E. P. Thompson and others? James Blaut's view is that it was Britain's position in the North Atlantic that allowed it to best plunder the New World and thereafter to buy its way into the world market using the loot that it had acquired. If this theory is accurate, why not also hypothesize that wealth in the hands of the British upper classes in this period not only gave Britain an entrée to the market but also funded the costs of maintaining a rather large proletariat, buying off in the process the radical trends of the seventeenth century, such as the Levelers? Given the long history of failed transitions to capitalism that the world had witnessed up to that point, this notion is a not uninteresting thought. Here was a country with access to a surplus that did not use the surplus to refeudalize as Spain, Italy, and most others did. It was thus not simply a question of the size of its economy as it was the choices made by the ruling class.

In terms of the size of its economy, China was larger than Britain, but, according to Samir Amin, its peasantry was more stable, and there was therefore much less pressure for capitalist transformation in the early modern period. It was the feudal form of the tributary system, the one with the lord living on the land, that lent itself to instability; China, like most other countries with a centralized tax-gathering system, was simply more stable.[27] Britain backed into its precocious position in terms of proletarian-ization from the failure of what went before, a failure that then somehow was dealt with and turned to account in the context of capitalism. The way it was dealt with, however, involved political choices.

Detailed studies of the British proletariat appear to support such a view. Certainly, they confirm the impression of size. As historian David Levine writes, it was in 1524–25 that King Henry VIII levied a tax to pay for his foreign wars. From the records of this tax levy, one can calculate that there were already some 600,000 proletarians (counting their dependents) out of a population of 2.4 million. By the middle of the nineteenth century, the ratio of employees and domestics to the total population had risen to four out of five (14 million out of 18 million).[28] As its ranks swelled, according to Levine, the proletariat indeed made demands—for example, for suffrage and an escape from poverty—but there was never any automatic connection between its growth and its class position per se. By the end of the nineteenth century, Lenin, a keen observer of working classes, was correct, I believe, in characterizing segments of the British working class as an "aristocracy of labor." Whereas today the term of art in modern-day historiography might be *penny capitalist*, the point would stand that there was more to the rise of the proletariat than orthodox theory has allowed for.

The role of politics has to be considered. The British ruling classes found the concentration of workers threatening. Although the unemployed and the poor may have been an easy target for legislators, it was the workers who were the real matter of concern. Had there been no working class, the British Civil War would have been much less threatening to the aristocracy. The lords realized they would need to act, to use the resources they had, to prevent it from ever recurring. To create a loyal underclass would be expensive, but it would be worth it. And, certainly, the cost of having a working class has to be acknowledged. Many ruling classes could not afford what the British aristocracy could and not having had the experience of the British Civil War would not have seen it as a priority. To keep a working class one needs to take on the expenses of maintaining a lumpen proletariat to intimidate it, the cost of the police, the cost of the prison system, the cost of the white-collar workers to manage it, and the cost of maintaining a cultural system to justify what they were doing to it.[29] Accumulation on a world scale in the age of colonization was enough to pay for these expenditures. Still, one wonders why Britain opted to keep this huge proletariat in existence for so long. Was the hope really one day to make it eventually pay for itself? This idea does not seem to have been very realistic. If it had been a real likelihood, others too would have created a mass proletariat; most never tried, and many appeared to regret even the smaller ones they had. It seems more likely to repeat the hypothesis that there was a political dimension. Proletarianization thus represented an economic reality while at the same time it was an experiment in molding the political and cultural order. It was an experiment that was partially successful but also partially a failure, at least if one looks at it as an attempt to create a lower caste of loyal, self-supporting subalterns like the mythical peasantry of old.[30] Eventually, as experiments go, it became simply too expensive for Britain to maintain when it lost the accumulation from its former colonies, decolonization spelling the death of the classical working class. Perhaps one could make sense of the Thatcher Revolution that way. Margaret Thatcher was the first ruler to apparently be indifferent to whether the trade union family would survive. In her period, one finds the renewal of ethnic nationalism and religious fundamentalism in the British Isles competing with class identity for the first time in centuries. Thatcher did not look back to victories and the empire but to England before the Civil War.

Proletarianization, then, is clearly an important part of modern capitalism. Clearly, it plays a role in counterhegemonic struggle, and clearly it is indispensable for an understanding of the dialectic. But as to the reasons for its size, ideological consciousness, or praxis, or what exactly constitutes the proletariat of some particular country at a given time, one needs to turn to politics. I raise these points because the stance of Western Marxism toward working-class matters has led it to disregard politics and instead to dwell on the size of the class as a marker of power and modernity and to write history accordingly, assuming not just the link but virtually the equation of proletarianization and the class structure brought about by economic capitalism. This in turn is assumed to produce a certain predictable class consciousness. The available evidence suggests that although there is a connection between the "point of production" and an aspect of proletarian class consciousness, another aspect of the proletariat's consciousness, one that is generally understated, relates to accumulation. Accumulation sustained the British working class. The empire was central to the accumulation process; when it collapsed, the working class grew weaker but more racist.

Where, then, does a wider understanding of basic categories lead one as regards the writing of world history? In the following two sections I attempt to provide a rough indication, doing so by turning to other applicable categories and attempting to expand their meanings as well.

MAJOR CATEGORIES AND PHASES USEFUL
FOR THE ANALYSIS OF EARLY MODERN HISTORY:
MERCHANTILISM AND ABSOLUTISM

If one looks at British wealth as a sign not just of material well-being but of vulnerability as well, if one looks at ruling-class history as a quest not just for luxury but for security as well, a security sought in worldwide alliances, then one needs categories that show the British experience to be comparable to others and not simply unique. For the sixteenth and seventeenth centuries, what one needs to show is a world in which a large number of ruling classes attempted to profit from the new world market but often failed and went into crisis, a world of plunder combined with one in which there was a rise of law and diplomatic relations, a world in which ordinary people faced increasingly insuperable odds in confrontations with their rulers.

Classical Marxists acknowledge these points but oversimplify matters by reducing the world history of this period to the transition to capitalism in one or two countries.[31] This makes the traditional liberal historiography built on mercantilism and absolutism a necessary supplement because it allows for more precision. Concepts such as mercantilism and absolutism, which arose out of the older historiography, allow one to explain the various strategies pursued by ruling groups in the different kinds of hegemonies around the world.[32] There were thus several different versions of transition.

Relying on what has been termed a middle-level approach, what one ought to give preference to today in discussing the first couple of centuries of modern world capitalism is the eighteenth century over the seventeenth century. The reason for this is that there has been a considerable amount of scholarly work on the "Crisis of the Seventeenth Century," and this work suggests some degree of acceptance of the idea of a worldwide crisis. Such work not uncommonly focuses on the phenomenon of miscalculations on the part of regimes adjusting to market conditions and on the disasters that then followed.[33] If the study of the seventeenth century shows the world in terms of its commonality and comparability, the study of the eighteenth century shows a widening division in the historiographical imagination between a West and an Orient. For most historians, the rise of the West at this point is well under way. To get beyond this impasse, I will reexamine the traditional categories of analysis used for the study of the eighteenth-century period—for example, the Industrial Revolution and Bourgeois Revolution—to see if they could be adapted for wider applications. Could one show that the Industrial Revolution had a political side and the Bourgeois Revolution an economic one? Could one then show that the so-called Fourth World was not something timeless and archaic and way out there but a part of the familiar, ever present dynamic as well?

The Industrial Revolution, though obviously an economic event and a British economic event at that, was also a political event and an international one as well, one in which ruling classes and influential centers worldwide adopted a strategic approach to consumerism to keep it going, whereas in Britain what stands out is not just the factories but the political role of the aristocracy in allowing the revolution to move forward. Similarly, the Bourgeois Revolution, when looked at closely, turns out to be an economic event and a global event and not just a political event of the West. Looking at these events in this broader fashion clears the way for them to be useful to world history and not just to the history of three or four Western countries.

In an article dealing with the politics of the Industrial Revolution, Michael W. McCahill notes that the British aristocracy had controlled subsoil mineral rights to iron and coal since the sixteenth century. With the great expansion of such industries in the eighteenth century, it is not surprising to find examples of joint ventures where the aristocrat was positioned to be a sleeping partner in the newer venture. McCahill went on to show how the aristocracy was thus able to continue to dominate the British power structure into the nineteenth century by reducing the new industrial class to a lobby, and then by playing its interests against those of the people of the home regions. If necessary, it could sacrifice its newer financial interests when it would enhance its traditional political power. It knew very well how to make use of public opinion, some of which was proindustrial, some not. Thus, where one might have expected in the eighteenth century to find titans of industry dominating politics, empirical studies show that, for example, the ironmongers at one point had no representative in the House of Commons at all. It even remains an open question as to whether the government was working to encourage or impede the revolution. Still, one might suspect that without cooperation between the landed classes and the new industrial classes industrial progress would have been much slower and more difficult than it was. According to McCahill, this rather more expansive interpretation of the role of the peers revises older views of historians, especially those scholars emphasizing the agrarian involvement of the British peerage and the political power thought to have been possessed by the industrialists.[34] The peerage had the power. If one encounters an industrial revolution or finds a large proletariat in Britain, one has to ask what interest the peerage would have had in it.

The eighteenth century also witnessed the flowering of the Bourgeois Revolutions, notably the American and the French revolutions. In studying these events scholars have generally emphasized their political nature, leaving aside the contribution of these events to the development of the market. Today, it is only the odd article that might pick up on an economic aspect. According to the author of one such article, one on bankruptcy law in eighteenth-century America, one learns that whereas the Puritans had stigmatized the debtor, making all debtors sinners, God being the "Great Creditor," this notion gave way by 1800 to a new more flexible vision from a capitalist perspective. At that point, the wealthy commercial debtor would no longer bear a stigma for his debt; only the poor debtor with personal debts would, as Benjamin Franklin made clear in the *Almanack*.[35] Such insights would seem to have implications for what we mean by "Bourgeois Revolution." If this is what the revolution achieved, then one can find quite a number of countries in the process of achieving the same thing, not all of them a part of the West. This point suggests some utility in the concept.

One now needs to recall as well that the Bourgeois Revolution had one other very general meaning: destroyer of nations. The Bourgeois Revolution provided the impetus for some nations to completely destroy other nations. With the widespread diffusion of capitalism and individualism, one man's gain was another man's loss. This destruction was what created the Fourth World, that is, the Bourgeois Revolution was responsible for the nations whose people had lost their homelands and who were often killed, the survivors, historians have noted, clinging desperately to some small remnant of what they once had, inserting themselves into the narrative of world history via their identity to avoid being utterly obliterated. So numerous are these people around the world and at the same time so distinctive, we term them the *Fourth World,* adding a historicization to the more familiar neoliberal usage, which reduces them to culture.

Of course, it is well known that the rise of states involved the killing of people who stood in the way, and it is well known as well that in times past historians have not infrequently justified its occurrence in terms of the advance of civilization. In more recent times, many historians, however, have come to see what the profession has done as somehow an intervention in history, its involvement somehow legitimating what states had set out to do. Gradually, too, the idea of Fourth World people as people who have ceased to exist as a part of history has been challenged by the increasing politicization of these people all over the world. For the historian, the question is then, who are these people? Until now there has been no academic consensus on this point; Fourth World is obviously a euphemism. We do not have a category for what one might term the victims of civilization (and it is doubtful that we really want one), but still we do not want simply a euphemism. In recent years *Fourth World* has been made to mean "environment defined," "identity focused," or subaltern. Obviously, this approach will not do. We do not need more polarities. The Fourth World is not the opposite of who we are; it is another part of the same mesh of which we are a part.

Whereas the period of the rise of the nation-state may have tended to correlate with a decline in the power of indigenous and Fourth World peoples, more recent history has seen a reverse trend. This is not to imply that the state is declining but that elements within society have grown alienated with the idea of the state. And in some cases Fourth World peoples have been able to benefit from this atmosphere of alienation. They have been able to avail themselves of educational systems and to gain some legal support for their causes, and they have marshaled a good deal of sympathy in the process. In recent times a growing number of scholars and lawyers all over the world actively support the rights of the Fourth World.[36]

Again, however, the field of history, given its origins and early development, remains a field identified with the nation-state more than do others, thus often lagging a bit when it comes to Fourth World studies. It has not been that common to find a history of the Fourth World, but even this situation is in the process of change. One of the first broad-scale attempts at such a history was by Anthony J. Hall, *The American Empire and the Fourth World: The Bowl with One Spoon* (2003). Hall begins his discussion with the contention that we cannot understand today's United States and its interface with the Middle East unless we understand the country's older interface with the Indians. Hall's point is that if there has been a pattern of conquest, a pattern of forcing a client regime onto a people, a regime that would agree to hand over its mineral assets, and if this pattern was repeated three or four hundred times over a century of dealing with Indian tribes, this pattern would instill a certain kind of political tradition. He may be right. In any case, if one wants to explain U.S. policy to Iraq, Palestine, or Lebanon in more recent times, an approach of this sort offers a more concrete form of analysis than the one commonly used that draws inferences from Puritan ideology or material interest.[37]

Hall's work is not only historical but comparative as well. He contrasts the differing outcomes for Canada and the United States of the Treaty of Paris of 1783 as it related to the position of indigenous people. Whereas in Canada the law upheld indigenous rights from that time on, in the United States it did not. Since 1871 U.S. law denied that First Nation people were even subject to international law and its scrutiny because the United States derived its power over such peoples by right of conquest. However, between 1776 and 1871 the United States had signed almost four hundred treaties with these so-called aboriginal peoples.[38]

The critical period in which American behavior was molded, in Hall's view, was between the Seven Years' War (beginning in 1754) and the end of the War of 1812. In this period, the Indians held the balance of power in conflicts between Britain, France, and America in terms of control of the upper Midwest and the Mississippi River valley. For this reason, Americans fought the War of 1812 presumably in order to preclude European recognition of Indian sovereignty rights, something that seemed to be looming. Tecumseh was killed presumably because the British were prepared to support his claims to sovereignty. Whether this level of power and influence ought to be ascribed to the Amerindians in this period is hard to know, but it points toward a growing inclusion of the Fourth World in the construction of the historical narrative and against the idea of understanding Amerindians as an unconnected, archaic culture. What works in favor of Hall's particular conclusions is the common assumption that the logic of modern hegemonies of most countries emerged from the struggles of this period. Hall puts particular emphasis on the importance of the Treaty of Greenville in 1795, signed by General Mad Anthony Wayne and Little Turtle of the Indian Confederacy. Hall notes that when Little Turtle and his family capitulated, the United States rewarded them. It became part of the pattern.

As Hall also shows, it is not that the United States of today has changed its approach to the Amerindian people all that much. There may be pockets of support and understanding, but the larger picture is still one of desperately poor Indians on reservations forced to acquiesce to having their lands used as toxic waste dumps, and further exploited by the casino economy. For Indian writers, even maintaining "intellectual sovereignty" is a challenge. At the same time, victimization would not be a useful or at least a very precise way to describe the lives of Amerindian activists such as George Manuel, the latter a figure who brought together leaders from all over the Fourth World in recent years.

How does one distinguish the Fourth World from the Third World? This question needs further clarification. The issue of paradigm is involved, but it is not simply that. On the day the Spanish arrived, the Aztecs were rulers of a tributary state parallel to others in the world, one that might have become Third World. Seemingly, its aristocracy looked at the coming of some powerful foreigners as a chance for alliances and for gain for themselves, the Aztec aristocracy here no different from many other ruling classes of the period. As history would have it, the Spanish took over the state, many Aztecs died, and the remaining ones were forced to accept Christianity and become a subordinate part of the new structure or accept being archaicized. For some historians, this event was the birth of the Fourth World in Mexico. Not everyone would agree with this view. The Zapatista, on the other hand, so often characterized as Fourth World in New Liberal scholarship, were never really displaced from their lands or from their role in the Mexican economy. Their political strategy, moreover, has tended to be one seeking alliances with the Mexican working class and with foreign progressives. Such a strategy fits a Third World–type situation better than it does a neoliberal Fourth World one.

To sum up, in this section the chapter introduced early modern history in terms of a number of structures and phases believed to have emerged sequentially following the birth of capitalism in the sixteenth century. It was in this context that the Rise of the Rich took place, and it was in this context that capitalism finally emerged triumphant. The explanation for this success lies not just in the rising efficiency in production in Britain but in the structure of accumulation and trade worldwide that, thanks to the New Men, sufficed to keep capitalism afloat. The New Men weathered the crises of mercantilism and made the Industrial Revolution work. Let us now take a deeper look at how they did it.

In the last section of the chapter what is hypothesized is that among the greatest achievements of the New Men of this period was one of developing an international system rooted in treaties, especially bilateral agreements. These agreements appear as the building blocks of what became in the long run an ever stronger market, providing as well a useful window for the historian from which to observe the world of mercantilism in the shorter run.

BILATERALISM: AN IMPORTANT PART OF THE POLITICAL DEVELOPMENT OF EARLY MODERN WORLD HISTORY

The development of the capitalist mode of production carries with it analytical problems, given its complexity and given the range of countries and commodities involved. Although this point is acknowledged, as a result of the narrow-way historians have analyzed the rise of capitalism, much has often been overlooked or understood in ways that closed off further questions. Take, for example, the understanding of the nature of diplomacy under capitalism—is it simply interstate or are there intraclass relations. Does diplomacy even matter?

Though it may be the case that the most obvious feature of diplomacy has generally been intergovernmental activity designed to foster bilateral relations, a perhaps less obvious but no less important feature of diplomacy is that diplomatic agreements also express interests shared among dominant elements. A hypothetical example should serve to make this point clear. The signing of a treaty often presages the arrival of foreign products or the export of raw products to foreign lands. This might appeal to the wealthier consumer classes. What it would mean for workers and artisans would be less certain. Among other possibilities, it might sharpen the class war. Certainly, rulers had to calculate such risks, which they generally did by making their treaty agreements appear to be congruent with the prevailing hegemonic logic, to minimize resistance. Taking up this less obvious feature of diplomacy, in this section I provide evidence of class issues along with national issues drawn from examples of such agreements between various countries of Africa, Asia, and the Middle East and Europe.

The subject matter is, of course, not new; what is new here is the approach. A more conventional approach would start from the European "Age of Exploration" or "Age of Expansion." It might emphasize coercion and plunder or intercivilizational or interempire contact; diplomacy would be little more than a way of rubber-stamping whatever the supposed reality was. Diplomacy in itself has no significance.

States, as the New Liberals remind us, often did not exist, so the idea of agreements between states does not make sense. Most people lived in territories or empires. To find otherwise, as I do, thus goes against a considerable tradition of scholarship, one that understands empires as great forces towering over their provincial components. To claim that in the history of the early modern world empire relations more often than not are subordinate in analytical importance to relations on a more local, national, and sometimes international level is therefore to make an assumption that does not find general acceptance. This assumption seems warranted, however, not only in terms of long-term outcomes but also in terms of how weak the bonds within most of the empires were most of the time. If the market needed commodities, one might assume those individuals who directly managed their production would be persons of importance, whereas emperors and other traditional rulers would be persons to endure. This reinterpretation of the narrative of power puts the focus on the provincial ruling classes, and in many cases even on contraband trade. As capitalism came to need more and more, it had to acknowledge the power of those groups and those countries that fulfilled its needs and include them in the profit making.

For provincial ruling classes in this period, political loyalty then involved a cost-benefit analysis. It was not a given. If the empire paid, they were empire men. If they could make more money by participating in contraband trade and ignoring imperial law, they did, sometimes thereby entering into the world of the New Men. Sometimes the choices of these provincial ruling classes proved to be a drain on imperial wealth, as was the case for the Ottomans, and sometimes it was no doubt even a part of what we have been terming the more general Crisis of the Seventeenth Century. Rulers of empires calculated on tax revenues they never received.

To survive in the face of these pressures, empires had to be flexible. One might recall that two empires that lasted a long time, the Russian and the British, were noteworthy for conceding considerable autonomy to most of the regions that demanded it. An example of an empire that was not able to be flexible was the Spanish one in the New World. As a result, it confronted a series of independence movements in the nineteenth century. At this point, Spain, to which one could add Portugal, entered a period of crisis. Historical sociology offers an explanation. For the Italian Road–type states, of which Spain is an example and Portugal another, the granting of autonomy or independence to a colony was a more difficult concession to make than it was for the British- or Russian-type states, because the whole hegemony rested on the supposed sufficiency of a single high culture. A granting of autonomy to some region would thus suggest an inadequacy of the empire's high culture. Basque separatists in Spain, the Zapatista in Chiapas, and the Nubians in Egyptian Nubia represent contemporary examples of this type of challenge.

Diplomacy and with it treaty making have existed since antiquity. What was it about the age of bilateralism that distinguished it from what went before? In this period, we find examples of treaty relationships reflecting the desire of the weaker ruling class as well as the stronger ruling class to ensure that market forces, consumerism, and even plunder continued to function smoothly. What had gone before lacked the level of shared concern for trade and market conditions; more commonly, the weaker party paid tribute to the stronger one. At this point, both stood to gain if the market continued to grow. As Chapter 4 will show, what transpired among nations even in the nineteenth and twentieth centuries retained these features of shared ruling-class interests, but by this point others were added to it. In this later period, bilateral relations continued to exist but in the context of multilateralism. A full account of bilateralism's decline and of the rise of multilateralism has yet to be written, so it is difficult to explain it in any detail. In very general terms, one could assume that the continuing development of the world market required a number of ruling classes to view the international market as being made up of a group of national markets, and it would therefore be important to stabilize all these national markets through collective understandings and if possible to deal collectively with problems that arose. This kind of understanding emerged only when a number of countries were well on their way to capitalist development in the nineteenth century. As this chapter shows in the early modern period, short-lived examples of multilateralism came and went, but for centuries bilateralism was the stabler form.

Early modern history did, of course, see a European expansion into Africa, Asia, and beyond, but many accounts also show that Great Britain—as well as other lead countries at different points—were constrained by factors not suggested by their technical capacity for expansion. Among these factors were constraints arising from law and diplomacy. Great Britain, for example, far from being free to do whatever it chose to do, as one might have expected from an imperialist country, was generally constrained to carry out negotiations, to pay lip service to the idea of law, and to pursue its interests in much the same manner as other much weaker countries. On occasion, it could pillage one place or another, turning it into a Fourth World, but even this lawlessness implied consent on the part of third parties. Moreover, judging from the texts of the various treaties that Britain signed from the late sixteenth to the mid-eighteenth centuries, what was demanded and what was conceded always had to be acceptable for public consumption at home as well. If this assumption is true, and it appears to be, then no country in this period, not even Britain, tried to function as if it were above the law.

In the original encounters of the sixteenth century in which the British Empire emerged from the activities of the Chartered Companies, the British often had the best weapons. But as interlopers in different contexts, they were outsiders in language and custom and were consequently dependent on others. Mainly, what they had was the bribe money and the firepower to get in. In most contexts, the British could thus win battles, but they could not win the peace unless they could find local New Men who would be interested in bilateral agreements; this was their goal, despite the constraints it imposed on them. Consequently, colonialism was something of an adventure, and in fact many wrote about it that way.

Another point one might notice is that in the years that followed, the British who went to the colonies were mainly all salary men; they lived off the tax revenue generated by the local peasantry and slave population. Wherever they were, then, they were dependent on groups that they supposedly dominated. This situation, to put it mildly, was an ambiguous one. It virtually obliged colonizers to take the position that they were on the side of law and civilization to justify why they were there to retain some basis for collaboration with the society. Equally, its collaboration also obliged collaborators to take the same point of view as well. This collaboration is how the Rise of the Rich evolved on the local level and how it got so involved with civilization and law.

Thus, we find not only bilateralism and civilization interrelated but so too bilateralism and international law. As a result, by considering the evolution of international law, we gain a sense of how bilateralism itself developed. As early as the seventeenth century, we find that international law was clarifying in some detail the rights of kings, the status of their countries, and even the rights of the nobility, here referring to the much maligned "Westphalian Moment."[39] Such laws must have been based on many kinds of understandings, which in turn must have implied serious communication among dominant elements over wide areas. Some of this communication doubtless dealt with the letter of the law, but some also must have dealt with such matters as how the law was to be upheld. In fact, upholding the law involved a great deal more than simply two parties signing a treaty. Here the role of the church and the missionary movement in propagating law must also be noted.

Another important point about international law is that it was secondary powers such as Italy and Spain that led the way, not Britain and France, the lead countries. It was Italian and Spanish diplomats in the sixteenth and seventeenth centuries who pioneered the development of the embassy and the office of the ambassador, building on earlier Arabic foundations. These institutions are thus often dated from that point, at least in European books. Moreover, whereas the Italians and Spanish attached importance to international law as a kind of ethics, the lead countries, such as Britain, France, and later the United States, did not. They often acted as if they were hemmed in by having to obey contractual agreements for the sake of managing their affairs.[40] For them, obeying laws was simply a part of the cost of doing business.

Bilateral relations was, then, a series of developments heavily influenced by the nature of the hegemonies involved. Countries following a particular form of hegemony adopted negotiation goals in their diplomacy congruent with their hegemonic logic. Let us examine this point beginning with tribal-ethnic states in Africa. Hegel used Africa as his example of people outside of history and politics. In more recent times, historians have shown that he was mistaken, but given Hegel's continuing influence their findings remain less well known. As noted earlier, we find a number of references to visits throughout early modern history by prominent Africans to Europe. One recent study of this subject discusses the arrival in Europe of trade delegations and students from West Africa in the seventeenth century. Such activities suggest the existence of other forms of connections as well. And, indeed, indications of such connections do in fact appear. For example, in the 1680s two West African courtiers were sent to Europe as hostages or as guarantors of a treaty. They learned French, gained French backing, and returned to their country to seize power. Despite the sketchiness of the detail, this account seems like the bilateral diplomacy of the New Men of a tribal-ethnic state. We appear to have a dominant local figure able to connect himself to a great power and thereby displace the existing power structure. This tribal-ethnic state approach could be contrasted with the form of bilateral relations more typical of Russian Road regimes. In this context, one finds Africans going to Europe as educators rather than for other reasons. Among the learned Africans to visit Europe was an Ethiopian scholar credited with contributing to the birth of Ethiopian studies in Europe. His trip amounted to a political visit. Ethiopia was a Russian Road state in the making, and it seems logical that its ruler might seize an opportunity to incorporate the state into the universal story line of elite culture as well as solidify its international position with other states. By the eighteenth century, it is estimated that more Africans, again probably mainly

West African, went to Britain than to other European countries, some stay-
ing because they were married.[41] As noted before, some were associated
with the abolitionist movement. It thus seems probable that early modern
African history, if one were to expand this discussion, could probably be
used to illustrate the prevailing strategies of the New Men, many of them
Africans, not "Euro-Africans," to refer to the dominant paradigm. What
the Rise of the Rich again shows is the emergence of groups that were con-
scious of their own interests and knew how to play the market game. Terms
common to scholarship such as *external regions of the world market* or
people without history simply do not convey this reality.[42]

As noted, Ethiopia was an African example of the Russian Road–type
of hegemony in the period of its formation. To continue with other Russian
Road regimes also in some stage of formation, one could turn to China,
Japan, the Ottomans in Anatolia and Persia, among others, and of course
to Russia itself. When we look at such states, we find all of them deploying
their caste and class strategies, all of them striving to protect the role of the
state as the essential arbiter of all important matters. Often, this resulted
in the decision to exclude foreign merchants from the local market. China,
for example, penned up foreign merchants in Macau; Japan followed suit,
imposing similar restrictions.[43] In these cases, it was not so much a matter
of a nonmarket system as it was a desire to not allow foreigners into the
market.

Scholarly perception of such strategies is predictable. A traditional
approach in Western scholarship would be one assuming that the nonen-
try of Europeans into a market would mean that a country such as China
would remain in stasis until this state of affairs came to an end. Ethiopia,
for example, was regarded as static. The visit of European traveler James
Bruce is the only bright spot to record for eighteenth-century Ethiopian
history in older Western books. According to a recent article in that vein
on Chinese history, it would make more sense in terms of periodization for
the researcher to go from the expulsion of the Mongols in 1368 to 1911
than to break for the formation of the Europe-centered world market.
The Ming dynasty leads rather more logically to the Qing dynasty up to
1911, the latter date symbolizing the breaking of the Confucian hold and
the rise of a Western presence. The 1500s, from a Chinese perspective, or

at least from an orientalist Chinese perspective, are not at first glance too revelatory.[44] But one might still suppose that every country has a double identity, national and global. A country could be closed to the West internally but still play a large role through a proxy in the world economy. Historians tell us that the Chinese economy in the sixteenth century was the largest in the world. If so, how could China not be a part of the development of modern history?

Another feature of the Russian Road that bears on bilateralism was the blurring of state and empire, as Russian Road regimes needed to create and maintain caste hierarchies. As early as the sixteenth century, many non-Han peoples became part of the Chinese Empire; Tibet, for example, was conquered and annexed in 1571. Thereafter, it existed as a fixture of the caste hierarchy. China, like other Russian Road states, had no interest in a Fourth World, as countries in other hegemonies had.

In bilateral negotiations with Russian Road states, a constant theme was the internal market. In such states, given their large peasantries and rather fixed internal markets, observers at the time and subsequently have found that capitalism seems to have progressed at a more leisurely pace than, for example, British capitalism. Thus, various authors have noted that in the Qing period Chinese producers did not have the same access to foreign markets that their counterparts in Britain did.[45] Scholars give various explanations for this state of affairs, among them that when such states confront pressure from the lead capitalist nations, they tend to close their markets to the outside world, working thereafter through trade ports, commercial minorities, overseas communities, or less direct circuits to prevent themselves being overrun economically, even at the cost of retarding their own capitalist development. Nor was this strategy that uncommon, as we may recall from the earlier discussion of mercantilism. Open markets were the exception, not the rule. Indeed, often, it was only the ideologists of the lead country who called for open markets, as Adam Smith did in *Wealth of Nations*. Nobody else did, though, and it is certainly not as if the UK always practiced what it preached.[46]

The Ottomans represented yet another variant of the Russian Road type of hegemony. They selected certain existing minorities to be commercial intermediaries with Europe, allowing them to build up foreign trade and contacts while limiting the entrance of other foreign merchants into the local market, as well as restricting (though not eliminating) the Muslim majority's access to European trade. Given how close the Ottomans were to Europe, this system was quite difficult to maintain, yet they managed it until World War I.[47] Should one then still consider the Ottomans "the Sick Man" of Europe?

Let us now turn to a consideration of the influence of hegemony logic on the bilateral relations that were evolving in this period. When, for example, the Ottomans had the upper hand in a particular political context and set the terms of a treaty, as at Pruth in 1711 with the czar of Russia, their express concern was the protection of the territorial nationalities that were Muslim in the Russian Empire. The Porte recognized that the Muslims living under the Romanovs—for example, the Polish Cossacks and the subjects of the prince of Crimea—would be suitable acquisitions, a point to which we will return. When the military outcome was reversed and Russia had the upper hand, as in the treaty of Kucuk Kaynarca in 1774, the Russians demanded to be the protectors of the Greek Orthodox subjects of the sultan, for similar reasons. The larger point here is that given the demands for further outlays that these treaties entailed, domestic public opinion would have to be supportive of them as well, and this was likely to be the case.

Even the provincial history of the Ottoman Empire saw international dealings done so as to appease domestic opinion. The case of Egypt comes to mind,[48] or at least it would if it were not for the paradigm issues.[49] Well-known details about Egyptian history ought to have led scholars to resist the Orientalist idea of the coming of the West in favor of bilateralism, but they have not. 'Ali Bey's attempts to gain Egypt's independence in the 1760s through his Italian connection or Alfi Bey's effort to gain British support in 1803 really happened and really presupposed bilateralism.[50] Both failed; neither had public opinion with it.

Turning now to Persia and its international dealing, we find the following. In 1598 the English soldier of fortune Sir Anthony Sherley reached the court of Shah 'Abbas at Qazwin.[51] Ostensibly the representative of the earl of Essex, Sherley was actually out to promote himself. He fits the description of the New Man. After some effort, he got the shah to appoint him as his diplomat to Europe, the shah offering capitulation agreements to facilitate his mission. This maneuvering was typical of the Russian Road, Iran keeping its secrets by using an uninformed foreigner as a diplomat, using capitulation as a way to offer market relations without really offering much access.

An older generation of scholars read accounts of the Sherley Mission to mean that Islamic society was closed and could deal in only a minimal way with Europe, an approach reminiscent of comments made by scholars on China about the Portuguese at Macau.[52] In neither case, however, does this approach seem convincing. If knowledge is power, then why not begin with the assumption that a Safavi ruler or his Chinese counterpart would think it was clever to send someone abroad who had nothing to reveal to others because he did not know anything?

By the early seventeenth century, Iran had to confront Dutch and British power and was not in a position to play one against the other to any great degree. Each received a capitulation treaty according to at least some of its dictates. Although these agreements were basically commercial treaties, we find in their text something of the difference in hegemonic logic one associates on the one hand with the Netherlands (a tribal-ethnic state) and on the other hand with the UK (a bourgeois democracy) and at the same time how Iran, a Russian Road state, pursued its own objectives as well. In the 1623 Capitulations Treaty of Shah 'Abbas with the Netherlands, the Netherlands demanded that if any Dutchman became a Muslim, the Netherlands reserved the right to seize him and his goods and deport him. If any Dutchman was found guilty of being in the company of a Muslim woman, he might only be punished by Dutch authorities. The Netherlands also reserved the right to buy local Christian slaves and take them out of the country.[53] This treaty contrasted with the Sherley Accord, signed six years later with Great Britain. In the English document of 1629, the apparent concern of the British as regards slaves was recovering runaway slaves as lost property, not specifically as Christians. Runaway slaves were to be handed over at cost except for any who were Muslim, this reservation no doubt an Iranian one. As concerned personal status issues, the document went on to specify ambassadorial responsibility for the deceased's children, assuming the absence of a family but not otherwise. It also specified that an Englishman had a right to safely convert to Islam.[54] This right was perhaps ahead of its time even for Britain, as it seems to have been considerably whittled away by the time of the 1675 Capitulations Act signed by Great Britain with the Ottoman Empire.[55] At that later point, an Englishman converting to Islam might expect his property to be seized by the British government, British society by this time beginning to consider Muslims, like the Irish, as a racial undercaste, as changes in the law suggest. By the 1670s, in what had become Restoration Britain, Muslims no longer enjoyed the same status they had in the Elizabethan period. Thus, British liberty no longer applied to Muslim converts to the extent it had even a half century earlier. From these examples, it is apparent that each side sought and received aspects compatible with its own public opinion.

As time went on there were more changes. By the Restoration period, British negotiators were stipulating that a British community abroad would live according to its own laws. From this decree it appears that the bourgeois democracy emerging in Britain was to be spread wherever the British went. An Englishman would no longer be free to live any other way. Thus, for a democracy, what stands out are the individual, his rights, and his property in the context of a certain racial hierarchy of which he is the top. This explains why the British did not anticipate allowing Persian merchants extraterritorial rights in Britain; it would have been a concession suggesting a granting of parity to a racialized other.[56] From a British point of view, the Dutch offered much greater reciprocity according to their agreement in 1623, suggesting, however symbolically, the difference between their hegemonies. For a tribal state, such as the Netherlands, the presence of an alien community did not carry the same baggage it did for the British. What was sensitive for the Netherlands were issues such as gender or religion. Once they were dealt with, it was simply a matter of having the Persians conform in a nondisruptive way to Dutch society. This contrast explains why they were granted a communal status via diplomacy, thereby allowing them to do business in Europe if they wanted to. Differences between Britain and Holland thus seem clear. Where an Englishman might choose to be a Muslim without problems as a matter of bourgeois liberty (at least for a good deal of the time), a Dutchman might face ostracism if he allowed himself to convert because tribal-ethnic lines were decisive for the hegemony in Holland, not bourgeois right. From a Persian point of view, none of it mattered too much because there was no threat to the state. Priorities had thus been preserved, and therefore domestic public opinion would likely be supportive. The Rise of the Rich evolved following such patterns.

As a third variant of hegemony, let us now consider an example of an Italian Road regime, France, looked at in terms of its dealings with tribal-ethnic states such as Lebanon and Tunisia. This too was a part of the Rise of the Rich. In Lebanon the French goal, perhaps because of the silk industry in Lyons, was to become accepted as the guarantor of the Maronite Christians, some of whom produced the raw silk that France needed. In 1649 Louis XIV, the "Sun King," succeeded in this effort, in effect becoming the guarantor of the Lebanese Maronites. Here seems to be the genesis of the culturalist approach to foreign policy for which France became known, France projecting its domestic hegemonic discourse into its foreign dealings and becoming not just the protector of various rulers of tribal states but also a source of the ruler's own high culture. Looked at the other way around, for the Lebanese political elite, merchants, landlords, and clergy of the period, there were many advantages to playing to the French, both in Lebanon and abroad. Thus they asserted the need for a protector, which would be in keeping with their own tribal-ethnic state logic. In return, the Crown would open positions for them in the church, in commerce, and in the university. French public opinion did not seem to react negatively to these initiatives.

Bilateral relations, as noted earlier, tended to be rooted in unequal power. How was this inequality expressed on a day-to-day basis without it appearing to be a threat to the weaker hegemony? How did the stronger party show its strength or remind the other periodically of its strength? Moreover, for whom was the display of strength intended? Was it to frighten the ruler of the weaker state or to frighten his subjects into allowing their ruler the freedom to collaborate with a stronger power? Whichever the case, it is clear that the technique varied. Two of the leading democracies, the United States and Great Britain, used gunboats, seemingly to intimidate the Deys, whereas the Italian Road regimes, of which France was an example, used culture to entrap them. Entrapment could work both ways. Often, rulers such as the Deys would require ceremonies and gift giving. In the French-Tunisian example in the early nineteenth century, a controversy arose that brought the issue to the fore. In this period, France was beginning its transition from being an Italian Road regime to being a bourgeois democracy. Apparently, as this took place gift giving became problematic. Paris became reluctant to being perceived as paying tribute, an attitude that collided with the attitude of the French consuls resident in North Africa, who dealt directly with the Deys and continued to believe they benefited from retaining the older approach. In an important interlude in the history of French foreign policy, the consuls demanded and received the right to keep giving the Deys presents. As a recent article on this subject suggests, technologically complicated and expensive gifts continued to be the way the French conveyed their power.[57] Correctly understood, the gift giving was far from paying tribute or appeasement. France was dealing with the rulers of tribal-ethnic states. These rulers appreciated such gifts as gift giving was how relations were solidified. For its part, France used culture as a component of its diplomacy with such rulers. The same approach might have had no utility in dealing with the United States or Russia and probably would not have been considered. It was not a question of the West and the Orient; it was a question of how to get the best results when dealing with a tribal-ethnic state.

From these divergent examples, it becomes clear that domestic hegemony logic was generally intertwined with foreign policy commitments. In some instances, this meant that to claim that a policy followed logically from local tradition was a good way for a ruler to make the pitch for some new foreign adventure. The public might balk at the prospect of paying some new levy to support any other kind of foreign policy, and opposition could easily rise up. Another point follows as well. Diplomacy works to overcome problems created by differences in hegemonic logic or ceremonial expectations.

CONCLUSION

This chapter set out to present an interpretation of the history of the world in early modern times using the framework of the Rise of the Rich. In doing this, it rejected a tradition in Marxist scholarship that considers the core of the subject of world history of the period to be British history and British history to be an internal progression rooted in class struggle. Equally, it rejected a tradition in liberal scholarship that saw each part of the world as a self-contained civilization into which the West intruded, which in essence amounts to the same thing. To introduce the Rise of the Rich paradigm and to show how it would differ from the Rise of the West, liberal or Marxist, the chapter entered into a discussion of two central concepts that serve to explain and interpret the development of modern capitalism: accumulation and proletarianization. It observed that current usage has limited these concepts to such an extent that they have come to be understood in very Eurocentric ways. The result is that it is easy to find a discussion of accumulation limited to a certain period or a certain locale or simply to economics with no reference to politics or to its actual larger significance. Proletarianization as a concept has suffered a similar fate.

The chapter then raised the question of how, with the materials at hand today, one could present the sequence of developments in world history, benefiting from existing scholarship but not defined by it. The solution proposed was to choose concepts based on how widely they were used and then try to adapt them to an even wider range of contexts. In most instances, the choices were concepts that had originated in the study of Europe but had already been applied more widely and had stood the test of time.

Methodologically, this approach was a departure from standard practice in at least two major ways. First, most specialists would assume that the study of world history reveals sharp differences between Europe and non-Europe and would work from that basis. I do not agree; difference here is put in the background under specificity. Second, most historians would then assume that even if Europe is much more carefully studied than other regions, the concepts one would use to study non-Europe must logically come from that material or else they are simply imposed. This methodological assumption is in turn based on a certain set of suppositions not only about the nature of the material but also about the nature of scholarly activity—for example, the supposition that the historian is simply a transmitter of what exists, not a creator, or that the historian does not impose but merely records. Here it is assumed the historian is, willingly or otherwise, a bit of both. Given where the field of world history is today, and how unevenly developed it is, it is presumed that one could learn about a country anywhere if the form of its hegemony was that which was familiar from some other context, be it from Europe or wherever; moreover, that as more examples from around the world are taken into consideration and more knowledge about them is accumulated, the original example of a particular form of hegemony would simply become one among a growing number. This methodology therefore is proposed as a short-term solution to the problem of imbalance and as a way to facilitate a change in the paradigm.

What most of the states of the early modern period faced was the problem of how to deal with the market. History for most of them moved from crisis to crisis—for instance, the Crisis of Seventeenth Century, the Bourgeois Revolution, the Industrial Revolution, and the birth of the Fourth World. The unusual feature of this series of events was both the number of crises and the fact that the transition to capitalism did not get derailed as it had earlier. Problems that had beset earlier attempts at the transition to capitalism were overcome this time, the chapter hypothesizes, thanks to the New Men. The New Men created or expanded both the market itself and the political and economic connections among the Rich. Without the New Men, it is difficult to imagine this period being part of a modern age. More likely, even the advanced countries would have slipped back into what Marx called the "Second Feudalism," as some in any case did. Without the New Men, states would not have been allied; accumulation would have been limited.

On examining the texts of a few of the treaties between European and Middle Eastern regimes from the period, we find the importance of hegemony logic in dictating various features of each side's demands. Rulers who involved themselves in commitments abroad faced a degree of vulnerability on the home front if the new treaty meant incurring additional burdens. To camouflage these burdens, the language and structure of the relations were designed to minimize these risks.

In Chapter 4 we pursue the subject of the Rise of the Rich from the years 1850 onward. In this period, hegemonies matured and developed complex forms of multilateral relations, in turn producing a series of crises leading to the present day.

THE AGE OF MULTILATERALISM

The World after 1850

IN A RISE OF THE RICH PARADIGM INTERPRETATION, the period from 1850 to the present, i.e., contemporary history, is the age of multilateralism, a period during which one sees the banding together of a growing number of the world's dominant elements in an increasing interdependency as they seek to promote market capitalism. It is a period in which one sees the rise and decline of several great powers, but at the same time one sees a new type of dispersion of power, one often drawing the great powers into conflicts or confrontations with each other in remote corners of the world as the alliance systems grow larger and more formalized. One thinks of Sarajevo. A century earlier the assassination of an archduke visiting Serbia would scarcely have caused a world war.

The Rich, it appears, can escape neither their roots in the nation-states nor the problems inherent in their class character. The result on the world scale is that they have become a class in themselves but not for themselves, while at the same time by virtue of the wealth and power they have accumulated they are confronted with ever increasing challenges. Competition among nations has also been ruthless. International law has sometimes been not much of an arbiter; dominant elements have often flouted it or redefined it in ways that defied the intent of its framers. The only real help likely to be proffered to countries in need is aid to sustain the market and stave off the rise of populism or nationalism.

In the absence of much apparent capacity for collective action, the Rich have evolved on an ad hoc basis, almost accidentally coming up with coping techniques in response to crises. Two of these techniques stand out and will be discussed in what follows. The first is rule by state of emergency. World-wide over the past century, more and more emergency legislation has been enacted and today is in use. The second involves anointing a great power, today notably the United States, as world policeman. Neither strategy has met with wide acceptance or enjoyed particular success. Critics claim that on a political level, these strategies represent desperation, that capitalism has run out of ideas. Although this opinion may overstate matters, there is some truth in it. If collective action is required even for the sake of human survival, at some point there may not be much that will be forthcoming as there will be no collectivity beyond that which would perpetuate the mar-ket. Where that leaves the perpetuation of the species is not clear.

One might well ask, how has humanity fallen into its present condi-tion? How has opposition to capitalism and to the world market failed so abysmally? Humanity's situation in early modern history was by no means this uncertain. As I have already argued, the reasons for the present condi-tion are essentially political ones, the result of a long series of political mis-takes made by opposition movements. What I found was that if one starts from the premise that the only counterhegemonic struggle is the struggle of organized labor, then one has made a historiographical choice and an incorrect one at that. As a result of this choice, the historian would likely concentrate on the gains and losses of organized labor. However, as mod-ern history has shown, this approach has repeatedly failed. Even the Rus-sian Revolution was ultimately such a failure. The workers' state arose, but the political stratification of Russia remained in place because it was never challenged. So one way, then, to explain humanity's current situation—here to repeat—is as the consequences of a series of bad choices when it comes to matters of emancipation historiography as part of the problem.

Still, the reader might ask, why approach the subject in this fashion? The subject of contemporary history is one we all know. Why not use some more familiar formulation out of the Hegelian tradition, such as "late capi-talism"? Why multilateralism?[1] Here one needs to recall that capitalism, though unable to redistribute wealth to the poor, has given back some of it to Third World ruling classes in acknowledgment of their power and the services they render to the market. Keeping this detail in mind, we can explain why not late capitalism: the answer relates to power and who has it. The advanced capitalist business structure of the core countries is only a part of the narrative of power in the world.[2] If one introduces that insight into the idea of late capitalism, one destroys the latter's rationale.

To tie these points together, I begin this chapter with an overview of the age of multilateralism, 1850 to the present. Multilateralism is found to be a brilliantly designed vehicle for capital accumulation. The chapter proceeds to show that as a result, multilateralism has engendered opposition, necessitating in turn the rise of the "world policeman" and rule by state of emergency. It then turns to consider this opposition. What opposition would result in such severe countermeasures on the part of the state? Certainly, it had to be more than that of the traditional independence movement, trade union movement, or communist party. There must be other kinds of opposition, opposition that must have some counterhegemonic potentiality. This would have frightened the state to take extreme measures. No clear conclusion can be reached about this hypothesis. The chapter concludes with observations about the challenges posed by the repoliticization of labor and the threat to the state posed by the growing importance of public opinion in the age of the Internet at the same time.

THE AGE OF MULTILATERALISM, 1850–PRESENT

This section presents the main phases of world history of the past 150 years as the age of multilateralism. It merges concepts from diplomatic, economic, political, and social history to create a periodization highlighting the stages of development through which multilateralism has gone. This section begins with a discussion of the term *multilateralism*. The term *multilateralism*, like the term *bilateralism,* is borrowed from the field of international relations, its meaning adapted for the purposes of a study of world history.

In IR terms *bilateralism* and *multilateralism* are terms that have a somewhat normative quality about them. Here by way of contrast, they characterize actual periods in history.[3] The age of multilateralism is thus intended here to be a description of the age of the capitalist nation-state and with it the growth of the internal market, these two developments made possible by the international alliances among dominant elements around the world; multilateralism in a more narrow sense is a characterization of the alliances.

A quick overview of the age of multilateralism would likely contain the following. It would begin with an account of the classical liberalism of the "Gilded Age." It would note the rise of rival power blocs before World War I; it would then note the development of "corporatist regimes" and alongside them the League of Nations. The corporatist phase, it is observed, lasted for some fifty years, into the early 1970s. During that period the United Nations would come to replace the League of Nations and the United States would come to replace Britain as the great power. This phase in turn was followed by a return to classical liberalism, bringing us to the present. To a certain extent, this latest phase is a repetition of the late nineteenth century, with rival power blocs and clashes of civilizations; to a certain extent, it is not. One can discern some change, and in the second part of the section, I will emphasize what specifically changed as capitalism encountered a political crisis.

The birth of the age of multilateralism came in the period 1850–80. In social history, this period is typically studied as the birth of the capitalist nation-state, the period in which the home market became fully developed. Where the power came from that allowed this market to be imposed on the different peoples of the world is generally left unexplored. Combining social history and diplomatic history, one finds that the birth of the nation-state coincided with what one might take to be a revolutionary period in diplomatic history. This period was marked by a sudden rapid growth of treaties, signed by an increasing number of nations. As the total of these treaties grew along with the number of signatories to them, so too did the power of those rulers who implemented them and modified them for local conditions, the latter including the Third World ruling classes. Although the latter may have been represented only in the various international conferences by observers, once the world bound itself to collective agreements and laws, they became copartners in the new order in interpreting and upholding them.

Hundreds of treaties were signed among rulers. These treaties were not simply an expanded version of the bilateral treaties of the sort found earlier, but a whole new system marked by consultation among the great powers as well as by interstate arbitration. A number of international conferences were held to resolve particular issues. Some of these conferences served to regulate shipping and maritime-related issues, such as fishing rights, whereas other conferences dealt with metrics, telegraphy, the post, the plague and sanitation issues, the creation of the Red Cross, and even the conduct of war. In 1890 the General Act of the Brussels Conference marked an important international step in trying to break the slave trade. In this period as well, the use of experts became more common, allowing technical work to proceed and freeing diplomats to carry on their work. Finally, beginning somewhat earlier but continuing through this period, one finds an acceptance of the idea of a supreme military commander, an idea that allowed for collective struggle. This move was necessary to combat Napoléon. Out of that struggle and following the Congress of 1814–15 came other far-reaching collective agreements, some involving a devolution of power, others ensuring the navigation of rivers, and still others protecting the rights of minorities.[4]

By the end of the nineteenth century, relative security on the level of the Rich had been achieved. The ruling classes of different countries started to congregate in public as in the Congress of Berlin in 1880 and at the League of Nations a few years later. The Rise of the Rich in the narrower sense of the term was thus quite visible. Tycoons, generals, and Afro-Asian rulers competed for attention in the media. By the end of the nineteenth century even those countries that had not previously had an aristocracy gained one thanks to the new possibilities of concentration of wealth and power afforded by the capitalist nation-state and multilateralism. Kevin Phillips, who has studied American wealth in this period, points to the sudden growth of dynastic families and even genealogy societies, showing how politics from that period was affected by the rather self-conscious role that certain wealthy families began to play. As Phillips notes, it was dynasticism that made this America of the Gilded Age so different from the earlier America captured by Tocqueville's description of a country of yeomen. Until now dynasticism has been something most Americans have taken for granted. According to a recent study, George Bush's family has had more intermarriages with European monarchies than John Kerry's, which the author of the study considers a relevant category of analysis in discussing rank.[5]

Just as there was nothing especially peaceful or diplomatic about the age of bilateral relations, the same could be said for the age of multilateralism.

Rulers may have felt a sense of security in their person and in their proper-
ties but not much else. If the old system of bilateral relations was marked
by numerous small instances of bloodshed, the new one in the nineteenth
century and beyond witnessed the beginning of the age of "total war," in
which warfare was much more lethal and involved many more participants.
Cooperation in some spheres could promote broader human welfare; cooperation in others could promote the opposite.

Another way of looking at this trajectory is to note that each step in
the development of multilateralism followed a crisis, and the same is true
today, to the extent that there still is development. In the late nineteenth
century, colonial rivalries led to a number of such crises. It would not be an
exaggeration to claim that beginning in this period more than once these
crises threatened the viability of multilateralism itself, forcing it to evolve or
fall apart. The Algeciras Conference of 1906 could serve as an example of
one such moment. At that conference participants realized that the expectation of reaching unanimity on an issue among all major states was no
longer realistic. At the same time, failure to reach some kind of consensus, especially on international issues, would have domestic repercussions.
One could anticipate that oppositional groups would see some advantage in
seizing the moment to stir up problems. In a sense what has followed could
be read as a footnote to that conference and that insight.

What resulted in the short term and often enough thereafter was the creation of blocs of countries. One bloc would take one position, and another
would take the opposite. As the crises in the Balkans and World War I
showed, however, the activities of the blocs could just as easily lead to wars
as it could to the prevention of wars. World War I proved this fairly defini-
tively. After the war, with the formation of the League of Nations came the
rise of a new mechanism of global conflict resolution, a kind of parliament
of nations. The league was an attempt to overcome the problem of blocs.

Before proceeding further, it is important to mention that from the
late nineteenth century onward, one begins to find the development of
parastatal organizations as well, adding another dimension to the subject
of multilateralism, one broadly associated with the political power of the
middle classes. Thus, for example, we find, in the later nineteenth century,
new international associations arising to regulate various issues of general

interest to states, to ruling classes, but also to interested parties, including the International Copyright Union, the International Institute for Agriculture, and the International Penitentiary Commission, among others.[6] These organizations for the most part still exist today.

Let us now turn to the League of Nations, the institution that symbolized more than any other the workings of multilateralism at that point in history, when liberalism was subsiding and corporatism was on the rise. The League of Nations began in 1919. It was composed of a council, a general assembly, and a permanent secretariat. It had various agencies and organizations attached to it. These agencies and organizations dealt generally with economic and financial issues. They also dealt with health, refugee, and drug issues and certain social problems, such as trafficking in women and children.

To discharge its responsibilities, the league acquired a permanent staff of international civil servants, becoming a professional organization in the process. Although history has not been kind to the league, one should acknowledge that it actually resolved many disputes, introduced the concept of the aggressor, and tried to inaugurate collective sanctions. There were, to be sure, limitations. The countries represented in its formal membership were mainly European and Latin American ones, but its vision and way of proceeding laid the groundwork for a future expansion of membership and of course brought observers from many other countries. The year 1945 saw the San Francisco Conference to write the charter for a United Nations, an organization that came to include most of the world's countries as members.

One initiative in multilateral diplomacy that has drawn a good deal of attention is the "Mandate System." The Mandate System arose because the league was left to deal with problems that no one state felt able to face alone but that called out for attention. What this development has suggested to historians—and it appears to fit with a multilateral analysis—is that the phase in which the great powers could truly proceed unilaterally was over. In recognition of this fact, colonial peoples formerly controlled by the Germans and Ottomans, the defeated parties during World War I, were put under the league's care, no one too sure who should deal with them or how. The league turned the victors in World War I into mandatory powers, bequeathing to them these ambiguities, a point to which we now turn, unilateralism henceforth more an appearance than a reality.

The idea of a mandate is an interesting if opaque one, one that has been capable of sustaining tensions among nations from the period of World War I to the present, tensions arising from different understandings of what a mandate was. Mandates were not supposed to be possessions in the sense of colonies. Following the adoption of the Mandate System, one country would be made to be responsible for upholding and transmitting the values of civilization to another on behalf of all civilized nations, the other being rated in terms of the progress it was making toward being civilized. Civilization was something assumed to be collectively shared by the advanced countries and enlightened elements around the world and something that could be transmitted in a finite amount of time.[7] Born in the Versailles Conference, the idea of the mandate has been commonly identified with Wilsonian idealism about the universality of human yearning for the benefits of civilization, but as academic studies have shown it also echoed the pragmatism of South African Jan Smuts, who also played a role in bringing about its genesis.[8] Smuts was no fan of international law or of the rising political influence of the anticolonial spokesmen, who tended to look at the world in terms of law. Thus, whatever its precise origins, in practice the mandate appears to have acknowledged the idea of rule by law but to have subsumed it under civilization. Perhaps one could claim that not too much had changed. The leading economic powers had never been very enthusiastic about international law. As the middle classes continued to grow in size and influence and as the influence of the Third World grew as well, the Rich increasingly found that they had to justify themselves somehow and that they might not be able to use civilization to do it. At that point, the idea of the mandate became useful. To justify owning a country, one could still claim at least for the short term that one stood for civilization. However, when it came to the matter of the long run or how a mandate was to be ruled, here of course conflicts would arise. Rule in terms of civilization unlike rule by law was not set up with transparent procedures. Not surprisingly, when anticolonial movements gained strength, the question of procedures or lack thereof became a matter of significance.

In fact, it could be claimed that the era of the Mandate System did not in any clear way solve the problems left over from the colonial heyday that preceded it. If anything, the system itself led to a series of crises for the leading colonial country of the day, crises that have yet to end. If Britain was to endorse the idea of the mandate, which it did, then the rationale for its continued colonialism was called into question; all its colonial ruling classes demanded independence or some other quid pro quo. This was a problem. The solution to it that the British proposed was the formation of the British Commonwealth. The Commonwealth would be a consultative organization, rooted philosophically in civilizationalism. It was tried, but it did not serve the purpose very well. A generation later, when the UK began to join the Common Market, the other members of the Commonwealth felt left in the lurch. It created other problems as well. In the Middle East, the Mandate System had raised expectations that were not to be met, and there was little the Commonwealth could do to address such matters. The Palestinian Question is a case in point. As the Palestinians came to realize that the real rationale for the Palestine Mandate System was to avoid granting their country independence, they became increasingly politicized.[9] The fact that some of the other mandates, such as Syria and Lebanon, became independent countries, provided the Palestinians with an irritating contrast to their own situation, especially since Syrian and Lebanese independence had more to do with the exhaustion of the mandatory power at a given moment than it did with the progress those mandates had made toward acquiring civilization.

The Palestine Question quickly became the locus classicus of the conflict between those segments of the rich supporting control of the world market by civilization and those supporting law. The former supported the mandate as a civilizing mission and later supported Israel's right to Palestine as a part of civilization, whereas the latter tended to support the mandate on a more contractual basis in terms of the right of national self-determination of the Palestinians. This very profound division explains why the Palestine Question remains unresolved year after year. And what this in turn suggests is that one could take the Palestine Question as evidence of the unfolding crisis of multilateralism of recent years. What the Palestine Question is is an example of an insoluble political problem because of the irreconcilability of law and civilization.

Looking back on the end of World War I, one wonders if Britain's rulers ever considered Palestine a mandate as opposed to a colony. The decision to offer the Zionist Movement a home there by Lord Balfour seems closer to the ideology of colonialism than to that of the Mandate System. The Balfour Declaration implied a sense of British ownership and hence a right to do what it saw fit to do. So too did the British reaction to the King-Crane Commission, the original inquiry to determine the views of the Palestinians about their future. The premise underlying the King-Crane Commission seemed to be one implying more the idea of a contractual arrangement. The Zionist Movement, for its part, on more than one occasion claimed to feel betrayed by the British, giving the sense that for them at least Palestine was a British colony and the British had been derelict in their responsibilities.

Palestinians, however, acted as if Palestine was more a mandate in the civilizational sense than anything else. Palestinian nationalism evolved under the British but more as cultural nationalism and civilizationalism than as a serious state-building project, crystallizing politically only in the 1950s after the departure of the British with the birth of the Palestine Liberation Organization (PLO). Why this is is not clear. Perhaps, it was simply the weakness of the Palestinian middle classes in that earlier period that allowed the country to be stuck in civilizationalism, or perhaps it was a deliberate strategy to gain what could be gained.

Mandates being what they are, Palestinian nationalists began their struggle as partial insiders to the world of the colonizer or civilizer. Unlike the North African *evoluées* and others, who were in a somewhat analogous situation, Palestinian nationalists, perhaps because of their belief that Palestine was a mandate, did not feel the need to seek European allies in their struggles as other anticolonial movements tended to. Even as late as 1948, Palestinians still appeared to be looking at their system as a matter of civilizational development, involving themselves in developing their educational system more than in developing their political infrastructure à la the Zionists. When the 1948 war came, no doubt most Palestinians were thus caught by surprise. On the other hand, the war did not seem to have been a surprise for the Zionist Movement. It was for them a war with a colonial power, one for which they had been preparing for a long time. Among the important events that occurred at that point was that the United States recognized Israel as an independent state. In recognizing Israel as an independent state, the United States seemed to move closer to the idea of Palestine as a British colony, one taken over by the Zionist Movement, and therefore to move further from the Wilsonian idea of Palestine as a mandate, as mandates cannot be turned over to any third party but only to the indigenous inhabitants. The acceptance of the idea that the remaining Palestinian homeland were territories whose disposition would be dealt with in the future further adds to the idea that Palestine was simply a colony.

This ambiguous legacy lives on in the refusal of most countries to recognize Palestinian statehood even on the land that remains to them in this supposedly postcolonial era, a point that is not easy to interpret outside of the context of a mandate believed to be still ongoing in one form or another. Yet this situation too is ambiguous, given that no one is claiming to be a mandatory power for Palestine. Still, how else can one explain the deferring of recognition of Palestinian statehood? Why else the deference to Israeli sensibilities, even when Israel shows no interest in assuming the formal responsibilities of an independent nation-state vis-à-vis its Palestinian inhabitants? One is left to assume in line with the mandate model that Israel inherited the mandate. As a civilized nation, Israel thus inherited the right of veto over whether the Palestinians are yet ready to be considered civilized and independent, inheriting in effect the privileges if not the responsibilities of a mandatory power. As a result, from a Palestinian perspective, the road to gaining national recognition, once that road was finally taken, has been pretty much nothing but uphill. Having recognized the right of Israel to exist even while Israel was occupying more and more land, land that presumably would be a part of their future state, Palestinians then found that recognition by the great powers would still be deferred until Palestinians ceased to attack Israeli settler encroachment. But since when do states recognize each other on that basis? Why, for example, should quarrels between Israel and the Palestinians preclude at least some countries from recognizing Palestine as an independent country and from signing treaties with it? One wonders if it means that Palestine in the Western imaginary is still in fact a mandate becoming civilized?

Something like this state of affairs appears to be the case by process of elimination: the Israelis do not want to assimilate more Palestinians. It is not just a matter of the Jewishness of Israel; it is a matter of security. Uncivilized people in this optic are by definition dangerous. Thus, we find that the right of return, a legal claim, does not apply to Palestinians but only to Jews. Other evidence points in the direction of civilizationalism as well. As American and Israeli politicians have put it in recent years, we have no partner in the peace process, implying that the Palestinians have not reached that stage of civilization yet, and no other government outside of the Arab world challenges these claims.

Israel's position, it could be hypothesized, mirrored the shifting politics of multilateralism of the era and this much to the distress of many individual Israelis. One recalls that after the 1967 war, a number of Israeli legal scholars pointed out the illegality of the occupation, and this had some impact for a while. However, soon thereafter, in the early days of neoliberalism, Israel, like most other countries in the world, experienced an upsurge in civilization sentiment that provided a rationale for what was occurring. And it was at that point one started to hear that "We have no partners in the peace process." Here, the Palestinian experience differs from most others', save possibly the Puerto Ricans or the First Americans, all three struggling with the problem of being "Fourth Worlded" by settler states.

Was it the weakness of the Palestinian middle classes before 1948 that resulted in the idea of the mandate becoming so deeply embedded? Whatever the case, in the 1948 war the Palestinians were scarcely a factor. While the Palestinian bourgeoisie said and did nothing, and this is scarcely an exaggeration, Palestinian society in general apparently expected that the Arab states or even the West would come to its rescue. For Palestinians, the whole premise of who they were was apparently bound up in this internationally recognized mandate. And this view continued not only through 1948 but then on through the Nasser years as well and even beyond, the rise of the PLO notwithstanding. In the 1980s, I myself encountered people in Ramallah still asking rhetorically in one meeting, "Fayn al-'Arab?" (Where are the Arabs who will rescue us?). One would have to interpret this as more congruent with the idea of a mandate than with that of a colony.

But how, one wonders, can leading countries even contemplate risking a predominantly civilizational approach, given the legitimacy of international law throughout the world and given as well what they themselves gain from it? In other words, even if the leading countries preferred civilization to law, most other countries do not. Indeed, from World War I until at least the 1970s, most of the Third World (except for a few right-wing regimes) as well as most European countries favored law in general and in later years the World Court in particular as the final arbiter of legal disputes, over simply the values of Western civilization.[10] In that period at least, the World Court seemed to be an institution rising in importance. In more recent years, that is, after 1970, it became clear that for whatever reasons there were limits to how far rule by law could go, that there still was a conflict between rule by law and rule by civilizational values. Evidence for this is that over the past twenty-five years, the United States and Israel, among others, have repudiated court decisions in areas of concern to them, such as in the use of nuclear weapons, in the right to undermine the sovereignty of Nicaragua, in the right to build walls around the Palestinians, and more.[11] It was not that they were above the law but that the law in their view was being misapplied, given the civilization factor.

After 9/11 this collision of ideas about the foundations of sovereignty came to a head. At this point, many Americans took the view that civilization was under attack by barbarians, that underlying 9/11 there was a clash of civilizations, a clash between one real civilization and a false barbarous one, that in such a situation the United States had to go it alone and do so in any way it saw fit, the law notwithstanding. As with the case of the First Americans, law would not apply in this case. Others disagreed. They took the view that the idea of Muslim terrorism was a gimmick used to keep justifying civilizationalism, to avoid rule by law, and to allow for emergency legislation and a militarized foreign policy, if not "business as usual."[12] They blamed the United States for stirring up violence in the world. In short, civilizationalism as a form of cement for multilateralism has not been working too well, unable to extend much beyond preserving a unity of the powerful by keeping Palestine in limbo. At best, it is a matter of balance. Clearly, too much civilization has its costs as well; a part of the Rich would feel excluded, the latter preferring rule by law and on some level even an independent Palestine. At the same time, too much law interferes with the development of capitalism—for instance, the New Men. But by the same token too little law fails to address the problem of the ethnic cleansing of the Palestinians that goes on because of civilization.

Looked at more positively, although multilateralism has not up to now granted rule by law an automatic priority, rule by law nonetheless plays enough of a role to put a damper on some of the more atrocious practices of the past. Wars might be more lethal today, but overall, atrocities are more open to criticism than they were earlier in history. The most atrocious acts of the premultilateral phases and the early multilateral phase, connected with the slave trade, the colonial genocides, Hitler and Stalin, and in a different sense the U.S. use of nuclear weapons, are criticized much more today than they were at the time of their occurrence. One can observe over the past century some movement away from such practices as rule by law has progressed. The use of war and genocide as policy options are now looked at more as crimes. Regrettably, one finds in more recent years in their place a rise of ethnic cleansing. Increasingly, perhaps it is now all that rulers can get away with.

Earlier, this was scarcely the case. The death and demographic havoc caused by the slave trade over a long period of time did not appear to have entered people's consciousness outside of Africa until the rise of the abolitionist movement of the late eighteenth century, and even then the slave trade was not looked at as genocide. It was simply something that was not part of British values. Although mass killings provoked revulsion at different times in the nineteenth century, it was not until the twentieth century that the concept took on the status of some kind of ultimate evil. This shift in thinking came about through a long transition. During it, the Andrew Jackson–type attack on the Cherokees and other such epic events tapered off, gradually becoming seen as excesses. On an international level, the turning point arguably was the decision in the Belgian parliament to no longer allow for there to be a Free State and to assume the responsibilities of being a colonial power for the Belgian Congo, taking the Congo out of the hands of the royal family in 1908. Thereafter, the old pattern tapered off even more.

Modern-day ethnic cleansing started to emerge after World War II and to do so in a conspicuous fashion. Of course, ethnic cleansing was not new, as the old history of the pogroms attests, but at this point it was—here to repeat—what states could sometimes get away with. The prestige of world law and the pervasiveness of international scrutiny that accompanied the continuing evolution of multilateralism had by this point made the leisurely extermination programs, which we associate with the past, impractical. Short, horrible periods of brutalization and killing on a smaller scale came in their place. This was the new ethnic cleansing. What has happened to the Bosnians, the Rwandans, and the Iraqis since 2003 reflects this shift to ethnic cleansing.

Beginning in 1948, acts of genocide along with ethnic cleansing were defined as a crime against humanity, and cases were turned over to the International Criminal Court. Thus, for example, in the past decade individual Serbians and Rwandans among others have been charged with genocide and been tried by this court. A few years ago General Sharon narrowly escaped being tried for the massacres at Sabra and Shatila. So although, no doubt, the same propensities to kill and mutilate one's enemies exist as before, at this point rulers fear giving into them beyond spasms. Evidence can be drawn from how such crimes are now committed. For the Serbians, the massacre of the Bosnians in the 1990s was calculated as something to be done very quickly, whereas in Rwanda the calculation seemed to be that there would be a little more time before the world would take notice because the victims were Africans. It is clear that neither the Serbians nor the Rwandans, nor the French backing the Rwandans, wanted to be considered as committers of genocide. When confronted, they did not try to justify their acts of ethnic cleaning in terms of being civilized or having a historical destiny on their side, as the Nazis and colonists did earlier. This might be taken as a hopeful sign that, contrary to appearances, international law does have an increasing enforcement potential. At the very least, there is certainly a growing possibility of lawsuits. Rulers contemplating major crimes today have to worry not only about their country's future but for the first time in a long time about their own as well.[13] We might conclude that despite the importance attached to the role of civilization, especially by the leading capitalist countries, and despite the recourse to rule by state of emergency, the recent history of multilateralism has also witnessed the growth of the rule of law buoyed in part no doubt by the growing power of Third World ruling classes, a point to which we now turn.[14]

As the market spread in the nineteenth century, power among the Rich became more dispersed. If Third World rulers were to enforce the New World Order, they could demand things in return. Rule by law in fact served as the language through which certain kinds of demands could be made. This point is illustrated routinely in the General Assembly in the United Nations, in parastatal organizations, in the Non-Aligned Movement, and even in the World Bank. Earlier, in the nineteenth century, Third World ruling-class power, if one was to generalize, was local power, meaning it was less oriented to international law, but in the age of multilateralism this changed.[15]

Perhaps it is not surprising to find as well that this growth in Third World power has often been a matter of concern to the First World. One needs only recall the American political discourse about the UN. It is so vehement that it often comes close to a critique of rule by international law itself. To much of the American establishment, it appears that nothing the UN has ever accomplished amounts to anything. Certainly, it does not compare to what the United States accomplished in occupying Japan and Germany at the end of World War II. Most American criticism of the UN is directed at the General Assembly, where of course one finds the greatest density of Third World representation and correspondingly the greatest concern with political rights. For some time, American administrations have been demanding a reform of the General Assembly. Not infrequently, these demands have been accompanied by economic threats, boycotts (as of UNESCO), and by occasional insistence on the UN's need to strengthen the Security Council as a prop against the General Assembly. Of course, in the General Assembly, the Third World put the United States on the defensive many times, this no doubt accounting for the U.S. position.[16] Overall, despite some progress in the area of law, multilateralism may be seen as troubled. It seems in some ways to be a victim of its own success, a point to which we now must turn.

MULTILATERALISM, PRIMITIVE ACCUMULATION, AND THE NEW MEN

We now turn to the subject of wealth and in particular the wealth accumulated by the Rich in the era of multilateralism, emphasizing wealth from primitive accumulation, the truly profitable side of capitalism. To begin, we naturally have to encounter the paradigm issue again. For liberalism, the growth of wealth followed from honest toil. Primitive accumulation is simply an example of corruption. For Liberalism, corruption is not part of the real economy. It is a catchall category for everything from criminality to the pursuit of national interest mixed in with many other things. This extreme imprecision has its explanations and justifications, but it is an obstacle to further development of the field of world history as regards the study of power and wealth.

My contention here is that if one categorizes individuals and organizations in terms of the acts they commit without reference to the context or the meaning of the acts, then from a scientific perspective one fails to truly understand these acts. An illegal business that uses terror in the service of world capitalism is not comparable to a Basque separatist organization that terrorizes Spanish policemen. Both may kill people, but it is not the same crime. In such matters, liberal positivism as a method no longer suffices.

The pursuit of a subject such as multilateralism's reliance on primitive accumulation illustrates this dilemma as well. For the most part the subject is likely to elude a positivist treatment. Multilateralism rests on primitive accumulation, but how would one show this to the satisfaction of a positivist? Unequal exchange does not "show" it; it is an inference one draws or at least one can draw. If one looks for works on rulers who facilitated primitive accumulation, one might find a few accounts of King Leopold and the Congo or something about "slash and burn" plantations, but even here there is no one source or combination of sources that would satisfy an empiricist. If one looks for works on those individuals who were involved in "unequal exchange," which is by far the largest part of primitive accumulation, not surprisingly again one finds no familiar work of scholarship to rely on. Most scholarly work assumes that today at least there is no such thing as accumulation and that whatever one takes to be accumulation might better be subsumed under either normal business relations or corruption, one or the other and certainly not both at the same time. Certain countries, in the Third World, for example, are corrupt, and certain individuals who are criminals do what they do and get what they get because they are corrupt. Although this point may be accurate, as an observation it does not shed much light on the larger picture in which primitive accumulation, that is, a providing of illegal services to world capitalism, exists but is scarcely definable in these terms.

Perhaps the way to proceed in this context is to demonstrate with an example or two that corruption and accumulation are not the same thing, that the liberal approach errs in conflating the two. To study primitive accumulation more efficiently, as the foregoing has made clear, one should focus on the activities engaged in by the New Men, as they are the group that represents primitive accumulation par excellence. Some examples of correct and incorrect usages of these terms are in order at this point.

To this end, let us begin with an example illustrating the misuse of the term *corruption,* the latter in this case being confused with the pursuit of national interest. To do so, let us turn once again to Egyptian history, Egypt often serving in Western scholarship as the textbook example of a country that is the opposite of the honest West—that is, it is a corrupt Oriental country. A consideration of a couple of well-known vignettes leaves one persuaded that what one finds both in the colonial period and thereafter might more accurately be characterized as a clash of interests between England and Egypt, as reflected in the scholarship and in the use of the term *corruption* in this case.

Looking at the Egyptian leadership in World War II and the motivations for its foreign policy might be a good place to try to find what we are seeking. World War II for many historians is the moment that defines our own contemporary world, and Egypt has its place in that history, one oftentimes constructed by various authors using the Oriental-despotism model to emphasize the ruler's supposed passivity and corruption or, worse yet, his indifference or unawareness of the great events happening around him. "Bribe me if you want me to fight the Germans" would be the portrayal of King Faruq in many academic works.

Read in a less orientalist way, one could draw from this account something quite different as concerned the ruler's real motivations at the time. This is much more than simply illegal personal gain. Egypt followed an "Italian Road" type of hegemony. Stability was maintained by playing the interests of the working class of the North against the interests of the peasantry of the South. The ruling class was composed of two regional wings. What seems obvious from the scholarly record is that both wings of the ruling class were maneuvering to achieve their ends throughout that period in history. The upper Egyptian wing represented to an increasing degree by the monarch was trying to stay allied to the colonial power in order to fend off the nationalist movement, which was for the most part concentrated in the Delta. The Delta, or North, was the developed region and the center of Egyptian nationalism, a point not lost on the British. It is therefore not surprising to find that the colonial authority even in its waning days was trying to slow this development and nationalism by perpetuating a southern feudalism and monarchism in collaboration with the royal family, the descendants of Muhammad 'Ali. The war constituted an atypical moment when the British needed a more broad-based support from Egypt and therefore turned to the nationalists.

In a recent account of the sort I am criticizing for its reliance on the idea of Oriental corruption and its liberalism more generally, the author never considers the role of dynamics of the sort mentioned here, much less national interest, noting simply that British war interests in fighting Rommel were continuously compromised by the corrupt nature of Egyptian politics. In order to mobilize Egypt, the British focus had to be to get the king to accept the Wafd Party, that is, the Egyptian nationalist party, as opposed to his cronies' party. Looking at the matter from an Egyptian point of view, one finds that King Faruq naturally had his own agenda. His reluctance to turn to the Wafd Party to form a government had a certain basis. He saw Egyptian participation in the war as threatening to his own position, indeed as more than a little reminiscent of Egyptian participation in World War I, when the nationalists marginalized the then king and positioned the country to move toward greater independence.[17] This interpretation seems to be much less that of the corrupt Orient than of some piece of a struggle going on in an "Italian Road" type of hegemony. It does not negate the presence of corruption as liberals define it, but it does not exaggerate it either.

Even in the 1970s and the years following, as one arrives in the age of neoliberalism, with the British-backed monarchy abolished in 1952 and the country led by the very pro-Western president Anwar al-Sadat, the presumption of corruption was still what stood out in conventional scholarship, as if it were a permanent attribute of anything Egyptian. In this period, Egyptian businessmen were beginning to make an impact in business in the core of the world market, and no doubt this involved the usual lobbying and politicking. Thus, for example, Muhammad Fayed acquired Harrods in London and Ramy Lakah acquired *France-Soir* and the Lafayette Press Group. For the reasons already suggested, Egyptian ownership of these enterprises involved controversy, at least in the European media, the latter constructing a controversy and somehow implying that there was a distinctively Egyptian form of corruption that had been brought to London and Paris, with Egyptians somehow importing their undesirable and dangerous oriental corrupt ways with them.[18]

What then of primitive accumulation and how it gets misinterpreted as corruption? Let us now put aside the discussion of the Egyptian pursuit of national interest and turn to this matter. To begin one may recall that previously it was claimed that since the sixteenth century, the New Men have played a very conspicuous and dynamic role in capitalism. From whatever nationality they hailed, they worked to expand the market in return for the rewards and privileges that would go with it. To this end, they engaged in activities others eschewed, and when discontented with what they received in return they shifted their loyalties and took their revenge; one contemporary term for this shift, now moving forward to the age of the Taliban, Halliburton, al-Qa'ida, and Blackwater, is *blowback*. However, such are the complex needs of the Rich today, there are many other players and many different versions of the same game.

So if one was to generalize, who are the New Men today? As in early modern history, so today some are Westerners, and some are Third Worlders. Today they range from junk bond salesmen who occasionally go to prison for their ingenious business strategies to bankers, speculators, entrepreneurs of various sorts, terrorists, the Mafia, pirates, warlords, soldiers of fortune, arms dealers, narco-terrorists and so on. Sociologically, they range from aristocrats to the underclass, and they still receive today more attention in the popular media than they do in scholarly writing. Perhaps, if the link between capitalism and primitive accumulation was seen by historians as more central, then the point put forward here about the interpenetration of the legal and illegal activity would be something one could take for granted, and the details would be better known. But historians do not see the link because once capitalism arrived at the Industrial

Revolution of the eighteenth century, accumulation was not even thought to exist, much less to play an important role. As a result most historians in the tradition of Hegel still find capitalism on an everyday level to be essentially legal and moral and corruption and primitive accumulation, if they take place, to be a departure. One can thus ask, can history, given such assumptions, effectively study capitalism?

Looking at world history as the Rise of the Rich, the contribution of primitive accumulation to the growth of the modern world market is a very straightforward matter. For the market to grow, it has to allow for plunder. It also has to provide all possible services for which there is a customer, and accordingly it has to reward even those individuals functioning on the margins of the law if they provide the desired services. So if regular banks and businesses are limited by national law codes and by investors' concerns with company images, there would need to be a way around such obstacles—and there is. This line of inquiry would seemingly have much to offer. For example, it would explain how modern capitalism has avoided stagnation and how it has been able to keep developing. It would explain as well how capitalism keeps attracting talent, functioning as it does in a sense as a meritocracy for a certain category of individuals.

Although this interpretation smacks of revisionism for today's historian, it would be less the case, one discovers, for a criminologist, especially one versed in current thought about "organized crime" or transnational crime. This field of criminology could therefore be one place world historians could turn to help distinguish primitive accumulation from corruption. In a recent study published on the meaning of "organized crime," the author, a criminologist, contends that "real crime history" or real corruption has always been tied up with the history of the political elite. A term such as *organized crime* is an artificial construct, a part of a paradigm developed for the study of crime in the United States and then uncritically adopted by scholars worldwide. This paradigm made out particular crimes or forms of corruption to be the work of foreigners, often foreigners from backward regions, as in the United States the rackets run by the Sicilian Mafia. The idea of calling this "organized" crime arose in the nineteenth century, and what in effect that characterization has done is cover up the fact that most of the most organized crime has in reality always been carried out by individuals in office or who are highly placed in society or the world system, not by marginalized immigrants. It is insiders and insiders alone who have had the means to carry out complicated large-scale crimes successfully. The utility of blaming Sicilians for crime in America apart from disguising this fact is that it allows for the development of a police state to control the minorities, one that would otherwise be difficult to justify, given the Constitution.[19] This claim about the political economy of corruption is more sweeping than what is required here. The point I want to make is that an analysis of primitive accumulation following the work of such scholars probably cannot be a part of mainstream history until there is a paradigm shift in the latter.

One could nonetheless illustrate what might become available for historians by considering some actual category of transnational crime in a little more detail. Piracy comes to mind. Piracy is, of course, also a subject long pursued by world historians and is thus very familiar. In the view of most historians, what one finds is that the concept of piracy, like that of the Orient or of corruption more generally, is something that serves as a foil for the idea of Western normality. In other words, it does not have any relationship to the officially sanctioned economy any more than does primitive accumulation. In contrast to the view of historians, a number of criminologists and law professors believe that piracy is a phenomenon with its own internal functionality and ties to global power structures and more.

Following their work, one discovers that piracy is in effect a recognizable part of the international economy. Piracy explains how uranium and oil change hands and makes some areas safer than others, thereby affecting the prosperity of entire regions. Although, of course, not all pirates are New Men engaged in primitive accumulation, piracy would be a logical place to look to find at least some of them. To do this efficiently, however, one's definition of piracy has to keep up to date with one's conception of capitalism. The author of a recent article on maritime law, for example, complains that the phenomenon of piracy as it exists today in law and in common understanding is still the one embodied in the UN Convention on the Law of the Sea drafted in 1982, one looking to the past. This outdated approach is problematic. Piracy is a part of today's structure; it is not something from the days of yore. Subjects such as piracy are thus in constant need of redefining. The 1982 definition, the author notes, emphasizes crimes on the high seas against ships and aircraft. There are, however, newer forms of piracy, ones yet to be recognized in law—for example, where it involves attacks in port and not just attacks by pirates on the high seas.[20] Yet it is a concern for someone writing world history, especially for someone concerned with Eurocentrism, that piracy is still conventionally studied only as corruption and rarely as meaningful economic activity, at least by historians; in other words, it is outside of history. The result is that one never seems to get beyond the Rise of the West, as the West has most of the economy defined as legitimate economy.

Two British criminologists who have been researching the term *transnational organized crime*, a term somewhat akin to *piracy*, have found that the Council of Europe's Classification of Organized Crime, issued in 1993, portrayed organized crime as a part of politics and as a part of economics but not as a part of society in any significant sense. They found this position logically unacceptable. Increasingly, they point out, the scholarly analysis of crime has been concentrated on how crimes are actually committed and what difference they make as opposed to the supposed immorality of the criminal. This framework leads in practice to the rejection of the idea of one legitimate market penetrated by criminal elements in favor of the idea of a spectrum of different but interdependent markets.[21] The emphasis in this newer work in criminology about the way crimes are committed and to what end appears to fit our discussion of the New Men, individuals who in yesteryear were not infrequently knighted if they lived to tell the tale for their contributions but often were simply hanged or jailed. The same situation still prevails today. For many players of the game today, working for countries such as the United States, it is uncertain if they will go to jail for their crimes or retire as pillars of their communities. Either is a possibility.

Unequal exchange, piracy, narco-terrorism, and other forms of illegal commerce are among the best-known types of today's primitive accumulation. Other types, however, also exist and in the age of neoliberalism appear to actually be on the rise. These forms include transnational service organizations, the term *transnational* finally gaining here a rigor it lacked in the New Liberal usage. These organizations are by definition criminal organizations. It is only "criminal" organizations that are likely to be transnational, as others are likely to be subject to some national law code or another. A couple of examples of activities of these transnational criminal organizations may serve to further dramatize the need for historians to distinguish between corruption and primitive accumulation, which is not to gainsay the point that primitive accumulation may involve corruption. The first example is the Bank of Credit and Commerce International (BCCI); the second is al-Qa'ida. Choosing these organizations over the producers of the savings-and-loans scandals in the United States, the individuals involved in bank corruption in Europe, or the junk bond geniuses is simply a choice, one that privileges the importance of the shift of the market to Asia and to new techniques over the creative use of already existing institutions within the Euro-American market.

BCCI was founded in 1972 in Pakistan with capital from the late Shaykh Zayid of Abu Dhabi, the Bank of America, and the CIA. The bank expanded the prevailing notion of full-service bank to include money laundering, bribery, support of terrorism, arms dealing, smuggling, and many other activities. In 1991 the Bank of England closed BCCI; lawsuits continued against the bank's guarantors until recently. Politicians around the world were affected by the fall of the bank, as of course were many other people, some of whom lost their savings in the pyramid schemes. A total of $358 million disappeared from the Faisal Islamic Bank of Egypt this way.[22] Insider dealing at BCCI was an art form. At one point in the 1970s, Egypt was in the process of buying six airplanes from McDonnell Douglas Corporation when Boeing moved in, managing a $90 million advance from Prince Zayid to shift the deal to Boeing. It worked. U.S. politicians on both sides of the aisle were intimately involved in BCCI. James R. Bath, Bush's close associate, has served as a member of the bank's board of directors. Jimmy Carter, Bert Lance, and Marc Rich also had links, as did many others. Thus, when Senator John Kerry set out to investigate the bank, he encountered so many roadblocks that he finally decided to turn for help to the New York district attorney, Robert Morgenthau. How did Morgenthau succeed in bringing the matter to light and making it into a "scandal" when Kerry failed? According to a recent analysis, by the late 1980s BCCI had outlived its usefulness and was probably therefore abandoned by some of its principal protectors. This loss of protection is what allowed the "scandal" to emerge. Revelations from the Noriega investigation concerning BCCI had the potential to embarrass Bush Senior, who was then the head of the CIA. The revelations raised the possibility that the bank would have to be closed. The bank lost even more support when its involvement in money laundering in Florida came to light, even more with the end of the Afghan war, in which it had been a key player, and even more as the importance of Pakistan to the great powers started to decline. To these events one might also add the end of the Iran-Contra transactions of which BCCI had also been a part.[23] References to its glory days when it even traded in nuclear secrets still surface from time to time.

Let us turn to al-Qa'ida. Although al-Qa'ida is not the same as BCCI, it too is a multigauge transnational service industry, though of course differing from BCCI in that it does not provide the same services or function in the same way. Al-Qa'ida functions with many subordinate units and sympathizers, each of whom operates in their own contexts, whereas BCCI was much smaller in size and closer to a traditional business. Arising in the late 1980s under the leadership of Saudi businessman Usama Bin Ladin in the context of the U.S. war in Afghanistan, which many of its original personnel had a connection to, it has managed over the years to function in a number of countries and to have linkages in many more. In other words, al-Qa'ida arose in the shadows of the American empire. Like BCCI, its ebb and flow have depended on its protectors.

Among al-Qa'ida's achievements, one might note its adaptation of a traditional way to move money untraceably around the world without reference to Western market institutions (the Hawala), its ability to achieve investment goals in ways that are very hard to trace, and its use of terrorism as a style of warfare that has worked for a number of years, among others. All these exploits require more study; clearly, the more conventional characterization of al-Qa'ida as Islamo-fascist does not get very far. Transnational would be more precise.

The fact that the attack against Bin Ladin in Afghanistan in the early 2000s by U.S. Special Forces failed, allowing him to escape, suggests that multigauge service industries such as al-Qa'ida still have supporters today, as they did at the time of BCCI. At this point, one can only speculate about who or why.

A recent study of al-Qa'ida by a security expert makes a useful distinction. In our times, Kimberley Thachuk claims, corruption is understood increasingly as a matter not simply of the host country but of international security whenever sovereignty has been suborned to create "states of convenience." Corruption at that point is no longer greasing the wheels of commerce or paying government officials; rather, it is a matter of criminal organizations that use terrorism to distort or suborn sovereignty domestically or internationally and thereby create for themselves a base to carry out conspiracies around the world. Thachuk sees this shift as a general phenomenon, leading her to lump together Halliburton with the Islamic movements of Southeast Asia. She notes as well how a half-dozen islands in the West Indies are becoming economically important because they launder money for such operations.[24] Looking at this range of activities as services rendered, one could just as easily look at al-Qa'ida, the narco-terrorists, the Mafia, BCCI, and others as groups in the process of working themselves into the world power structure through their service, just as the New Men of yesteryear did.

Where some nonetheless find novelty in these ventures, others find them to be derivative or even unsuccessful, or even find the Janus-faced world of al-Qa'ida to be privileged in a context where many others are doing roughly the same thing. A writer adopting the view of al-Qa'ida as an innovator would likely emphasize the strengths of its network structure and doctrines, noting how it promotes frugality and how it is able both to leverage wealthy donors who give money to charities as well as to create members skilled at running successful companies. Receiving money for charitable purposes seems to get al-Qa'ida around the problem of government inspection, which is associated with taxable income. Al-Qa'ida is revolutionizing currency transfer through mixing the Hawala system with modern banking. To accomplish all these things, al-Qa'ida makes use of a mix of methods in its financing, ranging from professional bankers to financiers and beyond. Thus, it can specialize in such areas as credit card fraud, document forgery, terrorism, and other criminal activities, which are of course sought out by certain clientele alongside its quite legitimate honey trade business.[25]

Adopting the opposite point of view, writers arguing that al-Qa'ida is nothing special have noted the permeability of network-style organizations, the Mossad–al-Qa'ida cell in Gaza often mentioned as an example, as well as the lack of effective goals and organization coming from the extreme decentralization. Such decentralization, it is argued by one writer, is a far cry from maximizing innovative capacity. Some critics point out that if one takes the treatment of women in Afghanistan or the attack on the Buddhist statues at Bamiyan into consideration, al-Qa'ida seems to be even below average. It ought to be acknowledged, though, that al-Qa'ida's services do not end there. The state in a number of countries has in effect abandoned many of its responsibilities, and as a result citizenship as an identity has become less fulfilling for many, especially in the younger generation. Partly for this reason, partly for others, the world is now filled with people who are actually dislocated or feel marginalized. In this situation a number of transnational entrepreneurs have entered the field of televangelism, cassette religion, and the like, bringing with them a certain acumen about what will sell given the needs people now have. Bin Ladin has been targeting a certain constituency within this market. His primary market, most agree, is made up of young Muslims, especially in the tribal-ethnic states and individual Muslims living uprootedly abroad. It is a very large market and one that appears to still be growing. "Join al-Qa'ida. America is the Great Satan. It will be defeated by the true religion of Islam. The Taliban defeated Russia, and Russia was a great power, so what then is a great power? America has declared war on al-Qa'ida, but what can it do?" This amounts to a service, a labor market being forged.[26] Somebody somewhere will probably pay to get access to it, and in business getting paid is all one wants.

In another version of academic commentaries on al-Qa'ida, Usama Bin Ladin is pictured as a charismatic individual, comparable to Che Guevara. Both go to where there are movements and action and lend their cachet. In both cases, there are pretty significant differences between what they claim to have done and what they may have actually done. Take, for example, the 2005 attack on the tourists in Sharm al-Shaykh, Egypt. The attack was initially attributed to Bin Ladin but subsequently was more strongly associated with the extreme alienation of the Sinai Bedouins, who have lost some of their lands with the expansion of the Egyptian tourist industry. Bin Ladin had merely lent his cachet. The conclusion drawn by one author is that a War on Terrorism concentrating on Bin Laden as an individual misses the widespread nature of the social crises of this period that produce certain opportunities for many local entrepreneurs and not simply for one well-known individual or group to come and lend its cachet. The article does not, of course, dispute that lending a cachet is a service.[27]

In sum, then, in addition to the empirical issues and the problem of sources and of establishing context, there is a problem of what position the field of world history is supposed to take as regards primitive accumulation and those individuals who engage in it. Can the field get beyond conflating it with the more universal phenomenon of corruption? Can historians see capitalism as driven by primitive accumulation? Here the basic problem is ultimately whether world history as a profession can exist apart from national history and the Hegelian tradition. Assuming that it could, a useful line of inquiry would be the one checking to see if the underlying cause of the crisis of multilateralism was that there is now too little primitive accumulation.

MULTILATERALISM IN A CRISIS STAGE:
THE RISE OF THE WORLD POLICEMAN CONCEPT
AND RULE BY STATE OF EMERGENCY AFTER 1970

We now return to the subject of multilateralism and the phase of crisis in the years after the 1970s, noting the two main approaches that multilateralism came up with in this period: the world policeman and rule by state of emergency. The hypothesis is that these approaches were and are nonspecific responses to the variety of problems confronting the Rich. Recourse to them would not produce the desired stabilization.

Crisis or *crisis stage* is a difficult term to use. It always needs to be defined in relation to some particular context. In this book, the term is used in two ways: to characterize moments in which multilateralism might have unraveled but did not thanks to one improvisation or another and then to characterize systemic crisis. We find examples of both meanings of the term in the events following the 1970s, but it is the latter that draws our attention.

The post-1970 period saw an immense economic accumulation in the hands of the upper classes with no concomitant mechanism for redistribution. Partly as a consequence, it saw a brewing political crisis on a world scale that would have to be confronted. Oil prices were on the rise; an ecological crisis was on the horizon. And, though none of the challenges was entirely new, what could be observed was that multilateralism was not showing an ability at this point to evolve in the face of such crises, or at least this ability was less in evidence. Earlier I noted the retreat from international law into civilizationalism and the inability of the multilateral system to resolve the Palestine Question. Now there were a number of other such intractable problems as well.

As concerns the idea of the United States as world policeman, the reader will recall from the earlier discussion of Neo-Gramscian international relations the claim that thanks to the United States the world is now suffused with democracy because although the United States is an imperial power, it is not like those empires that have gone before. Thus, according to neoliberalism, one could have a world policeman, but it would be one that would spread democracy and not one that would rob its colonies, as was the custom earlier.

Whether a historian agrees or disagrees with this view, he or she is likely to agree that the world policeman option represents a major political gamble on the part of many rulers in the world who acquiesced to it. Consider, for a moment, the seemingly momentous but curiously noncontroversial detail that U.S. law enforcement agencies and courts, including even its domestic ones, now concern themselves with the internal affairs of every other country in the world. Yet the role of world's policeman, an immense and highly controversial responsibility, was not the choice of the majority even of the population of the United States, much less the preference of other countries. The institution arose out of the needs of multilateralism; it was never even a topic of discussion in the United States until after the fact. When it became apparent what was going on, it was met by displeasure. The reason for its unpopularity in the United States, of course, is that the role of a policeman is a difficult and unrewarding one that it would involve all kinds of sacrifices. This situation would especially be true at the present time. The spread of fairly sophisticated weapons in recent times has made the world a rather more difficult place to police than it was a century ago. Whereas policing a world of strong nation-states, even well-armed ones, might be feasible if the rulers generally cooperated, policing a world of weak states that do not cooperate is like policing the waves of the sea. This picture is how one might describe the situation of the United States in what is being characterized as a War on Terrorism.

So what does a country, such as the United States, gain from being a world policeman or declaring a War on Terrorism? The answer appears to be twofold: first, being the world's policeman in a War on Terrorism is, contrary to what the Neo-Gramscians claim, a convenient way to justify neocolonial policies and pillage as relates to oil in Iraq and heroin in Afghanistan; second, a War on Terror opens up the possibility of increasing social control at home through rule via emergency legislation, which is something that the state itself increasingly appears to desire. This outcome is predictable. One need not impute megalomania to the rulers but simply note that inasmuch as the demands of multilateralism have less and less to do with the well-being of ordinary people, what is required by leadership is a position of strength. Experience shows that only from a position of strength can a ruler mold public opinion to acquiesce to his wishes. And rule by state of emergency gives the ruler a position of strength.

This point is well established; rule by state of emergency legislation has had quite a long history. Colonies, for example, were often ruled by state of emergency legislation and on that basis alone, as were weak states and failing regimes, especially those countries on the periphery. However, what one discovers is that in recent times the great powers, that is, the UK and the United States, are more and more relying on such legislation even to control the homeland. It is this point that draws our attention, as the democratic homeland is supposedly where the mode of production is at its healthiest—in other words, where capitalism could showcase persuasion as opposed to coercion. Today, apparently, even the democratic West has to be ruled as a colony.

In Britain emergency legislation drawn up for World War I was then used to break strikes and gradually evolved from there. After the war, Lloyd George, the prime minister, used the so-called Emergency Powers Act to break the Coal Strike of 1921, a strike occurring in a period of economic dislocation and considerable anticapitalist sentiment. The government invoked emergency powers, it said, so that women and children would not starve. Afterward, emergency powers were again invoked in 1924 in the London Tramways and Omnibus Strike of that year by Ramsay MacDonald and then again in the General Strike of 1926. At that point, parliamentary opposition arose. Later in 1948 and then again in 1949, the governing

Labour Party, much to the embarrassment of its rank and file, again felt obliged to use emergency powers to break dock strikes. The author of a recent article on this subject contrasts that use of law in the UK to that in the United States, where the government, constrained by the Bill of Rights, has been forced to operate on the basis of presidential prerogative. As a result, over the past fifty years, executive decrees have increasingly come to substitute for law. Such "legislation" prohibits strikes by dockers, policemen, and many others.[28]

This view distinguishing the situation in the United States and the UK is seemingly confirmed by yet another study of the nature of emergency powers found in the United States. This study by Jules Lobel notes that when the news broke in 1987 that the Federal Emergency Management Agency (FEMA) had developed a contingency plan to suspend the Constitution and impose martial law, there was little media coverage or public comment, even though the plan would involve the arrest of American citizens and legal aliens. Americans by this point had apparently come to accept executive prerogative as if it were law. And after a manner of speaking, it was law at least since 1950. In April 1950, the National Security Council (NSC) had issued Paper 68. NSC 68 made clear that the country would go through an indefinite period "of tension and danger." Most Americans apparently accepted this idea. Lobel notes that what took place was that with the help of a compliant judiciary, the executive branch steadily gained powers at the expense of the legislature and judiciary.[29] If imposing a state of emergency was this easy even in the bastions of liberty, moving on to being a world policeman or generating a cold war or a War on Terrorism would scarcely be that big a step.

MOVEMENTS IN CIVIL SOCIETY

To complete this discussion of "crisis," we now turn to the other side of the subject of the dialectic, that of the opposition, the opposition presumably the main cause of the crisis. For the sake of convenience, the subject of opposition is divided into two sections. The first deals with opposition more of less controlled by the state (movements in civil society), and the second deals with opposition less controlled by the state (movements on the margin of civil society). What separates the two, or more precisely what has separated the two until fairly recently, is a combination of class interest and hegemonic strategy. Were there to be a general unraveling of the hegemony in a moment of crisis, the two might very well come together. As far as what is meant by opposition "more or less controlled" by the state, we find that the issue is bound up in the link between the role of the middle class in civil society and the state. Here what is assumed is that the state needs the middle-class civil society to give the appearance that it is serving the society, and not simply itself. Crisis comes about and with it emergency legislation when the middle class declines to play its assigned role and or is simply too weak to do so.

Though state of emergency legislation might or might not be the optimal form of control of the middle classes, it was no accident that rulers turned to it and to the strategy of world policeman. The very evolution of multilateralism had worked to separate the realities and interests of rulers and ruled. Under such conditions, opposition to the status quo might well arise. If the middle classes began to show discontent and if their loyalty became a bit uncertain, the situation could be construed to require rule by state of emergency to keep the lid on.

That said, however, a state of emergency would be less than ideal. The whole purpose of civil society was to avoid such harsh measures. The state had designed civil society to divide the country between those individuals in it and those not in it. Those individuals in civil society, mainly the middle classes, would enjoy bourgeois freedom and the full benefit of the social contract; the rest of the society would not. Those in civil society could form movements; they could enjoy a certain freedom of speech. Indeed, the state even manifested an interest in their opinions. So why, then, was rule by state of emergency also necessary? Although the answer is not an entirely certain one, what also appears to be the case is that people in civil society are oppressed, as are people who are not in it. The entitlements they enjoy are not a right as much as they are a favor. The larger point about civil society, then, is that it is a strategy of divide and rule that few researchers have recognized as such, one that has given strength to the modern state, but one that the state is being forced to abandon to accommodate the continuing evolution of the Rise of the Rich.

This raises a variety of questions. If one has a breakdown of civil society and of middle-class life, is one then witnessing the gradual turn of the middle classes to the side of the workers and the underclass? If so, how would one study this? Although there is, of course, no one answer to these questions, one possible resource to try, which has received little attention until now among world historians, is public opinion polls and studies based on them. Public opinion polls do check on the middle class and the direction it is going. Of course, like other possible sources a historian might use, it will have its more useful and less useful features and bring with it its share of problems, but it does offer some fairly unique possibilities.

At the very least, a brief survey of available materials assures one that it is an already well-plowed field in scholarship. Indeed, one finds a number of scholars studying public opinion. Some of them seem to embrace its findings, whereas others acknowledge them but do not seem to take them too seriously. Some researchers, such as the American scholar and commentator Walter Lippmann, long concerned with public opinion, have taken the view that the incoherences and contradictions commonly found in public opinion are more or less a reason to dismiss it out of hand. How can such a thing be taken seriously by leaders? Lippmann's views, one might note, found quite wide acceptance among policy makers during the cold war.

The line of thought here is one proceeding according to somewhat different assumptions and needs. Incoherences and contradictions need not be looked at as manifestations of irrationality and grounds for dismissal; rather, they are something to be explained. They are in themselves evidence of something. Perhaps they are to be explained by existing power relations, that is, by the relatively weaker power position of the middle classes in relationship to the state. Instead of a clear negative or affirmative stance on some issue, what these less coherent responses might point to is dissatisfaction with or possibly a degree of opposition to official utterances, one that however cannot be expressed as such because of the power differential.

A hypothetical example might help make this point clear. Let us suppose there is some disagreement between two people of very unequal power, and let us suppose as well there is some difference in how each is expressing himself or herself in terms of thought processes or vocabulary.

What can then be observed is that the one in the weaker position often cannot fit his or her thoughts quickly and easily into the mold of expression of the one in the stronger position and may even be unsettled by the categories imposed in the conversation. This inability produces either silence or some degree of incoherence. Returning now to the societal level, one might then assume that this phenomenon of the pause, indecision, or incoherence is not to be confused with weakness per se; what it points to in modern history is the likelihood that the middle classes may be trying to follow their own agenda and to do so in a hierarchical situation. Nation-states especially in recent times are very hierarchical. For the historian who wants to portray the development of a phenomenon such as middle-class opposition over time, these incoherent opinion polls may represent the beginning. The appearance ultimately of an opposition movement out in the open is simply the final clarifying event. The real research question concerns the process that preceded it, and here public opinion might be of some use.

The use of public opinion as a source is, however, complicated because of the rise of the pollster and of the role that money plays in shaping opinion polls. The very need for the paid pollster and the spin, however, suggests the existence of underlying discord and gives the use of public opinion some credibility. Rulers may of course claim they ignore public opinion, but evidence suggests they are well aware of it. After all, public opinion is not only data that can be heeded, left, or manipulated but also a movement that can potentially be fearsome and unpredictable and thus cannot be ignored, at least over the long run. For the historian, whether the ruler claims to pay attention to public opinion or whether respondents claim to tell the truth is thus not a particularly important matter.

Another consideration is that not only is public opinion a movement, but it is a movement that could potentially break down the apparent separation between civil society and the rest by virtue of what it could reveal about either or both. If society were truly compartmentalized, then it would be virtually impossible for this breakdown to occur or for that matter for there to be a dialectic of ruler and ruled. It is for these reasons that the study of public opinion is chosen here as the place to initiate the study of opposition movements more or less controlled by the state.

To begin, one might want to return to the point that not all aspects of public opinion are of equal value for this type of research. Certain aspects of public opinion are simply a product of the logic of some particular form of hegemony, the society responding to the pressures exerted by that particular type of ruling process. The reader doubtless will recall, for example, the earlier discussions of the long-term opinions that the U.S. public has expressed about countries in various hegemonies and what it has meant for policy makers as a result.[30] Recall, for example, the discussion of the rather unrestrained hostility to Russian Road states, the rather contemptuous view of the morality of Italian Road states, the rather complete disregard for tribal-ethnic states (seen as incapable of causing trouble for the United States), and finally the blind trust in the goodwill of other democracies.[31] The sheer predictability of these views has been of some use to American politicians and others over the years, this aspect of public opinion shedding no new light on middle-class praxis per se. The same might be said where public opinion appears to reflect its own material interests or affirmations of identity independently of other considerations. An example would be middle-class views on tax policy. The same would be true as well where public opinion appears to reflect short-term support or opposition to something put forward by the state. Much of the public opinion of this sort is simply a surface reflex. Public opinion, however, has other features too. What I am suggesting ought to be the focus for world historians is not just the more straightforward side of public opinion research but that aspect of public opinion that is less clear-cut in terms of what it signifies, the reason being that we are living in a period of change. This fact makes the subject of class history a complicated matter, one half-buried and one very far from being a yes or no on a questionnaire. In a different period, a different approach to this material would be in order and indeed to this subject as well.

With these considerations in mind, consider the following example, an example when public opinion scarcely seems to take note of what is obviously a significant U.S. foreign policy program, one now a half century old. I refer here to Structural Adjustment Programs, or SAPs. What is interesting about this example, then, is the silence surrounding it. There is no immediate explanation for it. The policy in question is out in the open and regularly discussed in the media. Moreover, one may find a considerable body of writing on public opinion and U.S. foreign policy but not as far I can tell on this particular issue.

Structural Adjustment Programs are programs that the United States introduced after World War II as the centerpiece of its foreign economic policy; the programs carry on to the present, retaining much of their original importance. SAPs were designed to help develop the market, and they often involve lasting aid commitments on the part of the United States to various foreign countries. At the same time, features associated with SAPs contradict what one would assume were American core values about the equality of men and women. Despite this fact, public opinion has not been a factor in the passage of the relevant provisions of foreign aid bills or in their subsequent renewals. Certainly, no one has stood up and made the point that these programs are targeting women. The question, then, is why is public opinion silent when core values are being trampled on? It seems unlikely to be completely a matter of unawareness. At the same time, it seems improbable to imagine anything as simple as blind patriotism or class collaboration could explain it. The cold war as an issue is not particularly involved. Ignorance, patriotism, or fear of the Soviet Union may exist as factors, but they do not explain the absence of a public discussion surrounding a policy matter of this size and importance. It is as if the middle classes are somehow conflicted by this policy, that they are forced to confront conflicting values in themselves, and this renders them silent.

To pursue this hypothesis, one might try to eliminate other possibilities—for example, greed. Does silence mean support because the middle classes benefit from it? Certainly, this notion is not altogether implausible. Structural Adjustment Programs promote the expansion of free markets. For some middle-class Americans, this expansion encourages the stock market and this means more profit. Perhaps for them silence means approval for that reason.

To consider this possibility, let us look more closely at what these programs are achieving: market rationalization. Whatever is perceived to be an impediment to the growth of the market is something that needs to be removed. Here, as one might suspect, there is bound to be a political dimension as to what gets perceived to be an impediment. Thus, for example, the traditional noncapitalist economy in Third World countries tends to be given a pass, although it might well constitute the main impediment to the market, whereas it is the government entitlement programs that usually are perceived to be the impediments. Such programs tend to include welfare programs. According to neoliberal commentators, welfare programs detract from private-sector initiatives and therefore from the development of the market. Enter Structural Adjustment Programs. SAPs are in effect specific policy recommendations designed to facilitate entrance into the market. They are tailored to identify and eliminate whatever entitlement any state gave its people in the past in order to enhance the spread of the free market in the present.[32]

Here we come to the relevant detail. If one wants to shrink the budget of the state and expand the range of private-sector activities, then it may be necessary to drop state-subsidized health insurance, day care, elder care, after-school programs, or affirmative-action legislation. Women almost invariably are the ones who are expected to pick up the slack. This policy has been a disaster for women worldwide over this past generation. Only the very well-off and extremely poor remain unaffected. Of course, there have been attempts on the part of women to fight back with varying outcomes, but this is the general trend and certainly the most pronounced one in the tribal-ethnic states even more than in the others.

According to a recent article on the subject of SAPs in the Middle East by Valentine Moghadam, the development expert, it was Saudi foreign financial pressure on the Middle East beginning in the 1970s combined with the coming of SAPs to the region that not only destroyed the middle classes of a number of countries but also brought regime pressure to change women's dress and impose veiling and spatial and functional segregation, in the name of religion, the imposition of SAPs blending in with certain pieces of Salafi Islam (to generalize a bit the earlier discussion of al-Qa'ida). Moghadam's conclusion is that women in general and poor women in particular have become the shock absorbers of the new market economy of the Middle East and that nowhere was it more evident than in the tribal states of that region. And of course it was not just in that region or that form of hegemony alone.

So if that is the case, where does that lead us in terms of understanding Western public opinion and SAPs? Perhaps at this point one could imagine that, while there might be for some a material self-interest dimension implied in their silence, this would not actually reflect the views of others or even of a majority. One might suspect the majority actually might have misgivings about such a policy, not necessarily for the reasons outlined here but because marketizing a country, as NAFTA marketized Mexico, could result in it taking jobs away from the United States. However, if this is the case, it is not what one commonly finds in the opposition to NAFTA. Still to be precise, rather than focusing on a preoccupation with the attitude toward SAPs per se, the relevant issue to focus on might be how American public opinion regards the Third World worker in the United States. The views about SAPs would follow accordingly.

Adopting this approach, one finds a possible explanation for the silence around SAPs by looking at the concerns of the American middle-class family. What one finds is that near the top of the list of its concerns would be elder care, child care, and housework. The Third World woman service worker who performs these functions for the middle classes thus plays a very important role in their lives. For some, she makes their lives a great deal easier. If so, then for seemingly unrelated reasons the silence concerning SAPs on the part of public opinion might reflect not so much agreement on foreign policy, or a belief in women's subordination, or greed, or personal gain in some simple sense, but rather it would reflect dependence. This family depends on this woman and this realization is uncomfortable. The whole life struggle of the middle class is for security and autonomy only to wind up in dependence. This factor would explain the subtext that this woman has to enter the market because she had to be made poor. Possibly, she will emigrate. Perhaps she will emigrate to the United States. In sum, the more one looks into public opinion, the more one senses that it could be a resource that world historians might make use of in trying to understand the trajectory of the middle classes under multilateralism.

This point brings us to the conclusion that however one ultimately interprets public opinion concerning these aid programs, and there is obviously a good deal more to it than I am suggesting, it seems likely that the domestic point of reference has some salience. Where the middle classes will stand on SAPs and similar policies in the future may well depend on their position on the question of Hispanic immigrants, which in turn will be affected by the affordability of services such as elder care. How would their attitudes change if suddenly there was universal health care? Does a service workers union that organizes maids of Hispanic origin have a chance to gain middle-class allies under these conditions? Would it enhance its chance of doing so by pointing out the contradictions in the situation as related to gender? Would the development of a cross-class alliance be likely to lead to opposition to SAPs? These issues are unresearched, as of course is the larger one of whether the middle class is showing signs of breaking with the state and with the enticements of civil society. To sum up, public opinion research, with all the ambiguities it may contain, seems like an appropriate way for a historian to approach the subject of opposition that is partly controlled by the state.

Let us now look at opposition on the margin of civil society and less controlled by the state, opposition emerging from the collapse of a traditional industrial working class and from the rise of an immigrant underclass. This is the world of service workers, workers who provide services such as elder care.

OPPOSITION TRENDS ON THE MARGIN OF CIVIL SOCIETY

In this last section we examine opposition movements in effect virtually outside civil society. By "outside" I meant not just outside the organized working-class movements but movements closer to the nonorganized job market and the informal economy, movements whose oppositionality is thus partly the result of seeking an inclusion that the state does not welcome, in other words movements whose engagement in the dialectic is their everyday existence as much as anything else. My preference here would have been to use the term *mass society* or *mass movements,* but these terms have already been adopted for other purposes.

To begin, I lay out the conventional liberal and Marxist historiography of this subject, which typically runs along the lines of labor and capital. I juxtapose to this a contemporary example of the same subject, one making use of a ruler-ruled dialectic. To do this I focus on the rise of a new kind of worker movement, the social movement trade union as an illustration of the ruler-ruled dialectic today. The example discussed is that of Service Employees International Union (SEIU), a service workers union in the forefront of organizing unorganized workers, many of whom are women and many from a Hispanic background. The union has many sympathizers and supporters, not only in the trade union movement but even in the middle class. I take this fact to be evidence of the crisis in hegemony, the fraying of civil society.

The standard labor historiography reveals a different conception of the dialectic. For most Marxist historians, for instance, the preferred application of the dialectic, to the extent that it is applied at all, would be to the struggle of labor or capital in the interwar period of the twentieth century, to highlight the struggles of the AFL-CIO trade unions and the Communist Party with corporate capitalism. Movements of the nineteenth century like those of the present day do not figure in this account to any great extent. To question why this is the case makes one a populist, populism being a bogeyman. Of course, no one contests the point that trade unions, let us say in the 1930s, played a role in the dialectic, but clearly so too did the nonunionized worker, the underclass, and the middle class. The fact that one part of the working class was organized and another was not begs the question of how it was organized and what difference that made. W. E. B. DuBois, the historian and activist, introduced such ideas many years ago in his study of the post–Civil War period. They never penetrated deeply into American Marxism any more than did Gramsci's, though.

It is true, of course, that the movements of the post–World War I period were some of the largest movements in American history, movement capable of considerable militancy. At the same time, they collapsed for the most part within one generation, as is also well known, unable to deal with the birth of a short-lived aristocracy of labor created by Fordism or with token gains in civil rights. One wonders how it happened and what was the wider context in which it happened.

Approaching the dialectic as ruler and ruled, the record shows that there were a number of oppositional movements in the age of classical liberalism of the late nineteenth century, but as the Gompers-type "free trade unions" spread in alliance with the state, these movements were marginalized. Afterward, there was a long lull between World War I and the 1980s. This period witnessed the co-optation of the trade union movement. When the civil rights struggle rose after World War II, given the unfortunate timing, it could not forge deep links with the labor movement. The trade union movement did not see the wisdom in making such alliances and was in any case in a state of decline.

In the old liberal period of the late nineteenth century, by way of contrast, there were movements that not only challenged the state but lasted for a relatively long period of time. Some had roots in their communities and thus could not easily be divided or isolated, as later movements were. Some—for instance, the Knights of Labor, the Western Miners, and later the International Workers of the World (IWW)—were quite well known at the time nationally and even internationally. The state attacked these movements fiercely, using as its justification that these movements were anarchist.[33]

There are reasons this nineteenth-century radicalism is not well known. In most of the early literature, what one finds is mainly the perspective of the state on them until now and not much else. One learns, for example, about the Colorado National Guard, about the Chicago police aided on occasion by the Pinkerton Detective Agency, about the growing responsibilities assigned to the United States Secret Service through the late nineteenth century. Thus, for example in 1901–2, in the wake of the assassination of President McKinley, one learns that the Secret Service became the official guard of the president, the latter thereafter always having an official guard. The rise of the FBI (1908–10), one learns, led to the crushing of the IWW. This defeat appears to have been something of a turning point.

With the destruction of the IWW, the struggle continued, but its tenor changed; the state at that point was not seriously challenged. It had been able to force the trade unions to choose between legality and ostracism, and the trade unions had chosen legality. Most workers were thus cut adrift, and their trajectory drops from view, at least on the level of the historiography. Thereafter, the Gompers heritage of free trade unionism and Third International Communism of the American Communist Party served to reinforce this status quo against those groups and individuals who would argue for more inclusive and presumably more politically oriented types of movements such as had existed before. Garveyism performed a similar function in African American civil rights circles.

What is noticeable about the post–World War I period of U.S. history is the unions' assumption that only a political party could bring about change; a social movement could not. However, what is equally apparent from studies of the political history of the period is that labor had but little influence on any party, the Democratic Party included, and that third parties had little chance in the American electoral system.

In the 1930s, with the coming of the Great Depression, many people and not just workers realized that capitalism was the cause of their problems, and some became Communists. This shift did not threaten the state or capitalism to any great extent, though. Capitalists were not on the defensive. They never promised anything to anyone or appeared to feel any sense of remorse for the misery they had inflicted. In fact, only in a few European countries could one find anything even approaching some kind of a welfare system then or later. As the twentieth century wore on, therefore, workers in a few of the Western democracies grew richer thanks to the union movement or to government benefits, but virtually nowhere did their power grow. Power in the sense of organized power lay disproportionately on the level of multilateralism. Unions, given their form of struggle or perhaps in some cases their tunnel vision, did not seem to realize this and continued to measure their progress simply in terms of their income level. Only in the 1970s did some finally realize that such an approach would not suffice. But by that point, what would, unless they abandoned free trade unionism and gave up on civil society? At that point, capital flight and even an attack on trade unionism was the order of the day in many countries. The labor aristocracy was shriveling. By the 1980s, the attacks against organized labor grew more severe as new sites of production proliferated across the globe and as multilateralism began to rely on them. At this point, the traditional national unions lost much of their membership and with that their bargaining power. And as the unions lost ground, the organized working class found out that it did not have much to fall back on. This was the price to be paid for following Samuel Gompers and his narrow apolitical free trade unionism.

Since 1990 a new kind of unionism has begun to be visible. This new unionism is somehow reminiscent of the nineteenth-century trade unions and of the anarchist movements of that period, although so far it is less confrontational than they were. What makes it new or at least new to our own times is that it deals with social issues and not simply bread-and-butter union ones. This fact gives it some importance in a discussion of the ruler-ruled dialectic, as the social issues it deals with resonate throughout society.

These new-style trade unions, or "global social movement unions," as they are sometimes called, speak to the reality of present-day conditions in a way that neither the political parties, the mainstream unions, nor the civil rights movements do, the former all products of the corporatist period and all very much frozen in that mold. Some thus hope that these unions may be a harbinger of the rebirth of the Left.

Over the past few years, these social movement unions have been notable not only for their new ideas but for their new tactics as well. On a tactical level, they place themselves on the margin of the system, albeit the included margin, free therefore to attach themselves to various causes and issues that the traditional trade union movement would not have considered among their concerns. Two examples of these new union movements are taken up in this section, one from the periphery, one from the core, both from bourgeois democracies.[34]

Among the first and most important social movement trade unions was the Southern Initiative on Globalisation and Trade Union Rights (SIGTUR), an Australian and South African confederation dating from around 1990.[35] SIGTUR was and is largely made up of unions of dockworkers, or "wharfies," in countries such as Australia and South Africa,[36] and for that reason, it has been for some years in the forefront of the international labor struggle in the Indian Ocean region. SIGTUR's range of activities goes beyond this realm, however, into areas such as antiapartheid struggle, which explains its initiatives in South Africa taken in conjunction with COSATSU, the South African trade union confederation.[37]

More recently, the American Service Employees International Union, also confronting problems of race and class, began to adopt some of the same tactics as SIGTUR. How can Hispanic service workers in California, many of them women, ever fit into a society that is being racialized and "genderized" against them? This is the issue the SEIU faces, the issue being the flip side of the one discussed above concerning SAPs.[38]

Thus, one could assume, whether the SEIU or SIGTUR remains counterhegemonic or whether they simply remain a part of the larger trade union movement, both are important. The economic threats made by dockworkers in an internationalized economy or service workers in a service economy carry some weight, more perhaps than threats made by factory workers. A dock strike under prevailing conditions is an attack on the political structure and not just on some particular company's policy, distinguishing SIGTUR not just from traditional union struggle but also from other change-oriented movements such as the World Social Forum. A strike by maids not only hits at the tourist industry in California but also hits at the class order. Business meetings are disrupted. A traditional strike does not achieve any such thing. Moreover, the fact that these unions are connected to other issues opens the possibility that a dock strike or a strike by hotel workers might somehow spread. At the same time, the fact that SEIU is not a part of SIGTUR nor a part of the independent Mexican Union struggle but goes it alone in the United States seems to point in the other direction. One would think that no serious challenge to anything at this point is possible without an international connection. The United States is one arena of labor struggle among many.

As concerns the SEIU, the shift to a social movement unionism approach occurred gradually over the past generation as the union began to break with the tradition of the AFL-CIO. This point seems worth examining, as clearly the way a labor movement breaks with free trade union ideology is of some interest to a discussion of opposition. As this phenomenon is still in process, what is possible at this point is more a discussion of the stages of development of the SEIU leading up to the near present. A deeper analysis of the process of this transformation or its outcome will have to wait.

Looking back on SEIU in 1990, what one observes is that although it was less politicized in the traditional sense than other movements of the period—for example, ATTAC, the European coalition of trade unionists—it was clearly politicized, and politicized in some new way. Its politicism seemed to come from the way it confronted the political issues of the times, such as race, immigration, and gender, the union following its membership, many of whom came from the bottom of the American working class. Few other unions come to mind that follow their membership;

nearly all other unions simply lead and manage. This feature makes it more relevant for this discussion, given America's huge underclass, than the traditional American unions would be. Historians recognize that it is hard to interpret is the struggle of the American underclass. How does one interpret the struggle of workers whose work is barely acknowledged? The study of the SEIU provides a window on that world. One feature of the SEIU, which has stood out virtually from the beginning, has been the skill of its leadership in overcoming the racial and gender stratification imposed by employers. Each strike is therefore a political struggle as well as an economic struggle. Where most unions plan to withhold labor on some particular job site on a given day following the AFL-CIO tradition, the SEIU tries to undermine the employer's labor strategy of divide and rule. The traditional strike, in any case, would not be an adequate weapon for the SEIU. There are no shortage of scabs to do service work. This reality makes the SEIU so political.

In the mid-1990s, John Sweeney, the head of the SEIU at that more tentative point in the organization's history, became the head of the AFL-CIO, the old confederation in those years looking for new leadership. With the election of his "New Voices" slate, Sweeney tried to make the AFL-CIO rise to the challenges of the era. In his speeches, he called for a "level playing field" with the neoliberalism of the Clinton years. He failed to achieve anything near a level playing field. Moreover, his approach alienated a number of the confederation's member unions. Sweeney's failure, it thus appears, made clear the impossibility of reforming the "free trade union" movement from within or of succeeding with it as it was. Membership continued to drop, and internal divisions were not overcome. Sweeney's failure left the field open to the SEIU, especially its younger generation, to choose a different direction. The question was: which way they would go? Could the SEIU and similar organizations keep coming up with ideas on how to overcome the differences in the situation of Hispanic, black, and white workers in a context of such powerful racism as one finds promoted in the United States and without strong international alliances? In other words, could they survive? Perhaps they could. Perhaps their endurance is why we have the FEMA legislation, the Patriot Act, and other features of rule by state of emergency. With the passage of this legislation, what both the worker and the middle class encounter is an object lesson: watch out, it seems to be saying, or we will do to you what we did to the American Muslim community.

CONCLUSION

I set out in this chapter to show that contemporary world history, the period roughly from 1850 to the present, could be effectively understood as the era of multilateralism, that is, a continuation of and further development of the older bilateralism of the early modern period. From the middle of the nineteenth century onward, large numbers of ruling classes have been collaborating with each other, profiting from the expansion of the market, even if in many cases the states involved were so unstable that colonial occupation and loans were needed to keep their rulers in power.

What is clear from the history of the Rich in this period was that various disparate elements somehow cooperated with each other, thereby retaining the upper hand against potential challengers. As modern history progressed, however, the system as a whole appeared to become less resilient. It was no longer able to ward off crises easily. On the economic level, the problem was an old one that simply cumulated. It lay in the failure of capitalism to find a balance between accumulation and redistribution. This inability in turn led to excessive accumulation in the hands of the few, leaving the rest alienated. On the political level, the failure to resolve problems also became noticeable, as was found by considering the Palestine Question. The inability of the Rich to foster the creation of a Palestinian state after some half century or more might well be taken as an example of a systemic crisis. Another such example is the failure to respond to the onset of ecological crisis. The mode of production appears to be wearing down. The dialectic of history continues to move. Movements approximating antihegemonic movements are on the rise, even in countries such as the United States.

At its core, this chapter is an exercise in historiography. Mirroring or paralleling the crisis in the real world, there is a crisis in historiography. The field of world history still cannot break with Hegel. It is still in many ways an appendage of national history. This explains why one finds so much providentialism, Eurocentrism, and consensus history embedded in the writings in this scholarship.

In another context, one might imagine that historians would assume that if a state was afraid of its people and felt it was necessary to finance more and more security forces, this fact in itself was evidence of the working out of the dialectic in history. American historians by and large do not take that position. That point duly noted, writers in the Rise of the West paradigm are correct when they note the lack of a methodology that would allow them to pursue the dialectic of world history in an easy or predictable way. How does one pursue a subject if it appears to exist but it does not coherently express itself much of the time because it remains buried in structures like public opinion? This concern is valid.

What multilateralism seems to show until now, generally, is that mankind as a whole is capable of some degree of cooperation. This point is evident but barely so, as the only cooperation permitted has been among the dominant elements of today's capitalist world. Multilateralism taken out of its present historical context, however, might be seen as having inherently important aspects for some future potentiality of mankind. Faced as humans are with a rapidly changing environment, what other response would work but a multilateral one?

One of the contributions of multilateralism was that to a limited degree it fostered the development of world law. The development of world law has many important implications. For the field of world history, world law has an especially important role to play. It is the way the field of world history can get beyond national history. Because of world law, world history can look at the larger play of forces during some period such as World War II— and do so objectively without equating Hitler, Stalin, and Roosevelt but without collapsing into jingoism.

The next chapter brings my entire argument together. Too much weight has been placed in dominant historiography on Westerners and too little on the Third World ruling class in constructing the narrative of modern world history. The result has been that scholars have failed to correctly understand many major developments, even developments in Western history. Though this fact might be acknowledged to a degree, for the most part historians have chosen to retain the Rise of the West paradigm. It thus remains to be shown that Third World ruling classes in the age of multilateralism increasingly affect the daily life of the ordinary Westerner in his or her own society. It is not simply a matter of Westerners affecting the Third World but the reverse as well. The last chapter takes note of this foreign penetration, asking, is it still possible to write American history in the framework of the Rise of the West?

THE "RISE OF THE RICH" PARADIGM APPLIED TO THE CONTEMPORARY UNITED STATES

THIS CHAPTER LOOKS at contemporary U.S. history as a part of the Rise of the Rich. It tries to reconcile two seemingly contradictory features of this paradigm that coexist in contemporary history, one pointing to the role of the United States as world policeman, implying a certain centralization of power, another to the dispersion of power among the Rich. It is the first of these items that has received by far the most extensive treatment in scholarship, Marxists theorizing about imperialism and liberals theorizing about unilateralism, preemption, and empire. The Rise of the Rich paradigm leads one to hypothesize, however, that the second is of equal if not of greater importance than the first. Dispersion of power followed from the rise of multilateralism. It ultimately led, as this chapter shows, to the penetration of the imperial metropole by many states, even by some states on the periphery. This penetration in turn sharpened the opposition to multilateralism in the metropole, contributing to the government's turn toward an increasing reliance on rule by state of emergency.

The dispersion of power followed from the rise of multilateralism. It was in fact a logical outgrowth of the history of the past 150 years. Beginning in the middle of the nineteenth century, as more and more power structures collaborated with each other to uphold the market, power became more and more dispersed among their dominant elements. Over time their sheer number, their cultural diversity, and their geographical spread increasingly gave dominant elements on the periphery the capacity to leverage even the traditionally more powerful countries of the core. This was evident in the anticolonial struggles, but it did not end there. The rise of a number of countries in East Asia and South Asia in more recent years can be offered as another example of the consequences of this dispersion of power. The rise of these countries would not have been possible under the conditions of the old bilateralism of the early nineteenth century. The case of Muhammad 'Ali in Egypt bears witness to that fact. In his period in history, the option was not available. What changed the situation was the new geopolitics of the nation-state system that brought together a group of people and institutions all seeking power in the same way. To achieve the economic growth they desired, these people and institutions were obliged to develop close relations. After a century or more of such relations, the dispersion of power has become something increasingly taken for granted. Western industries more and more have found it in their interests to relocate in the Third World, and Western governments have increasingly found it in their interests to accept Third World people as immigrants. By the 1970s and 1980s and the years thereafter, one finds as a result a deindustrialization of the Western countries, a rise of global financial capitalism, and a growing penetration of the imperial metropole by foreign interests.

How did this foreign penetration of the American political economy take place? On whom could foreigners rely? Although doubtless each case had its own particular features, of general importance was the rise within the American power structure of a new institution, the foreign lobbyist. The foreign lobbyist is the New Man who made it and who now is legal; corruption and primitive accumulation are now more concealed. And much seemed to follow from that development. Over the past forty years, the foreign lobbyist has become a uniquely important vehicle not only for intraruling class dealings but also for creating access to Congress and state and local governments for foreign interests where none had existed before. The foreign lobbyist, some have noted, differs from other figures who also function in some kind of intermediary capacity, such as the ambassador, the international banker, and the lawyer. He works inside the structure in both politics and economics but largely outside the scrutiny either of the government or of the media. His income is not necessarily on the books. He therefore has certain advantages over others. A reasonable hypothesis is that the rise of the foreign lobbyist helped to bring about some of the major changes of recent years in countries such as the United States—for example, the creation of Rust Belt cities and the movement of industry to new locations—changes that would otherwise be unlikely to have occurred.

These changes brought in their wake, as a second section of the chapter shows, a resiting of jobs and a shift in the American job market to the South and the Southwest. The upper working classes and middle classes were heavily impacted. In a number of important industries, such as the automobile industry where this impact was especially noticeable, the driving force came from East Asia. In this period, Japan and Korea were among the most important clients of these lobbyists.

If foreign penetration had an impact on the existing job market, so too did it effect the future job market as a result of the deals—discussed in the third section—allowing for technology transfer. Heavily concentrated in the late 1970s, 1980s, and early 1990s, technology transfer obliterated whole sectors of the economy that had been employing many people and would predictably have continued to do so.

At this point, the chapter expands its purview, turning from a consideration of the industrialized countries and their penetration of the U.S. political economy to a Third World example of penetration, that of Mexico. What we discover in the fourth section of the chapter is that through its alliances the Mexican ruling class developed the power to dump its surplus labor on the United States, as well as the power to persuade millions of Mexicans to accept the idea of illegal immigration to the United States. The United States, it appears, has been caught off balance by this tactic. Despite its desire for a supply of cheap labor, it is clear that it is not in favor of the unlimited illegal migration being foisted on it but is so far unable to do much about it. It does not have the power to regulate the flow of immigration today that it did earlier in history when multilateralism was less developed. Not surprisingly, the issue has created an unprecedented level of controversy in American society, as the next three sections of the chapter show. The public wants to know why this immigration is happening. The United States is a great power; it should put an end to it. At this point, the chapter surveys semiofficial statements of the two governments supporting the status quo, then turns to the voices of opposition. Even the establishment-oriented AFL-CIO, one finds, is taking a stand. Its leadership says that what is needed is economic justice for all. In reaction to this stance of the unions and to other signs of disaffection with existing policies, a prominent spokesman for the state, as we will then see, recently issued a mass-market book seemingly designed to steer public discourse back along more "acceptable" lines of white nationalism, away from issues of class and justice. Anglo-Saxon America, the author claims, is being polluted by the arrival of so many Hispanics. This flood of immigration is, in his view, the crisis, and though one might agree there is a crisis, it would not be for the reasons he adduces. Certainly, crisis is a category in world history, which seems applicable. The question to be asked, as the next section makes clear, is whether foreign penetration and most particularly the immigration issue have significantly contributed to the already existing crisis or if what one witnesses today in countries such as the United States is simply a temporary problem as the racial hierarchy is being remodeled to make use of these newcomers. Taking a crisis-centered approach but in a somewhat different sense, the chapter then draws the book to a conclusion.

THE FOREIGN LOBBYIST IN WASHINGTON

There are two tiers among the foreign lobbyists found in Washington in recent years. First, there are those buried in the woodwork, serving the interests of Great Britain, Saudi Arabia, Israel, and other countries that have what are termed special relationships. Second, there are those who serve the rest. Acting as the representatives of dominant elements from around the world, the latter, although on the outside, are nonetheless well placed and frequently highly successful. By relying on foreign lobbyists, many foreign governments have developed a dual approach to dealing with the government of the United States, one that takes place on the level of the embassy in Washington and one that takes place on the level of the lobbyist. Foreign embassies serve national interests; their dealings are generally out in the open. Class interests, on the other hand, require a considerable degree of confidentiality and as a result are rarely public. An everyday example may serve to make this distinction clear. An ambassador agrees to have his country produce goods for a Western country. The deal is announced by the embassy to the media. Off the record, what has also been worked out is that he has agreed to lower the workers' wages. In return, there will be some side benefits for his government. How would this arrangement come about? My hypothesis is that it would be worked out in the office of the foreign lobbyist. This office would be a more discrete venue than the embassy. The lobbyist represents a secure backdoor form of communication, one that is especially useful for solidifying class interests as opposed to national interests.

One wonders, of course, how significant this could be. Does the existence of intraclass solidarity and backdoor dealing really make much of a difference in terms of the course of history, enough difference—as this book is implying—to warrant a change in the dominant paradigm of world history? The answer provided here is yes. Class interests trump national interests much of the time. If a ruling class of a powerful country suddenly turned against its own industrial base and destroyed most of the well-paying jobs that its citizens could hope to get, as happened in the 1970s and 1980s in the case of the United States, one would have to believe that there is something taking place beyond the bounds of what consensus history or the Rise of the West would lead us to expect. There is a class-solidarity dimension of which foreign penetration is an expression.[1]

To study the subject of the lobbyist, however one chooses to do it, one needs sources; this is a problem. The historian will find that most of the scholarship done thus far comes from the social sciences. Historical research on this subject is virtually nonexistent for most periods before the near present. One finds only a small amount of information on the foreign lobbyist for the nineteenth century, a bit more for the World War II and cold war eras, and then, for reasons to be discussed, more for the years of the Reagan Revolution of the 1980s and later. Much of the information we do find or find easily, however, seems to come from sources that a historian might prefer not to rely on. Take, for example, the information that a foreign lobbyist might choose to reveal in some exceptional moment—for example, when he decides to mobilize some local ethnic community or some other such constituency for the sake of added support. This situation would, of course, be the exception, and the information made available would have to be examined in that light. Most of the time the foreign lobbyist tends to rely on himself, his clients, and his contacts more than on the media or society at large, much less the world of scholarship. All of this has wider implications.

The subject of foreign influence, which is what the lobbyist represents, is an unusual example in American history of a subject that has yet to be studied in depth.[2] There are studies of foreign investment in the United States, studies of immigrant communities and their impact on foreign policy, studies of U.S. corporations and their dealings with foreign countries. All touch on the subject of influence. However, until now, one does not find anyone who is urging that the study of U.S. politics should consider foreign governments working through lobbyists to be a part of the U.S. political structure. Is the reason perhaps that the subject is considered too unimportant to be worth pursuing? Perhaps this is the case. Still, one might recall that many subjects, even subjects considered of fairly marginal importance to the study of American politics, are nonetheless meticulously covered. This subject, however, is not one of them. Perhaps, then, the issue is more than simply a matter of the availability of sources, as many such subjects present similar technical challenges. Perhaps the subject itself is nonintuitive, bordering on conspiracy thinking, muckraking, or some other ideologically driven activity. For many historians, such a subject would rightfully be one found in the domain of literature or journalism but not history. Mark Twain's *Gilded Age* may persuade one that American politics in the 1870s was really corrupt and in need of reform. He could write about such matters because he was a man of letters, not a historian. Others, social scientists, for example, have been able to bring some credibility to their studies.

If the function of the foreign lobbyist is to buy, bribe, or one way or another procure results for a client, this subject could be studied as political corruption.[3] And, as we saw in the last chapter, despite some limitations in that body of work, it could be a useful resource for historians, perhaps even a stimulus for them to take up the subject for themselves. This approach would certainly be feasible for the historian, but there is one other problem with it. The field of the political sociology of corruption, except for a few authors of the sort we cited in the last chapter, does not seem to be progressing at this time. Whereas there was once a good deal of attention paid to the field, in the past twenty years, with a few important exceptions, there appears to have been less and less new scholarly work. Why there has not been more is not clear. Perhaps it reflects the fact that times are corrupt, and perhaps as a result the research is less fundable at this point. Alternatively, perhaps scholars are wondering what the point of studying corruption would be if no one is interested in reform.[4] Perhaps, too, the problem is that such research calls into question the image of democracy. Whatever the reasons, we find that in the past few years some of the research of the 1970s and 1980s is being republished to fill the void.[5]

What we find in this somewhat older work is that scholars were trying out various approaches to explain why there still was political corruption and why reforms never worked. If an approach did not work, then it was abandoned. The liberal approach to the study of political corruption was tried out, it did not work very well, and so some researchers at least abandoned it. It simply could not be shown that some cultures tolerate corruption more than others, or that democracy is the least corrupt form of culture, or that more developed countries are less corrupt than less developed countries. Nor is there any point going on looking for evidence of systemic corruption in nondemocratic countries and simple malfeasance in democratic countries. Research in the 1970s and 1980s showed that in democracies, corrupt individuals were as plentiful as they were elsewhere. This realization, as we have previously shown, led to a certain amount of rethinking in the field. Ultimately, it served to point the discussion in other directions.

As a result of this rethinking, a historian using such material could expect to find evidence that each of the different forms of hegemony have a typical manifestation of corruption and that no one of these manifestations is necessarily more corrupt than another. Such work could be undertaken, and it could be eventually applied to subjects such as the foreign lobbyist. One notes, for example, that in tribal states information exists to show that bribes on the official level are often disdainfully called presents. As already noted, the Deys in North Africa wanted such presents from the French consuls. In bourgeois democracies, bribes are believed to be given by corrupt businessmen—or foreign lobbyists as the case may be—to corrupt politicians in what is believed to be an otherwise virtuous society, whereas in Russian- and Italian-type societies bribes are part of everyday life. Everyone is made to participate openly in corruption, so the corrupt activities of the dominant classes do not stand out.[6]

Given such findings, some researchers have concluded, corruption is clearly a part of the structure, and if so, then what is important is how one should categorize and rate the different forms of corruption in particular structures. According to one writer, whose views are not too dissimilar from those of the criminologists previously discussed, it is important to focus on the size and function of corruption in terms of a particular structure rather than how it may have been defined in any structure. Pursuing the subject in this fashion, corruption, it was found, depending on context, may be benign (for example, the cost of moving paper in the government, or the cost of "crony capitalism") or system threatening (such as narco-terrorism). If the context changes, hypothetically at least, narco-terrorism could be benign and the cost of moving paper system threatening.[7]

Such an orientation has not always prevailed, even in the social sciences. For a long time, in fields such as criminology, crony capitalism, to take one example, was looked at only as something to be reformed. In such work it was thought to be an endemic problem, especially of undeveloped countries and in particular of comprador bourgeoisies in such countries.[8] What crony capitalism reflected in the eyes of many scholars in those years, and still does for some today, is an inability of the political elite to separate itself from business matters and to allow for market logic to function. This inability makes it an obstacle to development and thus a threat.

Recent studies of crony capitalism, however, offer a more nuanced picture of the subject; their conclusions seem less predictable in advance. One recent work commenting on the situation in the Philippines and South Korea argues that given certain balances, crony capitalism is not necessarily an obstacle to growth. A recent study of Egypt's "32 Whales" suggests that crony capitalism was tied to political stability. It is not simply a lack of self-control on the part of politicians. The author of this study goes so far as to suggest that rather than starting from the assumption of the need for reform, research should be pursued along the lines of network analysis, that is, how the political economy is actually functioning in terms of networks, *crony* not being such an exact term. More provocatively, a study of crony capitalism in Texas with an emphasis on the "Texas Six-Pack" argues that crony capitalism was the tool allowing for the state's rise to national prominence.[9]

This gradual move away from labeling crony capitalism as corrupt to one in which the scholar tries to understand what is taking place from its context and what difference it makes is very hopeful. It would mean that it might one day become a useful theoretical term, especially if it could rid itself of its association with weakness. Crony capitalism is not a sign of weakness or for that matter of inefficiency; to the contrary, crony capitalism is something requiring some level of strength and efficiency. The question of what the internal dynamics are within crony capitalism that often give it its power or how it differs from state capitalism or various other related phenomena awaits further work. Suffice to note here that if one wants to examine the activities of people who play an intermediary role, that is, who trade in confidential political and economic information, as foreign lobbyists do, then crony capitalism might serve as some kind of framework. With these preliminary observations out of the way, let us turn to a consideration of foreign lobbyists in U.S. history.

Who were the first foreign lobbyists? What issues did foreign lobbyists tend to deal with in 1776 and thereafter? Concerning earlier American history, fragmentary information suggests that economic and political penetration by agents representing foreign interests date back to the founding of the country. Some of these agents may have been lobbyists, though it is unclear. The U.S. government, it appears, considered foreign penetration an important issue in a political sense, but it was not until 1938 that the first regulatory act was passed. At that point, there was a Nazi lobby to contend with whose representatives were purchasing war matériel.

After World War II, the national preoccupation became the menace of communism, which allowed lobbyists for the anticommunist Third World a point of entrance within the Beltway. The United States needed the support of these countries. One could recall here as an example the Taiwan Lobby. The Taiwan Lobby (then known as the China Lobby) succeeded for many years in garnering vast amounts of U.S. foreign aid as well as securing its foreign policy objective of keeping the Republic of China out of the United Nations. Perhaps for its part, it contributed to the cold war fervor of that era found in the United States. By the early 1960s, some fifteen foreign countries, mainly from the Third World working through lobbyists in Washington, obtained the right to sell sugar to the United States to replace the sugar that Washington would no longer buy from Cuba. These nations included a number of Latin American countries but also included India and South Africa. Their key target was a North Carolina Democrat, Harold D. Cooley, the so-called sugar czar.[10] How those lobbyists managed to influence Cooley would no doubt make an interesting story. One wonders if they were important in pushing for the embargo of Cuban products.

By the middle 1960s, congressional inquiries revealed that foreign lobbyists were less likely to try to subvert the government than they were to try to influence the legislative process. This revelation led to further revisions in the regulatory legislation governing foreign lobbyists, revisions that came to be known as the FARA Amendments of 1966. Follow-up studies of the efficiency of these legislative revisions, which were carried out in the 1970s, showed that the FARA Amendments achieved little; foreign governments continued to influence the legislative process. And surprisingly, at least until that point, there was little information about these lobbyists, the Justice Department rarely pursuing suspected infractions of the law. Indeed, there has always been an air of secrecy around the lobbying process, and there still is. For example, in a landmark case in 1976, a Washington law firm representing the Republic of Guinea, a country with bauxite interests, managed to hold on to most of its attorney-client privileges despite the foreign policy implications of the case. In the same period, it became apparent that former officials of the United States often took up lobbyist jobs in their area of expertise after their retirement from service in the government. This disclosure struck many as a conflict of interest. The Michael Deaver case of the 1980s falls in this category. Deaver was both a successful lobbyist for Third World interests and a close friend of the Reagans from his days of working in the administration.

In 1977 Congress, reacting to a groundswell of complaints from American businessmen who were losing out, took another step and passed the Foreign Corrupt Practices Act (FCPA) of 1977. This act outlawed illegal payments by overseas business.[11] Nothing was said about the role of the lobbyist who opened doors and facilitated deals in the United States, it simply focused on what was done "abroad." What catches one's attention on looking at the FCPA is that it scarcely tried to address the actual context of international trade, where if a corporation from one country failed to offer a bribe, it gave the advantage to a country that did. Thus, when the law was enforced, as it sometimes was, there were sensitive aspects to it. In light of these sensitivities, the Securities and Exchange Commission (SEC) decided to clarify that bribery by U.S. firms abroad made the carrying out of U.S. foreign policy more difficult because bribery suggested neocolonialism, and, furthermore, the nondisclosed payments to foreign leaders constituted illegal use of corporate funds to the possible detriment of the investor. Nonetheless, by the 1980s the Reagan administration itself was involved in violations of the FCPA in the Iran-Contra scandal. By the 1990s, the number of cases of violation of the FCPA actually pursued by the SEC had dwindled sharply. In 1999, when the German organization Transparency International issued its Bribe Payers Index, it showed that the United States ranked with countries with no regulatory framework at all. Third World leaders and others continue to extract bribes from American businesses and deposit them in foreign bank accounts. A historian might well reason that this was an indication of their power. Again, however, there is little public discussion of the intermediaries who may have brokered such deals.

A study of foreign lobbyists in Washington carried out in the mid-1990s by a political science professor showed that the majority chosen by foreign interests were white East Coast Protestants who had majored in political science—in short, their profile fit certain preconceptions one might have about the transformation to neoliberalism of that period. The major job responsibility of these lobbyists was influencing legislators concerning this or that special foreign interest, which tended to mean that the lobbyist's main communication was with the key committee members in Congress, *communication* a code word for possible political or economic pressuring.

This study also raised the question of how successful such efforts were and whether the success registered can be attributed simply to lobbying. These questions are interesting but difficult ones to pursue. In all probability, success, especially success regarding high-profile issues, came as a result of a variety of factors and not simply because of foreign money paid by a lobbyist. In such cases, and these cases are the ones about which we have the most information, pressure groups also played a role. Such groups already existed, and lobbyists would on occasion try to mobilize them. AIPAC, working on behalf of Israel and the National Association of Arab-Americans for Arab causes, may serve as a well-known example of such groups. What one assumes, however, is that although these groups could be mobilized out in the open for certain kinds of issues, daily relations would take place mainly behind the scenes.

As the foregoing suggests, most of what we actually know about lobbyists comes from a few cases that got in the newspapers by virtue of their controversial nature. The year 1981, for example, witnessed an atypically high-profile clash between the Zionist lobby and the Christian Right, on the one hand, and major segments of the America corporate structure allied with Saudi Arabia and the Arab-American community, on the other, over the decision of the administration to sell AWACS to Saudi Arabia. AWACS were advanced reconnaissance planes that could detect all air operations and defend Saudi oil fields from foreign low-flying planes, as from Iran, or in the Israeli view spy on Israeli air force activities. The passage of the bill in the Senate could be and was interpreted as a victory for the "Texas-Saudi axis." The AWACS sale was atypical in another sense. Usually, countries such as England or Israel or other bourgeois democracies rely more on placing people on the inside than the outside. As a result, even less is typically aired publicly.

From the 1980s on, as far as social science research shows, foreign economic penetration seems to have been expanding and so too was the institution of the foreign lobbyist. The two developments seem very likely to be interconnected. In this period, the traditional big-seven leaders of foreign direct investment (FDI)—the UK, Japan, the Netherlands, German, Canada, France, and Switzerland, followed by other countries—continued as before, and lobbyists played a role in this process.[12] However, with the continuing development of the New International Economic Order in this period, other investors arrived as well, some with considerable amounts of money, among them citizens of other Asian countries such as South Korea and then later China, Singapore, and India, as well as of other parts of the Third World and Israel.

Concerning Japan, studies suggest in rather general terms how its enormous investment in the United States in this period was appreciated by the American establishment. What exactly this gratitude meant politically remains uncertain. What one might be able to infer is that given the size of Japan's economic presence, it obtained entrée to the political process through its political action committees and lobbyists and the shaping of public opinion through the media and scholarship. What is certain is that

Japanese business was able to continue exporting year after year to the United States without ever confronting protectionist legislation that might have warded off American industrial ruin.

Here one might note that the lobbyists for Japan did have some advantages relative to others, as the Japanese government not only employed lobbyists but relied as well on a state-to-state approach, an approach one might expect a Russian Road regime to use. Working on the official level and through the official media, Japanese businessmen could reassure the reader of the American newspaper with reports of continuing sales of cars with the Ford logo, the typical reader little aware that the work itself was being increasingly done abroad and that the parts were increasingly foreign in manufacture. The union man knew better; between 1979 and 1981 one-third of automobile jobs were lost forever. Union struggle, as previously indicated, was extraordinarily ineffectual, given the stakes involved.

Of course, the East did not give up its paramountcy in the American political economy without some struggle. The American automobile industry as well as the United Auto Workers union mounted a salvage campaign through such initiatives as the domestic content bill. However, the Japanese car lobby fought and defeated the bill by creating a coalition of American interest groups, including even segments of the trade union movement such as the International Longshoremen's Association.

There has been up to now little connection drawn between the collapse of the industrial Northeast and the rise of the South and West, the latter now the preferred areas for foreign investment. One can surmise this shift was a process, the decline of the one allowing for the rise of the other. Whereas historically the core culture may have once been the center of American isolationism and protectionism, and may once have been economically weaker than the East Coast and the industrial Midwest, suddenly this changed. These two regions became stronger and their approach to geopolitics changed, evidence for which comes not only from information about factory relocation but also from what is known about the General Agreement on Tariffs and Trade (GATT) negotiations, the latter the very symbol of how capitalism worked in that period. As the GATT negotiations progressed, the core culture's regional priorities became increasingly embedded in the final position the United States would adopt. The defenders of GATT, who insisted on opening the market, wound up making an exception for soybeans, wheat, corn, and aircraft, products having a somewhat regionally specific quality. This position could not have been an accidental one. The only logical conclusion is that it reflected the rising political power of the historic American core culture, a phenomenon, we now understand, as beginning in the Goldwater-Reagan years.[13] It was their representatives who had the power to protect their region while inflicting the open market on competing regions, provided they could find international collaborators to help them do it. This combination of circumstances was how the penetration of the core of the world market proceeded.

During the period from the 1960s to the 1980s, the number of lobbyists working for other Asian countries (other than Japan and Taiwan) increased, among them the South Korean lobby, headed by the Washington-based rice merchant Tongsun Park. Park was, of course, Korean. As a conspicuously wealthy individual in Washington, Park was something of a role model for the wider group of registered foreign lobbyists. As a registered foreign lobbyist from a "tribal-ethnic state," Park adopted techniques that mirrored the already existing bilateral relations between South Korea and the United States. As the United States was South Korea's protector, he projected a desire for a client or friend relationship with American politicians. Behind this cover, South Korea's goal was to penetrate the American market with its industrial products. In addition, South Korea was also concerned with security issues. It felt threatened by North Korea, especially after the two events of 1968—the attack on the USS *Pueblo* that was not avenged and the attack on the presidential palace that was only narrowly thwarted.

During his tenure in Washington, Park, in contrast to most other lobbyists, threw lavish parties and by means of them worked his way into becoming a campaign donor to a variety of politicians. All of this activity, of course, served to ensure the continuing U.S. commitment to the armed forces in South Korea and the growth of Korean exports to the United States. Eventually, Park's success led to exposés that revealed his relations with Reverend Moon, a discredited prototype of himself. At this point, the Korean government appears to have decided that relying entirely on a "personalized approach" through a Moon or a Park might fail, and it shifted to a more broad-gauge approach to pursuing its interests in Washington. The

1980s saw the creation of two lobby groups rooted in the community of Koreans in America (the Korean-American Political Action Committee and the Korean Economic Institute of America), these organizations becoming a form of lobbying new for South Korea.

As for Park, what probably occurred was that he fell victim to a series of events beginning in the late 1970s back in Korea. In this period, strikes by women and workers against the dictatorship shook the regime. Following the predictable crackdown that followed, divisions in the Korean ruling circles appeared, leading in time to multiple centers of power. Once there were multiple centers of power, it was impossible for a figure such as Park to function as he had. One or another of these centers of power would be bound to want to see him discredited. Park was thus quickly off the scene.

The Saudi ambassador in Washington could serve as an example of another even more extraordinary figure, one blending the function of ambassador with that of lobbyist and guarantor of the special relations of the United States and Saudi Arabia. Coming from an even more coherent version of a tribal-ethnic state than the Korea of Tongsun Park, he was able to exploit the personal approach more successfully than could Park or for that matter anyone else.[14]

In summary, this opening section argues that the foreign lobbyist has been an important institution in modern American history, one that has been frequently overlooked by historians despite the fact that it has clearly played a role in American politics. Second, although relatively little is known about the foreign lobbyists, one could observe that hegemonic logic has been influencing the strategy that countries use in seeking to achieve their objectives through their choice of lobbying techniques.

To pursue the impact of multilateralism on the imperial metropole more deeply, one needs to also look at outcomes. What is the impact? Where, for example, did factory jobs go in the great shakeup of the 1980s, and why were factories sited where they were?

CONTROL OF FACTORY LOCATION

In this section and the next we take up examples of empirical terrains in which world historians would be able to pursue the subject of the growth of foreign political and economic influence in the United States, first examining the politics of factory siting and then that of technology transfer. These topics are, of course, generally studied by economists. The assumption here is that historians could study these topics as well.

Previously, we observed that there appeared to be a correlation between the increasing importance of the foreign lobbyist and the growth of job flight from the traditional industrial regions. On closer inspection the matter appears somewhat more complicated. The correlation exists, but it is not that simple. The terminology associated with job flight is not very precise, *job siting* is better, and as ever the role of the lobbyist is in the background.

Major competitors of the United States, such as Japan, apparently wanted to move factories out of unionized areas but to retain the advantages of remaining located in the American market, whereas it was the Third World countries that were interested in the relocation of American industry overseas, specifically to some particular country in the Third World. Thus, it probably would be more precise to refer to job siting rather than simply to job flight. That point noted, a look at the records suggests that foreign ruling classes, among them Third World ones, have enjoyed growing success in achieving their various objectives, which has sometimes meant that jobs long associated with the American economy disappeared from the United States in the 1970s and 1980s. Parts of this story are well known thanks to investigative work by the media and do not need to be belabored. Who has not read about the flight of the apparel industry to Central America and the Caribbean, the flight of Nike to Southeast Asia, and the worldwide production base of Wal-Mart, to give just a few examples?[15] Less, however, is written about the political significance of industrial relocations within the United States and the role that foreign money and political influence played in this process. This would certainly be a place to look to study foreign penetration.

Beginning in the 1970s, the rise of the new economy and the obvious importance of America as a consumer market encouraged a great deal of European and Japanese foreign direct investment. There is some documentation and commentary on this subject. Within this writing on FDI or more specifically IFDI (incoming foreign direct investment), factory location and the politics of jobs related to it receive a limited amount of attention. What one can infer from it is that foreign direct investment is a phenomenon as old as the United States itself and that it has never been a very large part of the economy in percentage terms, and that it began to attract sustained scholarly attention only in the 1970s when the United States was losing its competitive position. So far, few historians have adopted it as a theme. As a result, the significance of FDI in terms of the larger dynamics of modern American history still remains to be worked out.

As noted, studies by economists make clear that much of the FDI of the past twenty-five years first targeted the American South[16] and then increasingly the Southwest.[17] Given its growth in these locations, it is hard to escape the hypothesis introduced before that FDI might someday be understood to have been a part of the Reagan Revolution, as these regions are where and when the Reagan Revolution arose. What is more certain at this point is that FDI definitely played a role in the regional shift in the country's industrial base. And, given this point, a corollary proposition would seem to be that it should also be considered a factor in the formation of the Rust Belt.

What is commonly noted by social scientists is that during the 1980s, the South and the West rose, leaving the industrial Midwest behind, under the aegis of a renascent Republican Party. The possible role of foreigners in this process is not something commonly assumed. Thus, it would be, if such were the case, a new way of looking at the Reagan Revolution as well as a new way of looking at deindustrialization, the latter phenomenon generally regarded as more economic than political, though political it was. Consider, however, the following. If we assume capitalists prefer Republicans over Democrats, then why not also assume that capitalists abroad would notice that a regional shift in industry—say, from the American North to the American South—would hurt the Democrats but might help the Republicans?[18]

Although a number of studies on foreign plant location have appeared from the 1980s onward, for the most part it is difficult to use them to address these wider points. Most are rather narrow and technical in nature. They do, however, reinforce the point made earlier that foreign businesses prefer nonunion areas. This point would make a lot of sense if one assumed as well that the Japanese goal of foreign investment was at least partly one of weakening the Japanese unions back home. Apart from that, what is also well known is that the states that are the most nonunion are the ones that also tend to have right-to-work laws, to have fewer days of work stoppage, and to have lower pay scales, all of which are also attractive features from a business perspective. It is also the case that many of these states are located in the South. And although employers do prefer skilled workforces and southern education does not produce them, southern state governments do run widely appreciated specialized labor training programs at their own expense to meet the needs of potential investors. Sun Belt states have also benefited from their recent entry into manufacturing by being able to invest in the latest technology, in so doing outstripping the northern states that were burdened with their existing technology that was often appreciably older. Moreover, southern industry has generally tried to perform certain fixed functions and to avoid product development and innovation. Its factories tend as a result to be organized in a simpler fashion than are those of their northern counterparts—for example, they are more likely to be organized as a line flow than as a job shop. Finally, as southern factories are focused on producing already established products, they can use cost-cutting approaches such as just-in-time manufacturing principles, which save on warehousing and handling costs.[19] These factors doubtless all influenced decisions about job siting as well.

Incoming foreign direct investment, it was found in one study, went against the national trend of the suburbanization of industry of the 1980s and 1990s by remaining heavily urban. Thus, investors put their money into the cities, which became known in this period as the New South and later the New Southwest, cities that played a lead role in the rise of the Republican Party in the Reagan Revolution.[20] Still another study based on a questionnaire of chief executive officers confirmed that foreign companies did indeed choose particular states, their knowledge of these states in some instances coming from politicians and members of trade missions who had passed their way.[21] Specific locations within states, however, tended to be chosen with the help of state economic development agencies. Not uncommonly, the final choice came down to a bidding war between sites in two or more states. Other factors of importance in siting plants appear to be more technical, such as the factor of agglomeration. An already existing density, as in chemical plants in New Jersey, sometimes led to further investments of the same kind in the same area. Proximity to home base was also a factor in some cases. This factor gave California an importance to some Pacific Rim firms, New York State to some Canadian firms, and New York City to some Europeans ones. It helped raise these two states' IFDI to the level of Tennessee, Georgia, North Carolina, and Illinois, attracting fifty or more foreign plants a year, according to a study carrying up to the year 1987.[22]

In summary, multilateral politics and open-market capitalism drew foreign investment into the United States; it was bound to have some consequences, some of them in the U.S. proper and some beyond. Car factories owned by Japan opened in nonunionized parts of the American South and in Mexico; South Korea started producing steel for the American market. The American middle classes and working classes went into steep decline. The AFL-CIO went into crisis. Without deeper study, it is hard to know how significant foreign politics was in terms of what was happening. At the same time, it is hard not to imagine one is hearing the voice of the foreign lobbyist promising to secure loopholes in legislation if a company needs them.

TECHNOLOGY TRANSFER

The subject of technology transfer has already been referred to in terms of factory siting. In this section we will consider technology transfer more generally. We begin this section as we did the previous one, by noting the work done by economists and other social scientists on the subject and the relative absence of historical research. I will then summarize some of the findings of social scientists, emphasizing one of the main points, the decline of federal industrial regulation of technology transfer.

In the first half of the twentieth century, as economists have shown, the availability of technology reinforced the importance of certain locations in the United States; these locations often had a near monopoly of a particular technology—for example, a specific industrial technology. After the 1970s, however, with the onset of the New International Economic Order, the meaning of availability was transformed by the rising phenomenon of technology transfer. Technology transfer made technology available to the highest bidder, in effect foreign countries. Historical location meant much less.[23]

From work done by economists, one learns that technology transfer was and is officially controlled by government policy. This was the case for many years. However, as many have noted, in the 1970s and 1980s the existing policies seemed to have lapsed. At that point, the government abandoned its support and protection of sectors of the economy in which the country had had a worldwide lead, going against marginal utility theory if not national strategic interests, and doing so even where taxpayer dollars had paid for the initial research, thereby going against public interest. What appeared to some was that the government had to be feigning indifference to what was lost, that there had to be a political dimension, but it never came to light. Whatever was happening was always explained in economic terms, the latter shielding what one would have to assume to be the real politics of Reaganism.

Whatever the case, the abandonment of the advanced economy and of government oversight did not go unnoticed. In Congress, in the media, and on the level of governors and mayors, one found unending protests. Whether it was computer chips, tires, fighter plane technology, genetic engineering, or other critical areas of technology, it did not seem to matter. One by one, these sectors were sold to foreign countries. What else were their owners to do? How could new expensive products be profitably produced without support and protection? The presidents, one after another, defended the new policy, claiming, often rather sarcastically, that all commodity producers wanted to have themselves certified as critical to the national defense and worthy of protection. What was really needed, given the balance of trade, was to encourage foreign investment by keeping an open market and not discouraging foreign acquisitions or fussing about Rust Belts.

This manner of speaking leaves us with what one could term the paradox of the Reagan Revolution and its politics. How could it be so anticommunist rhetorically but so open to the communist regimes economically? This fact remains unfortunately a paradox. What we know unequivocally is that the conversion in the 1980s of the historic American core culture to an aggressive player in the multilateral world had certain benefits not only for South Korea and Saudi Arabia but for other regimes as well, including paradoxically the arch enemies of the United State, that is, the Soviet Union and China. How this situation came about, however, remains a matter of speculation. To woo allies abroad for his crusades, President Reagan offered many right-wing regimes the latest technology.[24] Doing so meant not just support in the cold war, but as an added incentive it often meant that American industrialists gained the option of new labor markets, in general nonunionized ones. Did it really bother Reagan that such technology could wind up in the Soviet Union through resales? Truly, one has to wonder about this point and wonder as well about what he meant by anticommunism. Could it be that Reagan promoted industrial technology transfer because he (or perhaps Nancy Reagan) did not want to see a union-based America? Was it a resurgence of sectionalism?

The contradictions in this about-face of an isolationist turned aggressive multilateralist were not lost on Reagan's contemporaries, even those individuals in his own circle. In a chapter of a collected work published in the 1980s, Richard Perle, then a fellow at the American Enterprise Institute, expressed his concern that Western technology was being used in more than five thousand Soviet military research experiments in one year alone. And although Perle concerned himself specifically with the Soviet Union, he might as well have noted how this technology was going everywhere. Some of this transfer was sanctioned by existing U.S. laws, some was not, being pushed through as a matter of dual-use technology or simply smuggled out and in. In any case, smuggling was certainly on the rise. Soviet technology smugglers became quite renowned in New York, and they were scarcely the only ones, although perhaps they were the best. In Perle's view, the United States was thus, inadvertently perhaps, saving the Soviets billions in research costs had they had to develop this technology on their own. Perle gives as examples the air-to-air missile, space shuttle technology, and computer systems, all of which the Soviets had appropriated. Zelenograd, Perle claimed, was the microelectronic capital of the communist world. If it did not exist, it would be cheaper for the U.S. military.[25]

In another chapter in the same volume, William Schneider Jr. acknowledged that the 1980s policy toward technology transfer marked a departure from the practices of the 1970s, the policy to the People's Republic of China on rocket technology being a case in point. As Schneider saw it, this policy eventually became more and more coordinated, involving many nations, thanks to the creation of the Coordinating Committee on Multilateral Export Controls.[26]

In yet another contribution to this volume, Victor Basiuk, a consultant to the U.S. government on Soviet science, technology, and national security policy, wrote that with the rise of Gorbachev in 1985, the USSR had become increasingly aware of the inefficiency of the command economy approach. Up-to-date technology made such decision making unnecessary. Soviet economic management appeared, to the leadership, increasingly inept; it was apparent that the country's growth rate was actually falling. For Basiuk, this failure raised a question: why worry about the Soviet Union and not China? Yet in 1985 twenty-seven categories of technology were made available to China. One wonders how this situation could exist.[27]

Was Reagan's cold war rhetoric simply a cover to allow him to drop Taiwan and pursue commercial possibilities with China? This is speculation, but consider the fact that whereas the Jackson-Vanik Amendment to the Trade Act of 1974 precluded communist nations from receiving most-favored-nation status, the president, with the approval of Congress, has continuously granted China a waiver to get around the amendment, with Reagan signing these waivers like every other president. Was it the skill of the mainland China Lobby working state to state that overwhelmed the Taiwan Lobby or some other part of the development of multilateralism? It is difficult to know.

What we do know is that in the context of the Reagan Revolution, with its blend of free-market capitalism and antiunionism, Detroit in effect lost the automobile industry as early as the beginning of the 1980s, and by the end of the same decade Pittsburgh lost its steel production. What these losses meant in terms of social change has been the subject of much journalistic investigation as well as some academic scholarship. According to a recent scholarly work on the subject of the deindustrialization of Pittsburgh by Dale Hathaway, the results for that city were sociologically catastrophic, as if a war had been lost. As Hathaway wrote in his study,

> The number of people (in 1987) who derived their income from steel had declined to less than four thousand, down from over thirty five thousand in 1981 and from eighty thousand in the 1940s. The mill towns, once so alive with the heavy throb of industry, now gave off the weak throb of welfare as if they were retirement communities. The degree of suffering

caused by lost jobs, mortgage foreclosures, suicides, broken marriages and alcoholism was beyond calculation. Many people especially the young left the Valley but middle aged and older workers unable or unwilling to migrate from the only home they had ever known went through the anguish of trying to start new careers. The standard of living, boosted to a high level by the United Steelworkers, was falling steadily.

In some cases, the families supported by these workers abandoned them.[28]

In the course of his research, Hathaway interviewed a Mellon Bank economist in Pittsburgh in 1986, someone who declined to have his name used but who provided the following insights from what one might term the multilateral or neocon wing of the Reagan Revolution. I paraphrase what Hathaway quoted from his remarks in extenso: You cannot fight the world economy, he stated. Our rising standard of living is threatened by the low wages elsewhere. Steel has been in decline for a long time in Pittsburgh, a factor being the aggressive and antimanagement orientation of the unions. From a bank economist perspective, the following was likely to happen. It would be necessary to generate high unemployment to deal with the unions. High unemployment would create an environment in which high wage demands would be impossible. It would take a while and require a thinning out of the valley's population. He regretted the turnaround would not be quicker, but he thought it was not likely. After several generations of working in the mills, the workers had developed a sense of stability and community, and their income had risen, causing them to forget their ancestors' struggles with hardship. It was time now to become reacquainted. The new source of steel would be South Korea; Congress would approve, and the president would appropriate funds for job retraining at government expense. America was changing. It was the Rise of the Rich.[29] Mellon, a Pittsburgh bank, was simply in Pittsburgh to do business.

The erosion of the American industrial base had an impact on many levels of life. Parents could no longer transmit to their children what had been meaningful to them under conditions where that way of life itself was disappearing. A kind of postmodernism or focus on the present of the sort discussed in Chapters 1 and 2 was observed to be affecting the new generation. The new generation, it appeared, did not want to connect itself to a past that had betrayed it. A sign of the times perhaps, the epic struggle of the United Steelworkers and of the other unions, the struggle that had brought many poor and exploited workers out of poverty, was scarcely mentioned in public education or the media any longer. Is it surprising, then, that even in this quintessential center of American industry, workers simply could not rally the kind of support needed to make a stand against capital flight? Sometimes they could not even rally their own families. As time went on, it was further revealed that maybe even segments of the working class had come to embrace the idea that real patriotism implied accepting the premise of market rationality.

What allowed for the sell-off is a subject that intrigues many researchers but also puzzles them. What some have noted is that it took place during a phase of finance capitalism and would seem that it was in actuality Wall Street and not Washington that approved or disapproved the sales, mergers, and joint-venture arrangements. Indeed, the statements made by various presidents at this point often seemed to echo what was already being said on Wall Street. Perhaps so. In any case, it had not always been this way. In the nineteenth century, the United States was ruled by finance capital. Yet in the Tariff of 1888, unlike in the GATT of today, the government protected its markets and national interests. Presumably, multilateralism then was still a lot weaker.

In summary, if foreign investment and the relocation of industry to the South or abroad could profoundly reshape American society, doing so with the apparent acquiescence of segments of all classes, and if major assets could be casually disposed of, does one not ultimately need a new explanation for how decisions were being made? Is it really simply market logic, as the dominant paradigm maintains?

What one might assume is that whereas bankers, Wall Street brokers, and foreign lobbyists were at the very least one part of the decision-making process, another and probably much more important part might have been the neoconservative political wing of the American power structure. What was done amounted to a choice; in the final analysis, the choice was a political one. In this period for the neocons, the loss of world technological leadership might have appeared to be a reasonable price to pay for gaining a decisive victory over the entrenched industrial interests of the country as well as over the unions. In 1888 this choice would not have been possible; it was possible now because of how far multilateralism had come. Focusing as neoconservatives do on the present and on the very near future, many doubt-less might have come to the conclusion that ridding the country of unions would pave the way for a more profitable and more trouble-free future.

LARGE-SCALE IMMIGRATION INTO THE AMERICAN LABOR MARKET AS AN EXAMPLE OF THIRD WORLD RULING-CLASS PENETRATION OF THE IMPERIAL METROPOLE

The development of multilateralism affected not only the production and distribution of goods and services but also the composition of the labor market and the society. In the case of the United States, nothing has impacted more heavily in recent years on the composition of the labor market and the society than the large-scale migration from Hispanic America, principally Mexico. In this section we take up this subject as a part of the discussion of foreign penetration, using the example of Mexico. What this migration demonstrates is the capacity of a Third World ruling class to resolve its problems by imposing them on a country of the core. How, one wonders, could it happen? Here one must turn to the historiography to find out.

In recent scholarship by historians and others concerned with the issue of migration, what one finds is a growing awareness that the United States has not been influencing Latin American governments at will, as was once thought. One implication of this newer work, as we shall see, is that the historian has to try to understand strategies pursued by Latin American and in this case Mexican politicians in order to actually understand the outcomes previously associated simply with U.S. policy. The immigration issue may serve as an example. Immigration was once taken to be something the United States demanded and received; today this view is much less common. Today, it is more commonly understood to be a subject that has an internal dimension not just in the United States but in Mexico as well. To enter into this newer form of analysis, we will examine what historians have written and what public figures are saying about the current immigration situation.

In historiography, the study of U.S. relations with Latin America has long been an established subfield in the discipline of history. The study of migration is a well-known part of it. In older scholarship on the subject of migration, we find that most authors adhered to the liberal paradigm in one way or another. Latin American countries were assumed to have been "banana republics." For better or worse, their governments were maintained by U.S. policies as a result of the Monroe Doctrine. If migration took place, it was because the United States demanded it. In recent years, neoliberal writers have done much to defend this older perspective by stressing the inevitability of globalization. In fact, they have made something of an icon out of the hardworking migrant who carries on true to his or her diasporic culture, thanks to modern technology.

Other scholarship, however, proceeds in different directions. Some of it, which is closer to the line of thought in this chapter, points to the fact that there has always been a considerable amount of Caribbean Basin influence on the level of the implementation of American immigration policy over the years. In more recent times, in fact, scholars are pointing to a growing ability of Latin American governments to make use of Hispanics in America as a political pressure group, one willing to work on their behalf like lobbyists.[30] Some of this scholarship goes so far as to look at this set of facts as pointing toward a reintroduction of slavery in the United States, one that is rooted in a de facto collaboration between the American and Mexican ruling classes.

To examine this subject as it is discussed today, we will now consider three influential discourses on the subject of Mexican immigration to the United States. First is the Mexican and American elite view of the subject of immigration. This discourse is the one that has had the upper hand in the public domain; it is the one promoting the benefits of flexible immigration on economic grounds. The second is the labor-oriented, "race to the bottom" view expressed by many workers, one that opposes large-scale immigration in the absence of economic solutions for the working class. Third is the culturally based opposition view, one running along the lines of American white nationalism, one that is now beginning to appeal to a segment of the American elite.

American and Mexican Elite Views

The first of the three discourses on Hispanic immigration considered here is that of American and Mexican elite views. Here the researcher finds views that one could interpret as being congruent with multilateralism. Though individual writers follow different tangents, they all appear to assume that immigration is a good thing both for the United States and for Mexico. In a recent study on the subject written by an American economist, the author claims that looked at through aggregate analysis, on the whole, continuous immigration has benefited the American economy. She meant by this selective immigration, not family reunification or amnesty for illegal immigrants who have managed to remain in the country. What has benefited the economy has been the acquiring of the skilled person, who immigrated legally. Selective immigration has not, however, been typical recently. Many recent immigrants have been arriving with few if any skills. What is needed, she concludes, is an electrified fence along the border to stop such people from coming.[31] Here she appears to be compromising with other trends of thought less in favor of immigration.

Implicit in much of this somewhat official writing is the view that although there are problems associated with immigration, most of them are caused by ordinary Americans, as a result of their racism and ignorance and not the policies themselves nor racism promoted by the government's implementation of its policies. Ignorance breeds irrational fear and racism. Mass fear, as one finds it today in American society, is an unfortunate factor with which the government has to contend. U.S. policy, another author argues, should not allow itself to be driven by such fear. It is a manifestation of ignorance to assume that the Hispanics who come will wind up on public assistance, as percentage wise this fear has not been borne out by the facts. Of course, there are "real" problems associated with immigration, but they can be solved. The author acknowledges that the recent trend of unskilled immigrant workers arriving and becoming concentrated in certain states has created a backlash, one coming from those workers whose jobs are threatened as well as those citizens who do not want their state taxes to pay for more community services and schooling. These problems can be remedied, the author believes, by the local society better educating the minorities and thereby overcoming the climate of racism. But in making such recommendations, she herself seems to be suggesting in a somewhat racially specific fashion that African Americans at that point in Houston perhaps will no longer want the unskilled jobs and the Mexicans could have them. The real problem she seems to actually be pointing to is the "ignorance" of the people of California, Texas, and Florida who do not want the job market to have a large number of jobs at starvation wages.

Another basis of support for the existing policy of flexible immigration is one strongly represented in academe and the media, as we saw in the discussions of New Liberal theory. For example, Saskia Sassens, a proponent of globalist interpretations and someone who takes migration to be a symbol of the age, writes that while the state "continues to play the most important role in immigration policy-making and implementation, it has been transformed by the growth of a global economic system and of other transnational processes. This has had as a practical outcome a relocation of various components of state authority to supranational organizations, such as the United States–Mexico Bi-National Immigration Commission or the institutions of the European Union."[32] It has also resulted in the emergence of a new privatized transnational legal regime for cross-border business transactions. The inference here is that what is taking place is a decline in traditional national sovereignty and a reshaping of sovereignty to fit the new transnationalist order. What the transnational market gains, the nation state loses.[33] In this optic, immigration is a mechanism of social change helping America to get beyond the nation-state phase. The state is not simply vesting its authority, it is growing weaker.

When one turns to official and semiofficial Mexican statements about the Hispanic immigration to the United State, the policy emphasis is on the interdependence of the labor markets as well as on the need for various reforms. It is necessary, for example, to overcome the problems of the failed system of border security and the problem of discrimination against Hispanics. Imperialism is also sometimes obliquely alluded to. As is the case with the American ruling class, so too with its Mexican counterpart, the stance is one of being above it all and of being motivated simply by humanistic concerns for the migrants. As with the American ruling class, so too with the Mexican ruling class, there is also some dimension of crisis lying behind the rhetoric adopted, and thus more is implied than actually spelled out or explained. Left unexplained, for example, is why large numbers of people are willing to risk their lives to try to cross into the United States simply to earn starvation-level wages, doing it again and again?[34] Yet another theme found in official Mexican discourse is that of labor-market complementarity. America has an aging population; it needs a source of young labor. An open labor market will provide it, and over time the market will achieve the needed equilibrium in terms of size and age group. This indeed may be the case, but such an equilibrium may not come anytime soon if so many Mexicans continue to die young.

Finally, there is the matter of emigrant remittances. Although the Mexican government has generally feigned indifference at what the emigrants supposedly choose to do with their earnings, one nonetheless finds a significant body of social science literature, some of it Mexican, appearing to acknowledge the fundamental role played by emigrant remittances to family and kin in the Mexican family economy.[35] In recent years, despite the official stance of being above it all, one clearly finds on occasion that the federal government and certain Mexican state governments have been trying to channel remittances from the United States back into specific local development projects under their aegis. In the 1990s, for instance, the Program for Mexican Communities Living Abroad found its way into the Mexican consulates of the United States.[36] At that point at least, state involvement in the affairs of the Mexicans in the United States was out in the open.

The subject of emigrant remittances as a part of Mexican scholarship, one might also note, is well established. It goes back to the 1930s. In 1931 Manuel Gamio (1883–1960), a pioneering Mexican social scientist, then in exile in the United States, published his well-known book, *The Mexican Immigrant,* in English. What its short-term impact in Mexico might have been is hard to know. However, as Prof. Arthur Schmidt pointed out to me, it was later translated into Spanish, supplemented by the research of Gilberto Loyo, and republished in 1969. This event could very well be taken as evidence that at least at that point, there was interest in Mexico in the role of the migrant's remittances in the home economy; perhaps the government had an undeclared policy even at that point.

In summary, according to the standard liberal world history, Mexico is obviously a Third World country. By definition, then, it is acted on by the West and not visa versa. There is no such thing as a penetration of the core by a periphery ruling class. A closer look does not find this position to be very precise. First, there is evidence of Mexico resolving domestic problems by exporting labor. Second, Mexico has allies in the United States. Not only are there businessmen who need Mexican labor, but there are also Mexican American groups who are willing to lobby for certain issues. Liberalism does not postulate that a Third World country would have allies of significance in the United States. For the Rise of the Rich, this is an example of collaboration and struggle between the ruling classes over a workforce.

Opposition to Immigration: The "Race to the Bottom" Trend

Let us now turn to the discourse in American civil society as regards Mexican immigration, taking up the views espoused by the rank and file of the AFL-CIO, and finally the white nationalist views as now found in the society and in some parts of the state itself.

The rank-and-file version of this opposition is often called the "race to the bottom" trend. The phrase conveys the idea of workers forced to accept lower and lower wages in order to compete for work, one group, country, or region played off against another. This interpretation of political economy is a widely held one among American workers. The union leadership as represented in the statements of Linda Chavez, an executive vice president of the AFL-CIO, however, supports a different position: equity for all is the confederation's official stance on immigration policy.

In recent years, the rank-and-file sentiment is found in a number of contexts, not strictly union ones. One finds it, for example, in the language of electoral and legislative politics in California, in the broadsides of lobbying groups such as FAIR, in studies of public opinion of the so-called man in the street, and forcefully articulated by African Americans workers in places such as Houston.

To illustrate the race to the bottom trend as it exists in the scholarly world, one could turn to the writings of Alan Tonelson. Alan Tonelson writes public policy studies for the U.S. Business and Industry Council, a voice for small business and labor. In *The Race to the Bottom: Why a Worldwide Worker Surplus and Uncontrolled Free Trade Are Sinking American Living Standards,* Tonelson speaks for Americans who are losing control of their job market. His book is a critique of NAFTA; it carries up to the year 2000. His critique of NAFTA and Hispanic immigration more generally is also in effect an attack on multilateralism. He asks, why does this ruination have to happen?

Tonelson argues that much of the support for NAFTA is based on a limited knowledge of and on limited research regarding what is really taking place in the American economy, this in large part because of a considerable breakdown in data collection and dissemination on the part of the government over the past generation, making economic analysis much more difficult than it had been before. Thus, what looks like one thing might in fact be something else altogether. He gives as an example the growth of the American export of spark plugs to Mexico following the passage of NAFTA. To some supporters of NAFTA, this example was evidence of how beneficial the treaty was for American workers. What the sale of spark plugs really meant, Tonelson shows, is that cars were being assembled there to be sold in the United States, cars once assembled in the United States, the sale of the spark plugs contributing to this process. Tonelson then gives another example. Commentators have noted that the passage of NAFTA coincided with a growth in the number of jobs in the United States. However, after some digging Tonelson finds that these jobs were overwhelmingly created in small businesses, only 1 or 2 percent of which depend on the globalized export economy. Most small businesses are oriented locally. To NAFTA supporters, this point, however, ignored the fact that most small businesses sell to large businesses and thus benefit indirectly from the export economy.

Here Tonelson's digging around draws one to consider another conclusion. Although it is true that small businesses sell to large ones, the larger context at this point in history is one in which corporations contracting to open factories in China—and China is the great new option for factory locations—are obliged to use Chinese suppliers and not American ones, so the growth of the global economy may simply obliterate these small businesses as time goes on, if current trends continue.

What Tonelson faced was a widespread refusal to believe him. How could Americans be poor and getting poorer? The Cato Institute went so far as to release a study disputing the view that Americans are poor; its conclusion was that there are very few poor Americans. One should judge wealth and poverty, it argued, in terms of what people possess. Where else do allegedly poor people own TVs, cars, and refrigerators? They may have huge debts and no jobs, but that fact is less important than what they possess. Pity the trade union official in this kind of climate who wants to argue from the experience of his workers and get himself heard! If Americans are actually well off, what difference does it make if another million immigrants show up? What Tonelson's book suggests is that the U.S. government is far less responsive to the needs of its citizens today than it was in the years around World War I. Tonelson may be writing in the language of the dominant paradigm, but what he conveys is supportive of the Rise of the Rich. He is describing multilateralism.

THE IMMIGRATION ISSUE AND WHITE NATIONALISM

Another perspective on immigration is represented in a recent book by Samuel Huntington. Samuel Huntington is commonly considered a "state intellectual." He has long been an influential political theorist and served as adviser to many presidents. In his 1993 article "Clash of Civilizations," he introduced the idea of divide and rule as a principle of conducting foreign policy. Since that time he has continued to develop this idea in other publications. In *Who Are We? The Challenges to America's National Identity,* Huntington picks up themes one associates with the populist Right about the Anglo nature of American culture threatened by Hispanization, using them to reinterpret the "race to the bottom" as a matter of cultural pollution of the American identity. Once again the hope seems to be, if one reads between the lines, one of divide and rule.

The book is framed as an appeal to American cultural tradition by someone apparently concerned with the maintenance of Anglo-Saxon cultural hegemony in the United States. It begins with a summarization of Thomas Jefferson's "American Creed." According to Huntington, this creed had defined the United States from its birth until the 1970s. Troubles arose in the 1970s when the intellectuals abandoned it as their compass in favor of multiculturalism, diversity, and Spanish as a second language. Huntington then recounts a Ralph Nader story from the 1990s to show that the problem of cultural orientation is not one simply limited to the academy. Nader had asked corporations to include the Pledge of Allegiance in their meetings; most refused to do so. Huntington tried to understand why. He turned to the subject of the process of Americanization, the process by which the immigrant traditionally learns English and civics. He found that it no longer exists. Following the onset of the contemporary Mexican immigration wave, he found that Americanization across the board was in abeyance. It was in abeyance, Huntington explained, as a result of a series of unique circumstances: the contiguity of the two countries, the number of those immigrants arriving in a short period of time, the degree of illegality involved, the subsequent regional concentration in the United States of Mexican immigrants, the persistence of the wave of immigrants legal or otherwise, the preexisting historical and cultural presence of the immigrant community in what is now their new home, the slowness of assimilation into the dominant American culture as a result of the nonadoption of English, and as a consequence the low level of achievement in formal education in the United States, the general result being a greater portion of the community living in poverty than was the case for other immigrant communities in the same time frame. Huntington also found endogamy to be a factor in delayed Americanization. Mexican Americans tend to marry other Mexican Americans, whereas other immigrants tend to marry outside their group. Finally, according to Huntington, in surveys identifying primary identity, Mexicans were at the bottom end of those individuals answering yes to the question "Am I an American?" Huntington, as one would expect, would not see this in terms of resistance to oppression. He would also no doubt dispute the idea that the "new white nationalists" are similar to the older white supremacists and nativists of the late nineteenth century. In his view, today's situation is unique, and in different ways he is right and wrong.

What Huntington's work actually shows is that with the evolution of multilateral relations, the emphasis on Americanization on the part of the state has, at least for the time being, declined. What is emerging as a result is a large number of unassimilated people. This is disturbing to Huntington, for he comes from a wing of the American political elite still concerned with the formation of the citizen as the guarantor of the state. There are for him no unassimilable people. The development of a multilateralism that allows for nonassimilation is therefore not such a good thing. Certainly, it is not a good thing for the hegemony.

Taking up Huntington's insights on the current situation, what is apparent as well is that the braceros are attempting to regain the borderlands. This strategy may work. At the same time, if they are successful in Hispanicizing the border states, it could weaken the struggle against multilateralism, as it would likely accentuate racial divisions and thereby strengthen the hegemony.

What Huntington and Tonelson are raising in their writings by implication is yet another question as well, one that is also worth pursuing. Does rapid deindustrialization combined with large-scale immigration and other challenges presented by multilateralism today exceed the capacities of the traditional hegemonies? Can these traditional hegemonies continue to evolve and cope with these problems? Or is it no longer likely because they have reached a crisis stage? In his book, Huntington appears to be exploring how anti-Hispanic racism could be made to bolster the American racial hierarchy. Tonelson appears to prefer going back to a more mercantilist past. Neither directly addresses the question of crisis. The next section takes up the issue of crisis, Huntington's essay opening the way.

CRISIS AS A CATEGORY IN WORLD HISTORY

This section returns to the issue of crisis as the term might be used in the study of world history. In Chapter 3 crisis was found to be a way to characterize the end of feudalism in two or three countries of Western Europe. It was a way to describe how powerful elements in the system often at war with one another inadvertently induced large numbers of peasants to flee to the free cities, which in turn coincided with other trends around the world and brought about the destruction of the feudal system in Europe and the rise of the capitalist mode of production on a world scale. In this sense, this crisis was a world historical one. The hypothesis here is that some analogies to the collapse of feudalism and the rise of capitalism can be found in our present-day situation. We have an international economic structure destroying the political bases that are its own foundation, that is, the nation-state. Large number of refugees from dysfunctional regimes are being created in the process. Leaving aside whether this shift will progress to another mode of production, one could argue that this situation is a crisis of the existing mode of production, its onset marked by the disjuncture between the economic and the political. Its outcome, here to repeat, is of course unknowable at this point.

Writers in the Rise of the West position would predictably hold otherwise. They would not define crisis in the same way and would certainly argue that modern history has no meaningful analogue in the past. They might claim that the "crises" that multilateralism faces today are comparable to the ones it faced in its recent past, and therefore what one should expect is a further evolution of multilateralism, not its collapse. This position, however, does not seem to be plausible. Earlier crises, as we have seen, arose between or among nations, whereas this one is arising in the idea of the nation-state itself. It is thus more analogous to the crisis of the feudal state than to anything more recent.

World historians have for the most part sided with the Rise of the West position. If one assumes, however, that a Rise of the Rich has taken place and a class in itself but not for itself is running the planet, then one might suppose that the Rich are trapped in the political system in which they find themselves, and for better or worse their progress is one of the main causes of the destruction of the mode of production. Richard Perle writing in the 1980s and Samuel Huntington writing more recently are examples of government officials aware of the crisis on the level of the state.

To demonstrate crisis in world history, it is not necessary to invoke eco-crises or Dark Age theory or some other external crisis but to simply look closely at failure on the national level. The nation-state is, after all, the bedrock of the modern world system. If one notes how the stratification system of some particular country once worked and then notes a progressive failure, one is confronting crisis. What one could assume as a corollary proposition is that a breakdown of the system of stratification in one or more nation-states would seriously disrupt the market, because it would disrupt multilateralism, and this disruption would be especially pronounced if the country in question was a part of the core and was a democracy.

Applying this set of assumptions to the example of the United States, one finds, in the years following the American Civil War, class was played against race as white over black. In time, this approach to stratification became the foundational logic of the modern state or the norm by which one could judge its subsequent history. For many years, it worked. In the 1870s with the arrival of a large number of Chinese immigrant workers, the system had to change a bit to accommodate this reality. Not only had masses of Chinese workers been brought in in a short period of time, but they were also ghettoized in Chinatowns. Soon the official discourse was that they were culturally unassimilable. This form of racial control was then simply added to the main Jim Crow–type white-over-black racism that was already in place. For a while, this modified system worked, but then it too began to break down, first as a few Asian Americans entered the trade union movement, then as a number of Asian Americans adopted the strategy of becoming "model minorities." By becoming a model minority, too many began to "whiten" too quickly. That occurred in the earlier twentieth century, and it forced yet further modifications in the system. At that point, the emphasis on a racially unassimilable caste was dropped, and in its place the "buffer race" strategy was introduced. One recalls from that point the waves of Italian, Jews, Irish, Slavic peoples and Middle Easterners who were considered not quite white.[37]

Buffer races, to clarify how this term is being used, were and are ethnic and racial groups brought in and situated so as to create frustration for African Americans and provide a buffer for whites. Their presence would allow whites to witness racial problems taking place among other groups, thus conveying the idea that where there were blacks, there were racial problems, that racism therefore was not a white problem, as reformers were maintaining it was. As a historian of race would know, this approach solved problems only in the short run. The difficulty was that the state could not keep any given buffer race in place for very long, any more than it could keep the Chinese unassimilable. The state may have brought in the Irish, the Italians, and the Jews to be buffer races, but none of them lasted as such; within a generation or so, they all "whitened," thus ceasing to be buffer races. The last attempt to construct a buffer race began in the 1960s. It saw the arrival of the professional classes of Latin America, East Asia, South Asia, and the Middle East. Today even these groups show signs of whitening. To slow this down, a desperate attempt to portray Muslims as terrorists is under way, reminiscent of J. Edgar Hoover's attacks on Italians as Mafia. In the face of these setbacks and perhaps lacking other groups to draw on and apparently unable in any case to sustain the deep racism of yesteryear, the bureaucrats running contemporary immigration policy have started to supplement the prevailing buffer-race approach with what appears to be a renewed use of the racial and cultural exclusionist one. If this is in fact what is occurring, then today would mark the second attempt to use the unassimilability strategy. One wonders if the state at this point expects that there would be a rise in racism against Muslims or Hispanics among white nationalists, as there was in the 1870s against the Chinese? If so and if it lasted, it would no doubt take the pressure off multilateralism. But is it likely? One would think the decision to approach Muslims and Hispanics this way, at a time when there already is a well-integrated Muslim and Hispanic middle class, seems counterproductive. The very existence of the latter serves to undercut the idea of unassimilability. Nevertheless, we now find signs written in Spanish as if to symbolize some permanent separation, as we find such signs written in Chinese. At the same time, an African American with a Muslim parent is a presidential nominee. This is evidence that the political system of one of the most stable and most influential countries in the world is in deep crisis.[38]

· · ·

BY WAY OF CONCLUSION, one of the weaknesses of capitalism on a world scale has been its inability to redistribute surplus beyond that which it redistributed to the ruling classes of the periphery. This inability has many ramifications. This last chapter provided one example, the penetration of the imperial metropole by multilateralism. Wealth is taken away from the periphery and invested in countries such as the United States. This led to foreign political influence in the United States, this in turn leading to problems for the American state. The American state is attempting to confront such problems through repression and through a further fine-tuning of its racial hierarchy strategy. However, these approaches are not working very well. Despite the support that multilateralism has afforded the American ruling class over the years, one still detects an air of crisis in U.S. politics. A certain kind of popular nationalism and antiglobalization is asserting itself around the immigration issue, which has counterhegemonic potentialities.

Other conclusions to be drawn from this chapter and from the book as a whole might be summed up as follows. Obviously, there is at this point a question of what paradigm to use in world history. With the emergence of social history, the old model of the Rise of the West lost much of its explanatory value. Some new way of characterizing the narrative of power is needed. This need is especially apparent for the study of modern world history. This book proposes the Rise of the Rich as an alternative to the Rise of the West. A sketch of world history along these lines shows a progression from bilateralism to multilateralism, the Rich gaining the power through their alliances.

A sketch was all that was possible. Given the limitations I bring to this work, there were simply too many problems to do more than that. Problems were encountered in source material and in the choice of useful terminology. In terms of what existed, there was a good deal of imbalance to overcome. In times past, historians carefully studied only one region, the West. As a result, there exists a fairly well-developed set of concepts for its study. For the study of other parts of the world, this is not the case. The concepts used often have limited applications at most. Often, they have been applied only to the country or civilization that gave rise to them. I proposed as a short-term solution to take whatever was strongest among existing concepts, especially the ones that have been applied to a number of countries, to see if it would be possible to keep adapting them to other cases worldwide. Concepts such as mercantilism, the nation-state, and hegemony seemed to be promising in this regard. Doubtless, there are others as well. In the long term, this approach, of course, will not suffice.

Despite the short-term problems, I proposed that adopting the Rise of the Rich was a worthwhile pursuit, because it could potentially resolve several problems in the field of world history, vexatious problems of long standing. These problems include how world history could escape from being Eurocentric without falling into polycentrism, how world history could effectively make use of the research done on national histories without becoming a prisoner of it, and how world history could acknowledge the historical agency of the lower classes and thereby overcome its tendency toward elitism.

In utilizing the Rise of the Rich as a paradigm, I also suggested that historians would challenge the perception of their discipline's supposed irrelevance to today's postmodern academe. New Liberals, as we have shown, take history to be a matter of stages, as, for example, the world before the invention of the computer and the world after it. In this optic, history as we know it in the history profession is little more than background material and is much devalued. The Rise of the Rich challenges this understanding of historicism. Computers may be useful technology. One cannot, however, meaningfully conceptualize world history around that fact.

There are a number of tacks a book such as this might have taken to present its argument. My approach was determined by one particular assumption more than others, that if the United States is where the Rise of the West paradigm is most deeply embedded, then for there to be a paradigm shift in world history, some attempt would have to be made to show that an alternative approach to American history would not only be successful but be superior. I attempted to dramatize this point by introducing the foreign lobbyist and the changes in epistemology that that implies. It would also be necessary to show, I thought, that there was a dialectic running through modern U.S. history, one not often made use of; in other words, one is not forced to approach the subject of American history from the premises of consensus, exceptionalism, and the West or from the straitjacket of labor and capital. For a work concerned with Eurocentrism, this strategy was no doubt an unusual one. More conventionally in a book of this sort, the author might have taken the United States as the imperial hegemon, doing so with the intention of concentrating on the details of struggle of the periphery. I actually entertained this possibility in one instance but then backed away from it. I found that through their struggle the Zapatista had managed to create a crisis in Mexico but that the strategy of the Zapatista up to now reveals its limitations. I also found that the Mexican state was strong enough to partly deflect this crisis by imposing hardship on many of its other citizens, forcing them to emigrate to the United States, benefiting as a result from its savings on social programs. The Mexican state, I found, was in crisis, but still holds on. The de facto expulsion into the United States of many Mexicans, which was also discussed, did not create a crisis for the U.S. power structure, as is commonly maintained by some U.S. historians. Indeed, one could argue, following the lines of this book, the new arrivals gave the government one last chance to fine-tune its racial hierarchy system and possibly slow down the crisis. Under such conditions, the "weak link" of capitalism, that is, the place where the current period of history will come to an end, crisis will surface, can no longer be assumed to be in the Third World, which is the common assumption; rather, it could be potentially anywhere. The collision of economic and political structures marking the onset of such a crisis is as likely in one country as another.

In attempting to stake out a claim for world history as a field of history distinct from national history, I took issue with two rules of historiography long upheld by the liberal tradition. The first concerns the absence of teleology, the second the absence of ethics in liberal scientific history. Neither teleology nor ethics contributes to scientific history in the view of most historians but, as regards to the field of history, this may be an exception. Teleology plays a useful role in world history. Given the variety of elements that enter into world history, the future is a necessary part of the conception of the past and of the present. The future plays an integrative role; it helps clarify the present and the past. I illustrate this point through the idea of the historical road. The historical road is simultaneously a part of the past, present, and future and thus retains its openness. Second, I argue that world history as a scientific enterprise is not separate from questions of ethics. It is not reducible to ethics, but ethics figures in it. In making this claim, I am taking exception to an assumption in history that to be scientific, one puts one's value judgments aside. What I claim is that although putting one's value judgments aside may suffice with small technical problems, world historians more often than not confront enormous problems, not small ones. To make sense of their materials, sometimes they favor one country over another, or one century over another, or one set of figures over another. Value judgments are inevitable, but how best to justify them in the context of historiography is usually uncertain. What often happens in practice is that the world historian confronted with organizing a text falls back on his or her own civilization for ethical guidance. At the same time, as every world historian knows, there are numerous civilizations and ways of judging and no scientific basis for insisting on one over another. This state of affairs has often cast the world historian in the position of the civics teacher who tells the student that he is right because everybody knows he is right, meaning in all probability that no one will read what he writes outside his own country. The escape from this dilemma—and it is a dilemma—is for the world historian to consider whether the ethical foundations of one's own perceptions could possibly resonate more widely.

Notes | *Bibliography* | *Index*

NOTES

INTRODUCTION

1. The Rise of the Rich differs from New Liberalism; for the latter, see the work of Antonio Negri and Michael Hardt, *Empire*. For a political economy reaction to it, see Atilio Boron, *Empire and Imperialism;* or Paul A. Passavant and Jodi Dean, eds., *Empire's New Clothes*. Negri and Hardt defend empire, claiming it is not imperialism. They attack Third World liberation, favoring world civil society as a counterforce to an American regime that has brought about what they term the suspension of history for all eternity. The Rise of the Rich problematic developed here regards the world as one of nation-states, the current empire with its designated policeman as one in which a niche position has been achieved as the result of the most recent crisis of multilateralism, a crisis allowing some American businesses a last great moment. It is not the end of history but a time of crisis of the capitalist mode of production.

2. For an introduction to more conventional history, see Eduardo Galeano, *Open Veins of Latin America: Five Centuries of the Pillage of a Continent;* and Jose Marti, *Inside the Monster: Writings on the United States and American Imperialism*. Such books over the years inspired one of the main American textbooks in world history of the past generation, Leften Stavrianos's *Global Rift: The Third World Comes of Age*.

3. R. A. Abou El Haj, "Historiography in West Asian and North African Studies since Sa'id's *Orientalism*," in *History after the Three Worlds,* edited by Arif Dirlik, Vinay Bahl, and Peter Gran, chap. 4, surveys mainstream Middle East history as an example.

4. Rise of the Rich merged with some political economy may be found in a recent book by the French socialist leader Lionel Jospin, *Le monde comme je le vois*. Chapter 5 deals with what Jospin calls the rise of the rich as science.

5. Researchers talented in finding their way around archives note a myriad of contacts and mutual influences among colonies and between colony and metropole. For example, see Brent Hayes Edward, *The Practice of Diaspora-Literature: Translation and the Rise of Black Internationalism*. This is representive of today's critique of Eurocentrism.

6. Frederick Cooper and Ann Stoler, eds., *Tensions of Empire: Colonial Cultures in a Bourgeois World*. See the editors' introduction, "Between Metropole and Colony: Rethinking

a Research Agenda," 1–58. This takes interelite matters back a few generations. For present day studies of world elites, there are numerous accounts. See endnote 7.

7. As a contemporary example of theory, see Leslie Sklair and Peter T. Robbins, "Global Capitalism and Major Corporations from the Third World." See also Leslie Sklair, *The Transnational Capitalist Class*. In this book, Sklair defines his subject in the following way: "The transnational capitalist class can be analytically divided into four main fractions: 1) TNC executives and their local affiliates (the corporate fraction); 2) globalizing bureaucrats and politicians (the state fraction); 3) globalizing professionals (the technical fraction); 4) merchants and media (the consumerist fraction)" (17). Sklair is most concerned with the first. He does not take on the role of the power elite and its criminal associations as in, for example, Robert Bryce, *Cronies: Oil, the Bushes, and the Rise of Texas, America's Superstate*. Other works also in the liberal tradition dealing with the world ruling class, meaning elite, include David Kowalewski, *Global Establishment: The Political Economy of North/Asian Networks;* and Morten Ougaard, *Political Globalization: State, Power, and Social Forces*. In hegemony analysis, as in my text, most of what one finds is fairly concrete because of the confrontation between actual social forces. In other words, there is the factor of class conflict. This factor is not found in liberal works where the determinacy of the market is more abstract, the present work thus closer to the rather more historically minded side of IR, such as Jeremi Suri, *Power and Protest: Global Revolution and the Rise of Détente*. Suri argues that the détente in the 1960s on the part of the superpowers followed class struggle in those countries. Somewhat close to the present text as well is Johan Galtung, "A Structural Theory of Imperialism," which stresses the commonalty of ruling-class interests across core and periphery. New liberalism is often very abstract or very concrete with nothing in between.

8. A classic analysis of the periphery is Samir Amin, *Accumulation on a World Scale: A Critique of the Theory of Underdevelopment*.

9. Jack A. Goldstone, "The Rise of the West—or Not? A Revision to Socio-economic History," esp. 191–92, shows that world history is not the only possible point of entry.

10. André Gunder Frank, *ReOrient*, enjoys its prestige thank to these conditions.

11. See Thomas S. Kuhn, *The Structure of Scientific Revolutions*.

12. See Paul Feyerabend, *Against Method*.

13. Opposing this, Micol Seigel, "Beyond Compare: Comparative Method after the Transnational Turn," restricts the role that comparative analysis plays.

14. Peter Gran, *Islamic Roots of Capitalism: Egypt, 1760–1840* and *Beyond Eurocentrism: A New View of Modern World History*. For the recasting of Middle Eastern and Egyptian history in these same terms, see, for example, my "Modern Middle Eastern History Beyond Oriental Despotism, World History Beyond Hegel: An Agenda Article" and "Egypt and Italy, 1760–1850: Toward a Comparative History."

15. Victoria E. Bonnell and Lynn Hunt, eds., *Beyond the Cultural Turn: New Directions in the Study of Society and Culture*, 1–34. The classic description of the period for

historians is Geoff Eley and Keith Nield, "Scholarly Controversy: Farewell to the Working Class?" Subsequently, they wrote a book-length exploration of class in contemporary social thought, *The Future of Class in History: What's Left of the Social?*

16. This book deals with modern world history and is aimed at that audience. It may, for that reason, trample on some professional sensibilities. As academic work has progressed, this field has had to compete with two other fields, global history and international history. Both have some claims on what is attempted here. World history in the traditional sense intended here concentrates on human societies and states and finds its dynamic and logic from within them. This book is such a work, and in this sense it differs from other works that try to put the human experience into some larger context, perhaps the natural history of the planet or the planet as a part of something larger. The latter, often called global history, introduces us to the idea of global ecological crises, such as the survival and extinction of different species. The present work does not follow this logic, but it takes world history at this point to be a field profoundly affected by thoughts about ecological disaster and stops at that point. The emphasis is more on who has power and who is therefore responsible and accountable for our response to crises. More recently, a third field has arisen, international history. Its center of gravity was originally the cold war and international relations. Gradually, as archives have opened up, first in the United States and then in the former Soviet Union, it has become possible to make the study of the cold war a normal part of the study of various national histories. This book has some claim on this field as well in its attempt to depict the contemporary world in terms of multilateralism.

17. The present book is not the first one to make such points, although it is perhaps among the first to call itself an agenda book. There has been an awareness of the problems of the metanarrative for some years, judging from the number of works criticizing Orientalism or calling for a rethinking of American history as a part of something larger than the traditional Western European context. Among recent books explicitly critical of Orientalism, one might note Dieter Senghaas, *The Clash Within Civilizations.*

18. With the rise of postmodernism, there comes a politics of the form in which works are written as well as in the claims they make. The narrative, for example, becomes a particular object of scrutiny. Though one might agree that the suitability of the narrative form is something to keep in mind, it is clearly not something to be simply dismissed, for it is a very powerful form of presentation. At the same time, if a narrative is Eurocentric, then it may not be useful. In theory at least, one should be able to separate the form (narrative) from the content (Eurocentric historiography). A corollary to this notion is that a narrative need not necessarily be a part of the "tyranny of abstraction," as some argue it must be, because abstraction need not necessarily be a tyrant. Again, it is the context that may make abstraction a tyrant, or alternatively, it may not. What makes for tyranny ultimately is bound up with how power is constituted and used. Thus, one need not fixate on abstraction or on the narrative per se unless the context is of that sort. Still, narratives have

in them, as many critics have also shown, some elements of teleology, which is also, with some justification, held against them. Again, however, in my view, such consensus may or may not be always justified. In a practical sense, who is not concerned about the future? Can we learn anything from the study of the past and present that would suggest what comes next? It would be a great service if historians could perform it. Teleology in the pejorative sense, then, I am assuming, is more a matter of being trapped in a one-way tunnel, whereas teleology in more enlightened sense might have a number of dimensions and possibilities. It could be emancipatory.

19. The most extreme foreign penetration is the case of the House of Sa'ud (see Craig Unger, *House of Bush, House of Saud: The Secret Relationship Between the World's Two Most Powerful Dynasties*). A few pages are devoted to Bush and Bin Laden.

20. Several writers have attempted to address the deleterious effects of a too narrow materialism and relate it to the problems of metanarrative, among them historians such as Eugene D. Genovese, "The Political Crisis of Social History"; and Keith Nield, "A Symptomatic Dispute? Notes on the Relation Between Marxian Theory and Historical Practice in Britain."

1. MODERN WORLD ECONOMIC HISTORY BETWEEN LIBERALISM AND POLITICAL ECONOMY

1. Several books introduce the key terms of New Liberalism, doing so in a critical way, none to my knowledge with the purpose of clarifying them specifically for historical research. The closest is Georgina Blakeley and Valerie Bryson, eds., *Contemporary Political Concepts: A Critical Introduction*. The concept of transnationalism in this chapter was chosen because of the concern here specifically with modern history. The concept of transnationalism allows for the discussion of migration, diaspora, and subalternity as well.

2. Mexico-North Research Network, Transnationalism Research Project Database, "On Transnationalism," 3–4. In business history, for example, terms such as *multinational* and *transnational* are often used interchangeably, but this practice creates problems. For an example of an article reflecting the very different perceptions of meanings of these terms, see Peter Hertner and Geoffrey Jones, eds., *Multinationals: Theory and History*, chap. 1.

3. The development of new derived applications of the term *globalization* goes on apace even while the term itself is criticized, including by its early enthusiasts. For example, see Robert A. Isaak, *The Globalization Gap: How the Rich Get Richer and the Poor Get Left Further Behind*. See also George Ritzer, *The Globalization of Nothing*.

4. Jed Greer and Kavaljit Singh, "A Brief History of Transnational Corporations." Another area of scholarship supportive of transnationalism comes from the study of the politics of cartels: for example, Gregory P. Nowell, *Mercantile States and the World Oil Cartel, 1900–1939*. On global elites, see also Kowalewski, *Global Establishment*.

5. See, for example, A. G. Hopkins, ed., *Globalization in World History*. See also Thomas Bender, ed., *Rethinking American History in a Global Age*.

6. Jonathan Beller, "The Cinematic Mode of Production: Towards a Political Economy of the Post-modern."

7. Sheldon Ungar, "Misplaced Metaphor: A Critical Analysis of the 'Knowledge Society.'"

8. Steven Brint, "Professionals and the 'Knowledge Economy': Rethinking the Theory of Postindustrial Society."

9. These points are all neatly summarized in James Petras, *The New Development Politics,* esp. chap. 5, "The Myth of the Third Scientific Technological Revolution." Petras is representative of a Marxist political economy position. Robbie Robertson, another theorist, is closer to a New Liberal position. He sees a gradual humanization of a triumphant U.S. imperialism, a position perhaps derived from the "humanization of the elite" idea found in German-school Marxism (for example, *The Three Waves of Globalization: A History of a Developing Global Consciousness*). Another center of New Liberal thought is Neo-Gramscian international relations. Its position is discussed at some length in Chapter 2. For a Marxist political economy commentary on Eurocentrism, see James M. Blaut, "Marxism and Eurocentric Diffusionism."

10. Petras, *The New Development Politics,* 59.

11. These points are amplified in Chapter 5 with materials on the foreign lobbyists. Information on direct foreign investment in the United States appears in Geoffrey Jones and Lina Galvez-Munoz, eds., *Foreign Multinationals in the United States: Management and Performance,* 2–3, 6–7, 10–11, 14–15.

12. Inderpal Grewal and Caren Kaplan, "Postcolonial Studies and Transnational Feminist Practices."

13. Patrick Manning, in *Migration in World History,* makes clear that migration has been a major part of history from the beginning of human life and is not something recent at all. I also wish to thank Adam McKeown here for clarifications on migration in an e-mail on December 26, 2005.

14. Larissa Ruiz Baia, "Rethinking Transnationalism: Reconstructing National Identities among Peruvian Catholics in New Jersey"; Gregory Benton, "Chinese Transnationalism in Britain: A Longer History."

15. Hilary Cunningham, "Nations Rebound? Crossing Borders in a Gated Globe."

16. Azza Karam, ed., *Transnational Political Islam: Religion, Ideology, and Power,* 50.

17. Maurice Roche and Rik Van Berkel, eds., *European Citizenship and Social Exclusion.* This section could be lengthened still further if we considered nongovernmental organizations and the popularized ideas surrounding their representation as international civil society independent from their sponsoring states (Kerstin Martens, "Mission Impossible? Defining Non-governmental Organizations"). However, such work is rather problematic.

18. Mexico-North Research Network, Transnationalism Research Project Database, "On Transnationalism," 3–4.

19. Mira Wilkins and Harm Schroter, eds., *The Free-Standing Company in the World Economy, 1830–1996,* 3.

20. Ibid.

21. Jerry Bentley has been serving as the editor of the *Journal of World History*.

22. In the United States the field of world history originally came to be known to many students through the several textbooks in the Marxist tradition written by the pioneering scholar Leften Stavrianos, who died in 2004.

23. For a general summary of Fordism, see George Steinmetz, "Regulation Theory, Post-Marxism, and New Social Movements."

24. William Lazonick, a well-known economist, summarizes what is wrong with the modern field of economics in the concluding lines of his 1991 book: "What is required to reverse the decline of economics as a relevant academic discipline is an innovative intellectual response. Instead of ignoring the history of capitalist development, economists need a methodology than can analyze it" (*Business Organization and the Myth of the Market Economy*, 349). In other words, it does not suffice to include politics, as liberalism does; rather, one must integrate it.

25. See Salim Rashid, *The Myth of Adam Smith*; and Jean Gadrey, *New Economy, New Myth*.

26. Nigel Harris's *End of the Third World: Newly Industrializing Countries and the Decline of an Ideology* prefigured a number of books that saw the Third World swept aside by globalism and transnationalism. Later came Alice Amsden's *Rise of "the Rest": Challenges to the West from Late-Industrializing Economies*. It has been difficult for Marxists to assimilate these newer ideas without a wider materialism.

27. The exception would be Neo-Gramscian international relations, which gets treated more fully in Chapter 2. For example, see Adam David Morton, "*La resurreccion del Maiz*: Globalization, Resistance, and the Zapatistas." Economism is the theme of another recent book, Teivo Teivainen's *Enter Economism, Exit Politics*. See also Peter Gran, "Gramsci el principal teorica de la transformacion socialista temprana."

28. Attempts to reintroduce politics more effectively into theory writings often seems Gramscian, cf. Eric Helleiner, "Post-globalization: Is the Financial Liberalization Trend Likely to Be Reversed?"; William I. Robinson and Jerry Harris, "Towards a Global Ruling Class? Globalization and the Transnationalist Capitalist Class"; and Linda Weiss, "Explaining the Underground Economy: State and Social Structure" and "Is the State Being Transformed?" See also Georg Sorenson, *The Transformation of the State: Beyond the Myth of Retreat*. A work spelling out the politics of globalism in quite a range of countries is Amy Chua's *World on Fire*.

2. MODERN WORLD POLITICAL HISTORY BETWEEN LIBERALISM AND POLITICAL ECONOMY

1. See, for example, John Mackenzie, "The Continuing Avalanche of Historical Mutations: The New 'New Social Movements,'" an article drawing from Ernesto Laclau and Chantal Mouffe, *Hegemony and Socialist Strategy: Towards a Radical Democratic Politics*, which argues

that the Left is in a period of expansion because it has gone beyond the phase of workerist ortho-doxy. It is up to the old Left to catch up and not be left behind by the new types of movements that now abound. The argument seems to boil down to a defense of New Liberalism.

2. In a review article, Marc Edelman, an anthropologist, writes that what stands out is a sense of bewilderment at the rapid paradigm change in the area of "theories of collective action" over the past generation. In his discussion of New Social Movements, he notes that this trend has scant use for ethnography and context ("Social Movements: Changing Paradigms and Forms of Politics," 309), citing how a work such as G. A. Collier's *Basta! Land and the Zapatista Rebellion in the Chiapas* looked at the rise of the Zapatista in terms of the local political struggles of the preceding decade and alliances that grew out of those struggles (292). He also cites June Nash, "The Fiesta of the Word: The Zapatista Uprising and Radical Democracy in America." Nash suggests that Marcos was staging what one could term a "War of Position" to conquer civil society, a line of thought scarcely considered in the NSM literature (293). Another issue to be noted is that of which political and social movements are studied and which are not. The Zapatista as a so-called progressive movement is considered a New Social Movement, whereas hate groups and right-wing movements are not. A social scientist makes this point, observing in a recent review of sociological writings on New Social Movements that right-wing movements are rarely studied, and that this undermines the utility of the NSM as a concept. The author finds this fact to be a central methodological flaw of most writings on NSMs and ascribes it to the leftist politics of those individuals who write about NSMs (Nelson A. Pichardo, "New Social Movements: A Critical Review"). A similar point is made in Edelman, "Social Movements," 293–94. Both authors also express doubts about how new NSMs really are, suggesting that old features of many movements are suddenly for the first time being given scholarly attention. They cite studies of nineteenth-century movements that appear to resemble the movements of today. A writer interested in studying middle-class movements of both the Left and Right is Fred Rose. In his essay "Toward a Class-Cultural Theory of Social Movements: Reinterpreting New Social Movements," Rose argues the need for more complicated theorization, one that should, for example, include "new class" theory. Where "new class" theories stress the class issue of middle-class movements, NSM theorists eschew class analysis, claiming these movements are "a defensive response to the encroachment of economics into other cultural spheres" (464). Rose also notes that European writers on NSMs claim that their work is a response to a new phase, one of disorganized capitalism, one in which the production process has "imposed new levels of control" (467). The strong point of NSM theories, according to Rose, is that they go beyond simply a class interest of the middle-class approach; they recognize change, and they avoid claiming to be approaching socialism. At the same time, they fail to acknowledge that specific class interests are being served, that social causes have a distributional dimension. For example, it is the middle class that gains the most from the prioritization of feminist or ecological movements (469). His conclusion is that the NSM approach to interpreting movements is too simple (470).

3. Ulrich Beck, *The Re-invention of Politics: Rethinking Modernity in the Global Social Order*, esp. chap. 5.

4. See, in general, Mikael Carleheden and Michael Hviid Jacobsen, eds., *The Transformation of Modernity*, 231–32, and in particular the article by Hauke Brukehorst, "Global Society as the Crisis of Democracy," 225–40.

5. See Linda Weiss, "Is the State Being Transformed?"

6. Carleheden and Jacobsen, *The Transformation of Modernity*, chap. 7.

7. Although Marxists have their troubles with the concept of NSMs, one might note that liberal writers have reservations about it as well. See, for example, Colin Barker and Gareth Dale, "Protest Waves in Western Europe: A Critique of 'New Social Movement' Theory," which looks at the role of both class and capitalism in recent European movements; and William K. Carroll and R. S. Ratner, "Between Leninism and Radical Pluralism: Gramscian Reflections on Counter-hegemony and the New Social Movements," which argues that although NSMs identify many issues, they basically fragment social theory in contrast to Gramsci. See also Paul D'Anieri et al., "New Social Movements in Historical Perspective"; and David Harvey, "The Practical Contradictions of Marxism." One could hypothesize that the concept of New Social Movements would have died had it not been for Islamism and Orientalism. For many, Iranian Islamism in 1979 was what gave credibility to the concept of the NSM. Approaching the subject more historically, one might, however, have one's doubts. Islamism need not be understood as an NSM. In 1979 the United States abandoned its alliance with the shah and allowed the opposition to come to power. The shah was leaning toward the Soviet Union, whereas the opposition was anti-Russian. This shift was presented by the media as an Islamic revolution as opposed to a cold war regime change; arguably, it was more palatable that way. Among many taken in by this was Michel Foucault.

8. Andreas Schedler et al., eds., *The Self-Restraining State: Power and Accountability in the New Democracies*. The commentary on events in Mexico is quite reserved; see chap. 6 and passim.

9. Richard Roman and Edur Velasco Arregui, "Worker Insurgency, Rural Revolt, and the Crisis of the Mexican Regime," esp. 131–33.

10. Gran, *Beyond Eurocentrism*, chaps. 4–6.

11. Marcus Green, "Gramsci Cannot Speak: Presentations and Interpretations of Gramsci's Concept of the Subaltern"; Peter Gran, *Subaltern Studies, Racism, and Class Struggle: Examples from India and the United States*. Like other theorists, Gramsci had his primary concerns and then a wider, more casual interest in many other matters. In more casual writing, he generalized his concept of the Italian "Passive Revolution" so as to apply it everywhere. "Passive Revolution" has now even entered the discourse of globalization (Adam David Morton, *Unravelling Gramsci: Hegemony and Passive Revolution in the Global Economy*). In my usage, Gramsci's Passive Revolution was a very specific moment in Italian history, one that he described at length and from which he drew much of his discussion of

later periods of Italian history. Passive Revolution, though particular to Italy, would thus apply to a few other countries as well, those following what one would term the "Italian Road." It is important to keep in mind that Gramsci was not in the habit of producing universally applicable concepts. His theory is middle-level theory. See in this regard his discussion of the Russian Revolution and its applicability to Italian conditions. This middle-level analysis is what is distinctive about his work (see my "Modern World History as the Rise of the Rich: A New Paradigm").

12. Stephen Gill, *Power and Resistance in the New World Order.* Gill's is not the first attempt to link Gramsci and Marcos. See Kathleen Bruhn, "Antonio Gramsci and the Palabra Verdadera: The Political Discourse of Mexico's Guerilla Forces."

13. Morton, *"La resurreccion del Maiz,"* 31–32, 47.

14. Ibid., 47; Donald Hodges and Ross Gandy, *Mexico Under Siege: Popular Resistance to Presidential Despotism,* 205. The more standard Left analysis has a kind of blame-the-victim quality.

15. See Stephen D. Morris, "Between Neo-liberalism and Neo-*indigenismo:* Reconstructing National Identity in Mexico."

16. Claudio Lomnitz-Adler, *Exits from the Labyrinth: Culture and Ideology in the Mexican National Space,* 247–50, makes similar points about Bonfil Batalla. This books open the door to a paradigm change in Mexican studies more than others.

17. Saskia Sassens, *Cities in a World Economy,* chap. 6, lends itself to this kind of reading.

18. Given the antifoundationalism of globalist thought, it is not surprising that scant attention has been paid to Gramsci's Southern Question in recent years. A rare exception that tries to enter into this theory is Timothy Brennan, "Antonio Gramsci and Post-colonial Theory: 'Southernism.'"

19. A notable example is Thomas Benjamin and Mark Wasserman, eds., *Provinces of the Revolution: Essays on Regional Mexican History, 1910–1929.* See also Thomas Benjamin and William McNellie, eds., *Other Mexicos: Essays in Regional Mexican History, 1876–1911.*

20. John M. Hobson and J. C. Sharman, "The Enduring Place of Hierarchy in World Politics: Tracing the Social Logics of Hierarchy and Political Change."

21. A basic source is Eric Hobsbawm, *Pre-capitalist Economic Formations,* 29ff, where the process follows from the breakdown of feudal society with the rise of towns and the evolving division of labor within them, Hobsbawm emphasizing the urban. Other historians, such as Rodney Hilton and Robert Brenner, have emphasized the rural roots of modern capitalism and C. L. R. James and others the role of global capital accumulation.

22. This point would apply to the well-known world history text of Stavrianos, *Global Rift.* See as well the response to Immanuel Wallerstein's attempt to look at the transition to modern world capitalism as a global event of a systemic sort in which the periphery of the world market had some of the elements of what Marx had called the "second feudalism."

Wallerstein was critically assessed by area-study specialists who have seen much greater complexity for their area. A well-known article by a specialist of Latin America is Steve J. Stern, "Feudalism, Capitalism, and the World-System in Perspective of Latin America and the Caribbean," with replies. See also Peter Gran, "Late Eighteenth–Early Nineteenth Century Egypt: Merchant Capital or Modern Capitalism?"

23. Louis Althusser, *For Marx*, chap. 6.

24. Whereas governmentality is often referred to, similar ideas in social science research rarely get the same attention. See, for example, Calvin Morrill, Mayer N. Zald, and Hayagreeva Rao, "Covert Political Conflict in Organizations: Challenges from Below." Such an article might even serve to valorize some of Foucault's points.

25. This use of Gramsci is critiqued in Joe Buttigieg, *Prison Notebooks*.

26. Perry Anderson, "The Antinomies of Antonio Gramsci"; Stuart Hall, ed., *The Hard Road to Renewal: Thatcherism and the Crisis of the Left*; Carl Boggs, *Gramsci's Marxism*, 11.

27. Gramsci's relation to the issue of Eurocentrism has routinely been wrongly cast. The short entry on Antonio Gramsci, "Hegemony of Western Culture over the World Culture," read as a freestanding narrative, sounds like a defense of coevality and Eurocentrism. A close reading shows it is part of the critique of Hegel and a claim for the necessity of the rise of Marxism, as well as a comment on the universality of Marxism. It does not suggest Eurocentrism. Gramsci was quite different from most other modern Marxists. For the reluctance of the Marxist tradition to go beyond the text and look at history in a more general sense, see Nield, "Symptomatic Dispute?"; and Genovese, "Political Crisis."

28. Gran, *Beyond Eurocentrism*; Anibal Quijano, "Coloniality of Power and Eurocentrism in Latin America." For a discussion of the hegemonism of democratic alliances, see Andreas Bieler and Adam David Morton, "Theoretical and Methodological Challenges of Neo-Gramscian Perspectives in International Political Economy."

29. Much is obscured by the long academic tradition of legitimating the study of certain features of history and calling the study of what might lie behind them or beside them conspiracy thinking, and hence dismissible out of hand. This way of proceeding, however, often hinders the development of new kinds of research. To give one example, academic tradition of this kind has been a barrier especially for social history, as social history depends on structural analysis and on assuming things one cannot see. An attempt to overcome this problem of how to ground structural analysis without having it appear conspiracy ridden is found in Peter Dale Scott's concept of "Deep Politics," most recently in *Deep Politics and the Death of JFK*. More typically, inferential reasoning appears as a subject in liberal philosophy journals such as *History and Theory*, where it tends to be attacked. See also Larry K. Griffin and Robert B. Korstad, "Historical Inference and Event Structure Analysis." Scholarly choice is a factor here. One wishes there was for world history what there is for IR. See, for example, Stephen Hobden, *International Relations and Historical Sociology: Breaking Down Boundaries*. More typical, however, is a collection such as Colin Elman and Miriam

Fendius Elman, eds., *Bridges and Boundaries: Historians, Political Scientists, and the Study of International Relations,* which describes authors in different disciplines keeping their distance from each other. In history, the most determined efforts to link social history and national politics and international relations probably are the works of the Bielenfeld School of History in the writings of such figures as Hans-Ulrich Wehler, author of many books, among them *The German Empire, 1871–1918.* In this work the German Empire is shown as arising from substantially internal causes, among them industrialization. Because it also deals with IR, Wehler's work goes beyond the older genre of study known under the rubric of "social imperialism," where the metropolitan elite solves its domestic social problems at the expense of the empire. Wehler has had disciples in the German academy. In the United States for an attempt to construct an internalist analysis of great-power-ism, see the previously cited book in international history by Jeremi Suri, *Power and Protest.* See also Paul W. Schroeder, "The Transformation of Political Thinking, 1787–1848." Schroeder identifies what he takes to be a transformation in political thinking from more linear (in my terms more bilateral) to more systemic (in my terms more multilateral) as one moves from the eighteenth century to the mid-nineteenth century.

3. THE RISE OF THE RICH IN EARLY MODERN TIMES, 1550–1850

1. See Jean Batou, *Between Development and Underdevelopment: The Precocious Attempts at Industry of the Periphery, 1800–1870.*

2. On island Southeast Asia, see Anthony Reid, *Charting the Shape of Early Modern Southeast Asia.* Reid centered Southeast Asian studies on the islands, making the dramatic rise-and-decline picture summarized in the text an important part of his narrative. He has his share of critics, among them historian Victor Lieberman. In *Strange Parallels: Southeast Asia in Global Context,* Lieberman accuses Reid of favoring the islands over mainland Southeast Asia, where one has more of the evolution of states of the sort commonly studied in comparative history (16). Even more severe a critic of Reid (and Lieberman, for that matter) are the editors of *Recalling Local Pasts: Autonomous History in Southeast Asia,* Sunait Chutintaranond and Chris Baker (169). Their approach is to look at island history as autonomous, as history freed from any larger pattern.

3. The whole area is now being intensively studied by students of world history. See, for example, Rene Barendse, *The Arabian Seas: The Indian Ocean World of the Seventeenth Century;* and Kenneth Pomerantz, *The Great Divergence: China, Europe, and the Making of the Modern World Economy.*

4. Pomerantz, *Great Divergence.*

5. John E. Wills Jr., "Maritime Asia, 1500–1899: The Interactive Emergence of European Domination," 97. Having made that point, one must acknowledge that until such a metaphor is in place, those individuals who are marginalized by the way in which history is currently conceptualized may see some advantage in trying to hold on to polycentric

approaches, lest their reality completely disappear out of world consciousness into the Fourth World. See, for example, Stuart B. Schwartz, "Expansion, Diaspora, and Encounter in the Early Modern South Atlantic."

6. John K. Thornton, "The Role of Africans in the Atlantic Economy, 1450–1650: Modern Africanist Historiography and the World-Systems Paradigm," 133.

7. These issues are discussed in an expanded fashion in his book, *Africa and Africans in the Making of the Atlantic World, 1400–1800.* More recently, see David Northrup, *Africa's Discovery of Europe, 1450–1850.*

8. Weston F. Cook Jr., introduction and conclusion to *The Hundred Years War for Morocco: Gunpowder and the Military Revolution in the Early Modern Muslim World.* A recent work on China appears to still move in the more traditional weapons-determinist direction, China using firepower since the sixteenth century but of a quality much inferior to Britain's (Bruce A. Elleman, *Modern Chinese Warfare, 1795–1989,* 6). The larger picture of the sixteenth-century military revolution in Europe seems to fit with the idea of a more proletarianized West. The infantry is progressively equipped with firearms and bayonets and as a result forced to learn new skills, which gives them an edge in fighting armies that lack these skills (David Eltis, introduction and conclusion to *The Military Revolution in Sixteenth-Century Europe*). One wonders about such factors as morale.

9. Georges Douin, "L'ambassade d'Elfi Bey à Londres (octobre–decembre 1803)." Ronald Ridley's *Napoleon's Proconsul in Egypt: The Life and Times of Bernardino Drovetti* contains a valuable summary of the last years of the Mamluks (1–40). The failed attempt of the English allied to the Ottomans making use of Alfi Bey to capture Egypt in 1806 is still a story in need of more research. For a recent defense of the Oriental-despotism line of interpretation for this period, see Joan-Pau Rubies, "Oriental Despotism and European Orientalism: Botero to Montesquieu." Rubies reviews prominent figures, upholding the model without reference to other voices or to the context in Europe of which these figures were a part.

10. For the wider discussion of "escape from the periphery," see the Swiss historian Batou, *Between Development,* including Muhammad 'Ali's attempt. For a general biography of Muhammad 'Ali Pasha, see Afaf Lutfi al-Sayyid Marsot, *Egypt in the Reign of Muhammad Ali.* For Muhammad 'Ali's use of his portrait, see Emily M. Weeks, "About Face: Sir David Wilkie's Portrait of Mehemet Ali." Weeks's article appears in *Orientalism Transposed: The Impact of the Colonies on British Culture,* edited by Julie F. Codell and Dianne Sachko Macleod, a work that pursues the "Easternization of Britain" in the colonial period, to paraphrase the introduction.

11. Mark Quintanilla, "Mercantile Communities in the Ceded Islands: The Alexander Bartlet and George Campbell Company."

12. See Henry Louis Gates and William L. Andrews, *Pioneers of the Black Atlantic: Five Slave Narratives from the Enlightenment, 1772–1815.* This book covers two influential works: Ottobah Cuguano, *Thoughts and Sentiments on the Nature of the Slave Trade* (1787); and Oladauh Equiano, *The Interesting Life of Oladauh Equiano* (1789).

13. The general synthesis of the period puts its emphasis on crisis more than on the commercial minorities (Geoffrey Parker and Lesley M. Smith, eds., *The General Crisis of the Seventeenth Century*). With the large body of writing on the commercial minorities appearing in recent years, this understanding will need to be reworked a bit. For whom was it a crisis, and who was it that benefited from such a crisis?

14. Most of the work in historical sociology has been concentrated here in the early modern period for whatever reason in figures ranging from Fernand Braudel and Barrington Moore to Haim Gerber, Immanuel Wallerstein, and Jack Goldstone, allowing a wealth of generalizations and hypotheses. See more recently the *Journal of Historical Sociology*.

15. On the Dahomey slave trade, Robin Law has written extensively. See his edited work, *From Slave Trade to "Legitimate" Commerce: The Commercial Transition in Nineteenth-Century West Africa* and "The Politics of Commercial Transition: Factional Conflict in Dahomey in the Context of the Ending of the Atlantic Slave Trade."

16. Gran, *Beyond Eurocentrism*, presents the argument that modern capitalism could produce only four successful types of hegemony.

17. See Fonna Forman-Barzilai, "Adam Smith as Globalization Theorist."

18. Peter Stearns, *Consumerism in World History: The Great Transformation of Desire*, deals more with the fact of than with the process whereby it came to be.

19. Gran, *Islamic Roots*, chaps. 1 and 6.

20. Daniel R. Headrick, *The Tools of Empire: Technology and European Imperialism in the Nineteenth Century*, argues the European technology dimension as an explanation. For the depopulation of Africa as a result of the slave trade, see Patrick Manning, *Slavery and African Life*.

21. See Rondo Cameron, "England, 1750–1840." This point is repeated and considerably amplified through lengthy economic analyses in Joseph E. Inikori, *Africans and the Industrial Revolution in England*, 316 and passim. Aggregating all economic contributions of Africans by following standard economic models may, however, not be the strongest way to combat Eurocentrism, as the text leads one to suppose, because it will still be considered only a small percentage of the British economy, given the approach to calculation of value.

22. See Ellen Meiksins Wood and Neal Wood, *A Trumpet of Sedition: Political Theory and the Rise of Capitalism, 1509–1688*.

23. Ibid.

24. I was alerted to this point by Jack Goldstone's critique of the New Left interpretation of the English Civil War, Goldstone's solution being to put more emphasis on demographic factors in explaining the events of England and of other countries (*Revolution and Rebellion in the Early Modern World*, 64–156).

25. Samir Amin, *Class and Nation Historically and in the Present Crisis*; James Blaut, *The Colonizer's Model of the World: Geographical Diffusionism and Eurocentric History*. For Robert Brenner, see a synthesis of his articles and books in Ellen Meiksins Wood, *The Origin of Capitalism: A Longer View*.

26. Teshale Tibebu, "On the Question of Feudalism, Absolutism, and Bourgeois Revolution."

27. Amin, *Class and Nation.*

28. David Levine, ed., *Proletarianization and Family History,* 88.

29. James Blaut, *Colonizer's Model,* chap. 4. On the "1492 watershed," see also Catharina Lis and Hugo Soly, "Policing the Early Modern Proletariat, 1450–1850," esp. 208ff, where the authors discuss problems of proletarianization in England and Western Europe. Perhaps it is significant that the subject of proletarianization has not led to much scholarly work since 1985. There are even some doubts expressed about its contemporary meaning. Can today's educated workers be termed proletarians? Sociologists Magali Sarfatti Larson, in "Proletarianization and Educated Labor," answers in the affirmative; Gordon Marshall, in "Proletarianization in the British Class Structure?" answers in the negative.

30. See E. P. Thompson, *The Making of the English Working Class.* Later, Thompson distinguished himself by writing about the peculiarities of English history and against English New Left Marxism. Some of his claims clearly point to weaknesses of the latter.

31. Why did Marxism in effect abandon its broader materialism and dialectic? The reasons have never been made too clear. Was it the critique of liberalism and empiricism that drove the dialectic underground, was it the continuous growth of knowledge in all areas that overwhelmed it, was it simply unfavorable political conditions in academe that prevented its development, or was it threatening to Marxism itself? I am inclined to the latter, preferring a more political explanation. Once Marxists solidified their relationship to the traditional trade union movement, the dialectic was an inconvenience and in practice abandoned. There is simply so much more to dialectical analysis than what is needed by the organized working class. It was not long before one found Marxists preferring the "mature" Marx, the Marx for whom dialectics was limited to the labor strike. For a different type of discussion of why Marx eschewed politics, see Allan Megill in a recent book, *The Burden of Reason: Why Marx Rejected Politics and the Market,* emphasizing the features of Marx's thought that seemed to predispose Marx against the subject of trade and politics after 1848. Though interesting, the approach does not allow the reader to understand why politics nonetheless played such a large role for many in the Marxist tradition, beginning with the young Marx himself—one thinks of Cabral, Mariategui, Gramsci, the Praxis school, and so on—and why clearly politics was indeed eschewed in latter-day Soviet and American Marxism.

32. Mercantilism has largely been studied until now in terms of Europe in the early modern period, the term entering Third World studies in recent years only as an accusation against regimes that raised tariffs (for example, Bruce Masters, *The Origins of Western Economic Dominance in the Middle East: Mercantilism and the Islamic Economy in Aleppo, 1600–1750*). An exception that considers Egyptian, Sudanese, and Senegalese examples of mercantilist regimes in earlier times is Samir Amin, "Trans-Saharan Exchange and the Black Slave Trade." Another term is *absolutist state,* sometimes used interchangeably with *mercantilism* (Richard Lachmann, "Comparisons Within a Single Social Formation: A Critical

Appreciation of Perry Anderson's *Lineages of the Absolutist State*"). *Absolutism* here invokes more of the political and less of the economic part of materialism.

33. For a discussion of the impact of the Price Revolution on various countries leading to the Crisis of the Seventeenth Century, see Jack A. Goldstone, "East and West in the Seventeenth Century: Political Crises in Stuart England, Ottoman Turkey, and Ming China." Niels Steensgaard, "The Seventeenth-Century Crisis and the Unity of Eurasian History," introduces some of the classical historiography of the crisis, a crisis concerning which there is now a large body of scholarship from different countries. One among many articles worth noting concerns Mexico. It takes up the possibly complicating factor of Mexico's colonial position and notes how for various structural reasons it does not in fact matter (J. I. Israel, "Mexico and the 'General Crisis' of the Seventeenth Century"). In a special issue of the journal *Modern Asian Studies* largely devoted to the subject, John F. Richards notes the delay of the onset of the crisis to around 1700 in regards to the Mughals, this fact perhaps attributable to the lesser degree of integration into the world market ("The Seventeenth-Century Crisis in South Asia").

34. Michael W. McCahill, "Peers, Patronage, and the Industrial Revolution, 1760–1800." Political ramifications are further considered in the next section, on bilateralism. The implications of the power of the peerage over the power of the industrial bourgeoisie were not lost even on the British New Left. See the well-known article of Perry Anderson, "Components of the National Culture."

35. Bruce H. Mann, "Failure in the Land of the Free," based on the author's book, *Republic of Debtors: Bankruptcy in the Age of American Independence*. Mann follows here an almost forgotten body of writing that once dominated American history writing in the age of Charles Beard and Mary Beard when the economic basis of the Constitution was the important subject. In citing Mann here and McCahill in the previous note, this section draws attention to the fact that the narrowing of the approach to these subjects was a matter of choice to historians over this past generation.

36. This topic is, of course, controversial terrain. For some it would be hard to imagine, indeed impossible. There is, after all, a powerful and highly technologically minded group of people who hold sway in the world, one whose mantra is the phrase "space colonies," and for these people the prevailing dichotomy between civilization and nature will live on.

37. Anthony J. Hall, *The American Empire and the Fourth World: The Bowl with One Spoon*, xxiii, 68, 74, 85, 88–89. This theory is a new hypothesis for Middle Eastern studies. At least a half-dozen books trace the roots of American policy in the Middle East to American character literature following the path in American studies laid out by Perry Miller in the 1930s. No book to my knowledge uses the pattern of conquest material the way Anthony does. An example of the resurgence of Fourth World issues can be found in an article on the UN: Mpazi Sinjela and Robin Ramcharan, "Protecting Traditional Knowledge and Traditional Medicines of Indigenous Peoples Through Intellectual Property Rights: Issues, Challenges, and Strategies").

38. Hall's line of reasoning was made all the more poignant when the blogosphere erupted with the news of President Bush's attraction to a recent book called *Imperial Grunts: The American Military on the Ground,* by Robert D. Kaplan, which makes the point that "Injun country" today is the Islamic world. This detail brings to mind Bush's own rhetoric after 9/11 about the nature of terrorists that, according to Hall, closely mirrored the anti-Indian rhetoric of the settler era (*American Empire,* 472–73). In a related discussion of the Aztecs in the text below, I am deducing the motives underlying the decision of the ruling council to invite Cortez to the Aztec capital Tenochtitlán (see Miguel León-Portilla, *The Broken Spears: The Aztec Account of the Conquest of Mexico,* chap. 8).

39. I connect law to capitalism. Another approach takes the clash of legal systems apart from capitalism as a building block of modern world history (see Lauren Benton, *Law and Colonial Cultures: Legal Regimes in World History, 1400–1900*). A recent article connecting law and political ambition to mercantilism with material from England and Holland is Thomas Leng, "Commercial Conflict and Regulation in the Discourse of Trade in Seventeenth Century England").

40. Given the interconnectedness of the modern world, terms such as *unilateralism* are much more difficult to employ than is commonly assumed. At this point, it may not even be a useful term to use. When we look at the rise in early modern history of the Dutch, French, or British, each carrying out its acts of aggrandizement, even then it seems more precise to suggest it was not the unilateralism of a great power, as it would have been in antiquity, but something taking place in a new context, a context in which it was understood that third parties were not going to interfere. What was happening at this point was that there was an implicit delegation of the sphere of influence, and as a result at least some of what historians have tended to term *great power unilateralism* following the "Rise of the West" model presumably could be better understood as prearranged behavior emerging in an increasingly collectivist context, one that was arising out of and was the outcome of the bilateralism of early modern history. A well-known example would be the pope's division of the New World between Spain and Portugal. This split was never directly contested by England or Holland.

41. Northrup, *Africa's Discovery of Europe,* esp. chap. 6. Northrup is controversial for some because he studies Africans and tries to make sense of what they were doing. See also Hans Werner DeBrunner, *Presence and Prestige: Africans in Europe.* This work collects information for the study of 154 Africans in Europe between 1450 and 1918. The author was criticized for failing to study what they were doing in Europe. On Germany and Ethiopia, a short work is Eike Haberland, *Three Hundred Years of Ethiopian-German Academic Collaboration.*

42. One strand of this debate took place over the meaning attached by the Hawaiians, supposedly a people without history, to the coming of Captain Cook to Hawaii. For the time being, the debate appears to have wound down with Gananath Obeyesekere, *The Apotheosis of Captain Cook,* and the reply, Marshall Sahlins, *How "Natives" Think: About Captain*

Cook, for example. This debate could be compared to the one between Edward Said and the defenders of Orientalism. Sahlins's discovery that Cook was made a god settled the matter of their primitivism for him. He would not consider the proposition that in tribal-ethnic states, the more gods, the merrier, as Obeyesekere pointed out.

43. Kai Cheok Fuk, "The Macao Formula: A Study of Chinese Management of Westerners from the Mid-Sixteenth Century to the Opium War Period."

44. For a major article on these dilemmas, see Jack A. Goldstone, "The Problem of the 'Early Modern' World." The reader interested in pursuing the rise of the tribal-ethnic state out of an old empire might consider using Austria under the Hapsburgs. The Austrians under the Hapsburgs and then thereafter looked with apprehension at changing ideas of women's status beginning in the Enlightenment and continuing thereafter. The writings of Sigmund Freud about women might serve as a latter-day example of the writings of a regime intellectual who manifested the tribal-ethnic state anxiety about women and power.

45. Laura Hostetler, *Qing Colonial Enterprise: Ethnography and Cartography in Early Modern China,* chap. 1; Xu Dixin and Wu Chengming, eds., *Chinese Capitalism, 1522–1840,* 377.

46. Kenneth Pomeranz, in *Great Divergence,* gives an assessment that the strategy allowed China to carry on without open markets until the opium wars of the nineteenth century. See also R. Bin Wong, "The Search for European Differences and Domination in the Early Modern World: A View from Asia." Neither goes into the issue of proletarianization, but they do show China as more parallel to than different from Europe. For both, Europe is Western Europe, especially England, and not Russia.

47. Jacob Hurewitz, *Diplomacy in the Near and Middle East,* 28, 39–40, 54.

48. Amira Sonbol, in *The New Mamluks: Egyptian Society and Modern Feudalism,* shows the continuing influence of Mamluk tradition until today.

49. See Gran, *Islamic Roots.* Recently, historians Andre Raymond and Muhammad 'Afifi published an edition and translation of the original text of Isma'il al-Khashshab, who took notes at the meetings of the council Napoléon formed to help him rule when he got to Cairo, *Le Diwan du Caire, 1800–1801.* As the discussion in the Diwan shows, a kind of Rise of the Rich set of dynamics was in process.

50. This methodology is a revisionist approach to the subject. So far, the main work of revisionism of early modern Ottoman history is Rifa'at Abou El Haj, *Formation of the Modern State: The Ottoman Empire, Sixteenth to the Eighteenth Centuries.* In both liberal and Marxist accounts, the Ottoman Empire is typically presented as an example of an empire that declined from the sixteenth century until the revolution of Kemal Ataturk in the early twentieth century. Yet rather than decline, one might note change. See also Gran, "Modern Middle East History," which also eschews the rise-and-decline approach.

51. Hurewitz, *Diplomacy,* 15. A more orthodox discussion of mercantilism in Persia in this period, one using the term in a more purely economic sense, would put a focus on Persia's export of silk to Europe, its acquiring of bullion from Europe, bullion originating in

the New World, and its spending this bullion in India on various commodities (Willem Floor and Patrick Clawson, "Safavid Iran's Search for Silver and Gold").

52. Orientalist Bernard Lewis has long supported this approach. For a recent work reaching quite different conclusions, see Nabil Matar, *In the Lands of the Christians: Arabic Travel Writing in the Seventeenth Century*.

53. Hurewitz, *Diplomacy*, 16–17, 30.

54. On this point, see Nabil Matar, *Islam in Britain, 1558–1685*.

55. Hurewitz, *Diplomacy*, 18–20.

56. Ibid., 20–21. For a discussion of the collapse of a Muslim community (Moroccans and Algerians) in Britain, see Nabil Matar, "The Last Moors: Maghariba in Early-Eighteenth-Century Britain."

57. Christian Windler, "Tributes and Presents in Franco-Tunisian Diplomacy."

4. THE AGE OF MULTILATERALISM: THE WORLD AFTER 1850

1. Some general propositions about economic capitalism are noted here. First, capitalism is a complex phenomenon for a historian to work with; reducing it to an economic phenomenon, even if it is one's ultimate focus, does not help. Second, the traditional itinerary of human progress as portrayed by Hegel on through Engels and beyond, which is economy-driven, offers little to a world anticipating the imminent collapse of a planet's capacity to sustain human life. As a result, teleology from having been a secure part of Marxist history now is more of a question mark. For some, this leads to an aversion these days even to asking how the past has led up to the present, as to ask that question is to deprive oneself of the pleasures of nostalgia. In taking a contrarian position, I would insist it is precisely this kind of self-conscious questioning of how we got here and where we are going that is a service history can render. Third, everyone who studies capitalism has a stake in the outcome of debates over terminology. Take, for example, the term *proletarianization*. Whereas a writer in the Western Marxist tradition, such as Chris Harman, *A People's History of the World*, finds a growing proletarianization of the world and a desire on the part of those individuals who are not to become proletarians, a writer such as the African economist Guy C. Mhone, *The Political Economy of a Dual Labor Market in Africa: The Copper Industry and Dependency in Zambia, 1929–1969*, argues for the analytical importance of the dual economy and its culture. Dual economy is not the same as proleterarianization; it is closer to uneven development or semicapitalism. For our purposes, the dual economy exists, and it exists because of the use of the Third World for purposes of capitalist accumulation. As many have noted, the function of the Third World is to bleed, not to develop. Why, then, expect there to be a growth of the proletariat? See, for example, Randolph B. Persaud, *Counter-hegemony and Foreign Policy: The Dialectics of Marginalized and Global Forces in Jamaica*. The growth model, however, is the one that pervades every aspect of the analysis of capitalism. One finds it conspicuously present, for example, in the "end of the Third World" trend. For example, see Thomas L. Friedman, *The*

Earth Is Flat: A Brief History of the Twenty-first Century, who foresees the digital divide replacing the First World–Third World divide. See also Harris, *End of the Third World,* which proceeds by conflating the historic Third World of the nineteenth century with the periphery of today and with the extent to which Third Worldism is in fashion as an ideology. See also Guy Arnold, *The End of the Third World.* More recently, the *Third World Quarterly* produced a special issue, edited by Mark T. Berger (25, no. 1 [2004]), looking critically at the term *Third World.* Of particular interest was the contribution by John Saul pointing to the difficulty of the African National Congress seeking to lead the Third World while linking itself so closely to Western capital. Equally valuable was David Moore's comment about how primitive accumulation is now called "global public goods." My claim is that so long as there is capitalism, there will need to be a Third World of some sort to allow for accumulation. Three books, somewhat Eurocentric but important for understanding the Rise of the Rich, are Holly Sklar, ed., *Trilateralism: The Trilateral Commission and Elite Management for World Management,* 2–3; Michel Crozier et al., eds., *The Crisis of Democracies: Report on the Governability of Democracies,* esp. 37–43 (Crozier's book was a report to the Trilateral Commission); and Paul Wolfowitz, ed., *Managing the International System over the Next Century.* Today Wolfowitz is a prominent figure in the Trilateral Commission, concerned with the peaceful integration of the Asian countries into the market without a return to the world wars of the twentieth century.

2. Robert Mayer, "Marx, Lenin, and the Corruption of the Working Class." The subject of politicization of the middle strata in the age of neoliberalism is more commonly approached in terms of what is called alienation studies. Alienation is commonly thought to have risen across the board after the mid-1960s. For a review of the literature, see David L. Weakliem and Casey Bosch, "Alienation in the United States: Uniform or Group Specific Change?"

3. A well-known writer taking multilateralism in a normative sense is John Gerard Ruggie, ed., *Multilateralism Matters.*

4. Gerald Mangone, *A Short History of International Organization.* Another useful book, one documenting much of the narrative section of this chapter, is Martin H. Geyer and Johannes Paulmann, eds., *The Mechanics of Internationalism: Culture, Society, and Politics from the 1840s to the First World War.*

5. Kevin Phillips, *American Dynasty,* chap. 2.

6. John Boli and George M. Thomas, eds., *Constructing World Culture: International Non-governmental Organizations since 1875.*

7. The idea that there is a European civilization was solidified during the Napoleonic years (Stuart Woolf, "The Construction of a European World-View in the Revolutionary-Napoleonic Years"). It played a role thereafter. Woolf was not so concerned with how politically divisive and complex the maintenance of the idea of civilizationalism was in later years. For a different kind of account of the rise of the idea of civilization, see Gerrit Gong, *The Standard of "Civilization" in International Society.*

8. Pitman B. Potter, "Origins of the System of Mandates under the League of Nations."

9. Benedict Kingsbury, "Indigenous People in International Law: A Constructivist Approach to the Asian Controversy."

10. Michael Adas, "Contested Hegemony: The Great War and the Afro-Asiatic Assault on the Civilizing Mission Ideology."

11. For an example of how controversial the idea of being bound by international law was for the United States, see Robert D. Accinelli, "The Hoover Administration and the World Court." On how the Soviet bloc used law, as in the Nicaragua crisis, against the United States as a rationale for the United States shunning the court, see the essay of a law professor at the National Defense University, Harry H. Almond Jr., "World Court Rulings on the Use of Force in the Context of a Global Power Struggle."

12. American writers have long appeared to shy away from the study of "business as usual," for example, or the American who accepts the bribes. See, for example, Kyle Rex Jacobson, "Doing Business with the Devil: The Challenges of Prosecuting Corporate Officials Whose Business Transactions Facilitate War Crimes and Crimes Against Humanity." The Jacobson article is a contemporary part of a longer history about which one only occasionally hears. There has long been foreign business influence, legal or otherwise, sometimes piratical or even terrorist. It would be so useful to have some single work that systematically pursued the subject of the influence of foreign money, threats, bribery, and so, but as yet there is none. Political scientist Andrew M. Scott wrote *The Revolution in Statecraft: Informal Penetration*. For some examples of foreign bribery here and there, see Mira Wilkins, *The History of Foreign Investment in the United States to 1914*, 413, 831, 914 (German chemical interests around World War I), 823 (Bayer Aspirin around 1912), 921 (British insurance companies in 1881). The subject of bribery becomes embedded in accounts of businesses in the United States owned by Axis powers as well as the dealings of U.S. companies with the enemy during wartime. For the latter, see Robert Franklin Maddox, *The War Within World War II: The United States and International Cartels*.

13. For a critical book review noting the problem of conflating the two terms *genocide* and *ethnic cleansing*, noting as well that there is yet to be a useful work on ethnic cleansing, see Sanya Popovic, "Review."

14. One detailed study is Martin Indyk, "The Politics of Patronage: Israel and Egypt Between the Superpowers, 1962–1973."

15. Third World power as a component of the development of multilateralism is a huge subject. One could do worse than to revisit the colonial theorists of indirect rule for evidence of the political influence of the Third World elite, as for example the canonical work of the 1930s, Lord Lugard, *The Dual Mandate in British Tropical Africa*. This posthumously published book is part of a genre that if read between the lines would show a steadily evolving dimension of Third World power in the period of colonialism. For more recent times, the Third World Approaches to International Law Project (TWAIL) is another terrain to

enter into, as here the rules of the game are discussed. See the somewhat contrarian piece, David P. Fidler, "Revolt Against or from Within the West? TWAIL, the Developing World, and the Future Direction of International Law." Another obvious place to look would be the literature on international organizations. See, for example, the rising participation of Africans in the General Assembly of the United Nations in Christopher O'Sullivan, "The United Nations, Decolonization, and Self-Determination in Cold War Sub-Saharan Africa, 1960–1994."

16. Jeffrey Laurenti, "Grand Goals, Modest Results: The UN in Search of Reform."

17. This topic is the theme of Michael Doran, *Pan-Arabism Before Nasser*. Many scholars turn to World War I, where the interplay of Western needs and local aspirations emerged, and they make this point their watershed for where to begin modern Middle Eastern history. This time frame does not take one far enough back. For Egypt, as the text implies, multilateralism is apparent as far back as the era of Khedive Isma'il in the 1860s. Events around or after World War I point toward a further development of multilateralism at that time: for example, the establishment by Great Britain of the Protectorate in Egypt in December 1914 "for wartime reasons," U.S. interwar oil policy in 1920–23 with its demands for an open door, and so on. For a discussion of how various elite Egyptian intellectuals came to deal with life in Paris in this period, another part of the Rise of the Rich, see Sa'id Lawindi, *'Ama'im wa tarabish-misriyun 'ashu fi Baris*.

18. The scholarly issue of importance is of course much broader than simply a few individuals mentioned in the text. For the emergence of the new class generally, see Malak Zaalouk, *Power, Class, and Foreign Capital in Egypt: The Rise of the New Bourgeoisie*. Part of what Zaalouk covers is the money to be made from dealing with USAID and it contracts. Many people made a fortune this way. Large-scale projects, another author maintains, usually found their way to American firms, whereas commodities went directly to the Egyptian bourgeoisie (Marvin Weinbaum, *Egypt and the Politics of U.S. Economic Aid*). U.S. policy to Egypt has apparently been "genteel" compared to its policy to Mexico, where loan money has had rapid repayment as a condition no matter how devastating it was on the standard of living (James Petras, *The Left Strikes Back*, 195). A comparative study would be useful.

19. Michael Woodiwiss, introduction to *Organized Crime and American Power*. Earlier there had appeared a somewhat historiographical article revealing that this "new" theorization about the confluence of white-collar and organized crime had appeared in the literature years back, but the article was apparently overlooked at the time (Dwight C. Smith Jr., "Paragons, Pariahs, and Pirates: A Spectrum-Based Theory of Enterprise"). My colleague Mark Haller wrote two foundational articles, "Illegal Enterprise: A Theoretical and Historical Interpretation" and "Historical Roots of Police Behavior: Chicago, 1890–1925."

20. Dana Dillon, "Maritime Piracy: Defining the Problem."

21. Adam Edwards and Pete Gill, "The Politics of 'Transnational Organized Crime': Discourse, Reflexivity, and the Narration of 'Threat,'" 260.

22. Jonathan Beaty and S. C. Gwynne, *The Outlaw Bank: A Wild Ride into the Secret Heart of BCCI,* 112. The decision here to discuss BCCI and al-Qa'ida is related to the paradigm issue underlying the book as a whole—one of getting beyond East and West. If this book was set up to present a more comprehensive account of the "New Men," then drug dealers might have to be given pride of place. See, for example, Menno Vellinga, ed., *The Political Economy of the Drug Industry: Latin America and the International System.* A monograph on the role of the New Men and their contribution to market expansion as a part of modern capitalism would definitely improve the general quality of political economy scholarship on world capitalism at this point.

23. Nikos Passas, "The Genesis of the BCCI Scandal."

24. Kimberley Thachuk, "Corruption and International Security," 143. For a particular concentration on al-Qa'ida and Southeast Asia, see Barry Desker, "Islam in Southeast Asia: The Challenge of Radical Interpretations."

25. Mark Basile, "Going to the Source: Why al-Qaeda's Financial Network Is Likely to Withstand the Current War on Terrorist Financing."

26. Brad McAllister, "Al-Qaeda and the Innovative Firm: Demythologizing the Network."

27. http://www.rense.com/general37/cost.htm. The story is not over. In July 2006 the Bush administration announced the closure of the Alec Station CIA unit that was in charge of tracking Usama Bin Ladin (http://thebluestate.typepad.com/my_weblog/2006/07/bush_administra.html).

28. Cornelius P. Cotter, "Constitutionalizing Emergency Powers: The British Experience." Some interrelate the domestic and the colonial, including Nasser Hussain, *The Jurisprudence of Emergency: Colonialism and the Rule of Law.*

29. Jules Lobel, "Emergency Powers and the Decline of Liberalism." Various Third World countries also have long-lasting states of emergency. Examples drawn from Africa and Egypt point toward long use of these practices. See John Hatchard, "States of Siege/Emergency"; and Diane Singerman, "Egypt."

30. The study of public opinion as a social movement is not a developed theme. For various reasons, political scientists have long taken public opinion to be a validation of democracy and not a force in its own right. This idea goes back to John Locke but extends up to the world of the bloggers of today. An example of a current researcher who takes it to be a validation of democracy is Paul Burstein, "The Impact of Public Opinion on Public Policy: A Review and an Agenda" and "Why Do Social Movement Organizations, Interest Groups, and Political Parties Seem to Have So Little Impact on Public Policy?" arguing that politicians routinely give more credence to opinion polls than to appeals from groups. If this approach typifies the liberal mainstream, in Marxism writers such as Herbert Schiller or Daniel Schiller point to the influence of the media on the shaping of public opinion, finding it to be how the system validates what it wanted to do in the first place. The media persuade in the sense that Gramsci's state intellectuals persuade. The text agrees that this direction is

an important way to proceed but notes that the overall conditions in contemporary society so affect the views of individuals that what the media say or do not say does not have much weight outside of the democracies. In countries with a significant peasantry, which is the majority of countries in the world, mass media have little utility, as there is no trust to begin with. Even in the Western democracies, however, the use of public opinion for the purpose of validating state programs in recent years has had its ups and downs. A way to form an impression of the dilemma of a state trying to give the impression of being shaped by public opinion is to study the growing dependence of the political order on pollsters paid to produce the desired effect (Susan Herbst, *Numbered Voices: How Opinion Polling Has Shaped American Politics*). The need for the pollster industry could be construed to mean that the state is not getting its results, this point in turn lending credence to the idea of public opinion today as a movement. See, for example, Ivan Steiner, "Primary Group Influences on Public Opinion," on the determinants of public opinion. As primary groups go, so goes public opinion. In noting the volatility and incoherence of public opinion, the text is not trying to bring back Walter Lippmann and his dismissal of the utility of public opinion in democracy but suggests that one needs to study the mix of coherence and incoherence as a clue to how societal interests may be being pursued. For a survey of the literature, see Ole Holsti, "Public Opinion and Foreign Policy: Challenges to the Almond-Lippmann Consensus Mershon Series, Research Program, and Debates."

31. Different forms of hegemony construct the "other" in quite predictable ways (see Gran, *Beyond Eurocentrism*). For democracies, see John H. Kautsky, *Marxism and Leninism, Not Marxism-Leninism: An Essay in the Sociology of Knowledge*. Kautsky, writing from the perspective of bourgeois democracy, claimed that Lenin writing as a Russian did not understand Marxism as Marx intended it. For another such example, one could look at the English-language Gramsci commentary literature found today. In it Gramsci is not studied on his own in his Italian context; rather, he is read and interpreted according to the needs of the English-speaking world. Thus, for example, one can read widely and still find little reference to the oppression of Sicily and Sardinia, the regions Gramsci analyzed at such length as the Southern Question. Yet without an appreciation of the fact that Gramsci was a southern Italian and was writing to locate his region in the larger struggle, it is difficult to imagine what he is writing about. At the same time, this contemporary use of Gramsci could scarcely be accidental. Indeed, a moment's reflection suggests that if we accept Gramsci's Sicily on his own terms, our understanding of European liberation struggle might have to begin there, and this would certainly not fit with our version of social theory. For this reason, perhaps, Gramsci is "critically" acclaimed (Anderson, "Antinomies of Gramsci"). Anderson's article in effect closes the door on the Southern Question as a category of any importance.

32. For women fighting back, see Zeinabou Hadari, "Qur'anic-Based Literacy and Islamic Education: A Basis for Female Empowerment in Niger." More generally, see Valentine Moghadam, "Gender and Globalization: Female Labor and Women's Mobilization."

33. For an attempt to see these struggles in a wider context, see Frits Van Holthoon and Marcel Van Der Linden, eds., *Internationalism in the Labour Movement, 1830–1940,* esp. 304–36.

34. There is an immense bibliography of materials old and new on the class war and counterhegemony in general terms. Some of it has been referred in previous chapters. Some examples are cited here of more conventional material to provide contrast with the new trade unionism being discussed in the text. An influential contemporary voice of the British New Left is Chris Harman. In "The Workers of the World," he argues that the percentage of the world that is proletarianized is steadily growing and that the theories of the world that see some radical changes leading to a service economy linked by computers lose sight of the larger picture. What underlines this line of thought is the slightly millennialist idea that the era of confrontation is upon us; as more and more people are defined as proletarians, the revolution is bound to happen. For more of the same, see also his *People's History of the World.* For views of counterhegemony closer to the neoliberalism paradigms discussed in Chapters 1 and 2, see Peter Evans, "Fighting Marginalization with Transnational Networks: Counter-hegemonic Globalization," which notes how groups linked through the Internet can leverage for change, how migrants to Los Angeles earn money to send home, how anti-Nike campaigns can help work conditions, and finally how NAFTA may open the door to some real labor cooperation north and south of the border. Such cooperation, he correctly points out, would help against the white racism that is also on the rise. See also Owen Worth and Carmen Kuhling, "Counter-hegemony, Anti-globalisation, and Culture in International Political Economy," which discusses the struggle over popular culture, mentioning the work of the Birmingham School. Owen Worth, "The Janus-Like Character of Counter-hegemony: Progressive and National Responses to Neo-liberalism," points to the rather contingent nature of the prevailing IPE theory (see Chapters 1–2). It is not, as he writes, that it lacks a historical schema covering the past, but it is rather too simplistic. Robert A. Rhoads, "Globalization and Resistance in the United States and Mexico: The Global Potemkin Village," applies the discussion of counterhegemony to the role of student activism and New Social Movements. For a recent example of studies of protest on local levels, see, for example, Michiel Baud and Rosanne Rutten, eds., *Popular Intellectuals and Social Movements: Framing Protest in Asia, Africa, and Latin America.*

35. Robert Lambert, "Labour Movement in the Era of Globalization: Union Responses in the South."

36. Noting some limitations, see Anita Chan and Robert J. S. Ross, "Racing to the Bottom: International Trade Without a Social Clause."

37. On SIGTUR, see Robert Lambert and Edward Webster, "Southern Unionism and the New Labour Internationalism"; and Jeffrey Harrod and Robert O'Brien, eds., *Global Unions: Theory and Strategies of Organized Labour in the Global Political Economy,* 199–201, dealing with the 2001 South Korea initiative. As SIGTUR has developed, it has come under increasing fire from the established labor establishment. For example, an ILO publication argues that COSATSU, the South African Labor Confederation, which is a main component of SIGTUR,

has very little global consciousness or linkage (Andries Bezuidenhout, *Towards Global Social Movement Unionism? Trade Union Responses to Globalization in South Africa*). Among other predictable criticisms are the ones concerning the relation of SIGTUR to the South, to class, and to socialism. Lambert tries to respond, describing the South as a region "defined by authoritarian stateism and corporate dominance, often coming out of colonial or racial oppression," a political as opposed to a purely economic definition (Lambert and Webster, "What Is New in the New Labour Internationalism? A Southern Perspective").

38. Meanwhile, Andrew L. Stern rose in SEIU ranks and in the process adopted ever more radical tactics; a collision with Sweeney finally accrued (Aaron Bernstein, "Can This Man Save Labor?"). For parallels elsewhere, see Geoffrey Wood and Chris Brewster, "Decline and Renewal in the British Labour Movement: Trends, Practices, and Lessons for South Africa." See also Peter Olney, "To Renew, Labor Must Look at Its Foreign Policy," esp. 15.

5. THE "RISE OF THE RICH" PARADIGM APPLIED TO THE CONTEMPORARY UNITED STATES

1. Several researchers have studied the restratification of society, their work lending credence to the choice of the Rise of the Rich here. See Kevin Phillips, *The Politics of Rich and Poor*, esp. chap. 5 on America's shrinking share of global wealth. See also Denny Braun, *The Rich Get Richer;* and George Marcus, *Lives in Trust: The Fortunes of Dynastic Families in Late-Twentieth-Century America*. The international dimension comes in anecdotally.

2. Jay Sexton, "Toward a Synthesis of Foreign Relations in the Civil War Era, 1848–1877," suggests this type of subject remains to be worked on. Matias Romero, *Mexican Lobby*, the odd book, covers the Civil War period.

3. Other approaches to Third World ruling-class power are doubtless better known but are not useful here, given the task at hand. See Sally Morphet, "Multilateralism and the Non-Aligned Movement: What Is the Global South Doing and Where Is It Going?" emphasizing the Non-Aligned Movement; and Denis Benn, *Multilateral Diplomacy and the Economics of Change: The Third World and the New International Economic Order*.

4. An older but still useful book of this sort is Neil Jacoby, *Bribery and Extortion in World Business: A Study of Corporate Political Payments Abroad*.

5. The 2002 edition of *Political Corruption*, edited by Arnold J. Heidenheimer and Michael Johnston, contains many articles originally published in the 1960s and 1970s.

6. Stephen Lovell et al., *Bribery and Blat in Russia*, 271.

7. Pat Choate, *Agents of Influence: How Japan's Lobbyists in the U.S. Manipulate America's Political and Economic System*.

8. An authoritative statement of this position is Anne O. Krueger, "Why Crony Capitalism Is Bad for Economic Growth." The evidence provided throughout the book that Krueger's chapter appears in does not, however, all support Krueger's view.

9. David C. Kang, *Crony Capitalism: Corruption and Development in South Korea and the Philippines;* John Sfakianakis, "The Whales of the Nile: Networks, Businessmen, and Bureaucrats During the Era of Privatization in Egypt"; Bryce, *Cronies.*

10. Chung Hee Lee, *Foreign Lobbying in American Politics.* Michael Johnson, "International Corruption via Campaign Contribution," concentrates on the United States as well.

11. Wesley Cragg and William Woof, "Legislating Against Corruption in International Markets: The Story of the U.S. Foreign Corrupt Practices Act."

12. Mira Wilkins, "Foreign Companies in the U.S., 1945–2000," 25. For Japan specifically, there is the work by an economist, Pat Choate, *Agents of Influence.* Samuel Huntington, "Why International Primacy Matters," esp. 79–80, claims that in 1989, 250 Japanese government agencies and corporations had Washington lobbyists. Canada was in second place with 90. Their estimated expenses were more than the expenditures of the next six largest spenders. In the area of political and cultural influence, Japanese investments in Hollywood led to a veto on movies critical of Japan, led to influence in research at Harvard, and led to the defeat of political candidates with positions hostile to Japanese business through the political action committee called AUTOPAC.

13. Information about the international dimensions of the new alliance, apart from the Texas oil connections, can be drawn from Bruce W. Jentleson, *With Friends Like These: Reagan, Bush, and Saddam, 1982–1990.*

14. See Unger, *House of Bush.*

15. Chan and Ross, "Racing to the Bottom," 1014.

16. This topic brings us up against another historiographical issue, a more difficult one, the need for new theories and hypotheses to overcome problems of incomplete information. Martin Tolchin and Susan Tolchin, authors of *Buying into America: How Foreign Money Is Changing the Face of Our Nation,* like many other writers cited in this book, make the point about how difficult it is to get precise information about the interconnection between the American economy and the world economy. This point of lack of information comes back endlessly, as if it were an attribute of neoliberalism. Perhaps it is. For example, apparently, in the 1970s when the Arab oil elite wanted to recycle their petrodollars back into the United States, they did not want it known exactly who was going to be involved. Perhaps this illustrates my point: the wealthy and powerful people of the new liberal age simply demand and get more privacy, which makes a researcher's task harder and harder. See Ibrahim M. Oweiss, *Impediments to Arab Investment in the United States,* 9. Jonathan Crystal, *Unwanted Company: Foreign Investment in American Industry,* is the unusual author dealing with the political side of investments. Crystal begins from economic explanations for firm behavior, finds they do not always work, and turns to politics. He finds that not all firms with international interests on the East Coast sat back without complaining as the foreign direct investment came in. Some did, but some did not. Local, more nationally minded firms did complain. Crystal's findings make the matter more interesting but even more complicated.

17. Kenichi Yasumuro, "Japanese Multinational Location Strategies," 226.

18. Although there are a number of American politicians from the Midwest and the West who have taken the view of foreign political control coming via foreign money, one finds fewer academic writers who do so. An exception could be found in the several coauthored books of Tolchin and Tolchin, such as *Buying into America*, referred to before.

19. Roger W. Schmenner, "Geography and the Character and Performance of Factories."

20. Douglas P. Woodward and Norman J. Glickman, "Regional and Local Determinants of Foreign Firm Location in the United States."

21. Robert W. Haigh, *Investment Strategies and the Plant-Location Decision: Foreign Companies in the United States*, 31–32.

22. Jan Ondrich and Michael Wasylenko, *Foreign Direct Investment in the United States*, 138.

23. Martin Tolchin and Susan Tolchin, *Selling Our Security: The Erosion of America's Assets*, 4. According to Pat Choate, in *Hot Property: The Stealing of Ideas in an Age of Globalization*, even more technology is simply stolen.

24. Scholars adopting the liberal paradigm often proclaim that the meaning of this period was that it saw the end of Third Worldism. See, for example, the special issue of the journal *Third World Quarterly* 25, no. 1 (2004) on the supposed end of Third Worldism.

25. Richard Perle, "The Strategic Impact of Technology Transfer," esp. 4.

26. William Schneider Jr., "Technology Transfer and U.S. Foreign Policy."

27. Victor Basiuk, "Technology Transfer to China."

28. Dale A. Hathaway, *Can Workers Have a Voice? The Politics of Deindustrialization in Pittsburgh*, 26–27. The classic overview on this subject remains Barry Bluestone and Bennett Harrison, *The Deindustrialization of America*. Many books take up the unraveling of society caused by mass unemployment. See, for example, Norman T. Feather, *The Psychological Impact of Unemployment*.

29. Hathaway, *Can Workers Have a Voice?* 178ff.

30. Marc R. Rosenblum, "Moving Beyond the Policy of No Policy: Emigration from Mexico and Central America."

31. Augustine J. Kposowa, *The Impact of Immigration on the United States Economy*, 177ff, chap. 12.

32. Saskia Sassens, "The De Facto Transnationalizing of Immigration Policy," 49.

33. Gary P. Freeman, "The Decline of Sovereignty." Quite opposite views are expressed about the power of the state as we have noted. See, for example, Jean-François Bayart et al., *The Criminalization of the State in Africa*.

34. Jorge Bustamente, "Undocumented Migration and National Security," 27.

35. Dolores Byrnes, *Driving the State*. Scholarship on Mexico is corroborated by the results of similar studies conducted elsewhere. For example, Suzanne Paige states that despite attendant risks, Turkish development plans were made "increasingly dependent on

labor export" (*Exporting Workers: The Turkish Case*, 36). This point is also put forward in another study, one partly devoted to south-central Anatolia, the primary labor-export region of Turkey. The author concludes that development politics were consciously connected to the remittance money but (and?) that the region was never allowed to move ahead (Jeffrey A. Courtemanche, "Economic Outcomes in Labor Exporting Regions: A Comparison of the Moroccan Rif and Central Anatolia," conclusion and bibliography).

36. Manuel Orozco, "Globalization and Migration: The Impact of Family Remittances in Latin America." For a detailed look at the Guanajuato one, see Byrnes, *Driving the State.*

37. Clearly, American nationalist sentiment against Mexicans is at a high level. James McKinley Jr.'s 2005 story in the *New York Times,* "A Guide for the Illegal Immigrant," about the Mexican government publishing a manual advising illegal immigrants on how to survive in the United States added fuel to the fire. The stereotype of Mexican corruption is, however, never far from the center of most American-oriented commentary. For a discussion of corrupt border police, see Ruben Andersson, "The New Frontiers of America." For corruption on a higher level, see Larry Elders, "How Does Mexico Treat Its Illegals?"

38. Before the SEIU Stephen O. Yokich, president of the United Auto Workers who died in 1998, was an example of an American trade unionist who tried to work with Asian unions. By the time Yokich arrived on the scene, Japanese and Korean capitalists, however, had other options in Asia and could run away from their workers. So far, most Japanese and Korean workers, like most of their American counterparts, have not tried to go beyond workerism to deal with hegemony issues. A deep history of the struggle against hegemony-driven racism has yet to be written.

BIBLIOGRAPHY

Abou El Haj, Rifaʻat. *Formation of the Modern State: The Ottoman Empire, Six-teenth to the Eighteenth Centuries*. 1991. Reprint, Syracuse: Syracuse Univ. Press, 2005.

Accinelli, Robert D. "The Hoover Administration and the World Court." *Peace and Change* 4, no. 3 (Fall 1977): 28–36.

Adas, Michael. "Contested Hegemony: The Great War and the Afro-Asiatic Assault on the Civilizing Mission Ideology." *Journal of World History* 15, no. 1 (2004): 31–63.

Almond, Harry H., Jr. "World Court Rulings on the Use of Force in the Context of a Global Power Struggle." *World Affairs* 148, no. 1 (Summer 1985): 19–25.

Althusser, Louis. *For Marx*. New York: Pantheon Books, 1969.

Amin, Samir. *Accumulation on a World Scale: A Critique of the Theory of Under-development*. New York: Monthly Review Press, 1974.

———. *Class and Nation Historically and in the Present Crisis*. New York: Monthly Review Press, 1980.

———. "Trans-Saharan Exchange and the Black Slave Trade." *Diogenes* 45, no. 3 (1997): 31–47.

Amsden, Alice. *The Rise of "the Rest": Challenges to the West from Late-Indus-trializing Economies*. Oxford: Oxford Univ. Press, 2001.

Anderson, Perry. "The Antinomies of Antonio Gramsci." *New Left Review*, no. 100 (1976–77): 5–78.

———. "Components of the National Culture." *New Left Review*, no. 50 (July 1968): 3–57.

Andersson, Ruben. "The New Frontiers of America." *Race and Class* 48, no. 3 (Jan. 2005): 28–38.

Arnold, Guy. *The End of the Third World*. New York: St. Martins Press, 1993.

Arnold, Terrell E. "The Costs of Blaming al-Qaida." http://www.rense.com/general37/cost.htm.

Baia, Larissa Ruiz. "Rethinking Transnationalism: Reconstructing National Identities among Peruvian Catholics in New Jersey." *Journal of Inter-American Studies and World Affairs* 41, no. 4 (1999): 93–109.

Barendse, Rene. *The Arabian Seas: The Indian Ocean World of the Seventeenth Century.* Armonk, N.Y.: M. E. Sharpe, 2001.

Barker, Colin, and Gareth Dale. "Protest Waves in Western Europe: A Critique of 'New Social Movement' Theory." *Critical Sociology* 24, nos. 1–2 (1998): 65–104.

Basile, Mark. "Going to the Source: Why al-Qaeda's Financial Network Is Likely to Withstand the Current War on Terrorist Financing." *Studies in Conflict and Terrorism* 27 (2004): 169–85.

Basiuk, Victor. "Technology Transfer to China." In *Selling the Rope to Hang Capitalism,* edited by Charles M. Perry and Robert L. Pfaltzgraff, 131–54. Washington, D.C.: Pergamon-Brassey, 1987.

Batalla, Guillermo Bonfil. *Mexico Profundo: Reclaiming a Civilization.* Austin: Univ. of Texas Press, 1998.

Batou, Jean. *Between Development and Underdevelopment: The Precocious Attempts at Industry of the Periphery, 1800–1870.* Geneva: Droz, 1991.

Baud, Michiel, and Rosanne Rutten, eds. *Popular Intellectuals and Social Movements: Framing Protest in Asia, Africa, and Latin America.* Cambridge: Cambridge Univ. Press, 2004.

Bayart, Jean-François, et al. *The Criminalization of the State in Africa.* Bloomington: Indiana Univ. Press, 1999.

Beaty, Jonathan, and S. C. Gwynne. *The Outlaw Bank: A Wild Ride into the Secret Heart of BCCI.* New York: Random House, 1993.

Beck, Ulrich. *The Re-invention of Politics: Rethinking Modernity in the Global Social Order.* Cambridge: Polity Press, 1997.

Beller, Jonathan. "The Cinematic Mode of Production: Towards a Political Economy of the Post-modern." *Culture, Theory, and Critique* 44, no. 1 (2003): 91–106.

Bender, Thomas, ed. *Rethinking American History in a Global Age.* Berkeley and Los Angeles: Univ. of California Press, 2002.

Benjamin, Thomas, and William McNellie, eds. *Other Mexicos: Essays in Regional Mexican History, 1876–1911.* Albuquerque: Univ. of New Mexico Press, 1984.

Benjamin, Thomas, and Mark Wasserman, eds. *Provinces of the Revolution: Essays on Regional Mexican History, 1910–1929.* Albuquerque: Univ. of New Mexico Press, 1990.

Benn, Denis. *Multilateral Diplomacy and the Economics of Change: The Third World and the New International Economic Order.* Kingston, Jamaica: Ian Randle, 2003.

Bentley, Jerry. "Cross-cultural Interaction and Periodization in World History." *American Historical Review* 101 (June 1996): 749–70.

Benton, Gregory. "Chinese Transnationalism in Britain: A Longer History." *Identities: Global Studies in Culture and Power* 10 (2003): 347–75.

Benton, Lauren. *Law and Colonial Cultures: Legal Regimes in World History, 1400–1900.* Cambridge: Cambridge Univ. Press, 2002.

Bernstein, Aaron. "Can This Man Save Labor?" *Business Week,* Sept. 13, 2004.

Bezuidenhout, Andries. *Towards Global Social Movement Unionism? Trade Union Responses to Globalization in South Africa.* Geneva: International Institute for Labour Studies, 2000.

Bieler, Andreas, and Adam David Morton. "Theoretical and Methodological Challenges of Neo-Gramscian Perspectives in International Political Economy." *International Gramsci Society Newsletter,* no. 13 (May 2003): 9–18.

Blakeley, Georgina, and Valerie Bryson, eds. *Contemporary Political Concepts: A Critical Introduction.* London: Pluto Press, 2002.

Blaut, James. *The Colonizer's Model of the World: Geographical Diffusionism and Eurocentric History.* New York: Guilford Press, 1993.

———. "Marxism and Eurocentric Diffusionism." In *The Political Economy of Imperialism: Critical Appraisals,* edited by Ronald H. Chilcote. Lanham, Md.: Rowman and Littlefield, 2000.

Bluestone, Barry, and Bennett Harrison. *The Deindustrialization of America.* New York: Basic Books, 1982.

Boggs, Carl. *Gramsci's Marxism.* London: Pluto Press, 1973.

Boli, John, and George M. Thomas, eds. *Constructing World Culture: International Non-governmental Organizations since 1875.* Stanford: Stanford Univ. Press, 1999.

Bonnell, Victoria E., and Lynn Hunt, eds. *Beyond the Cultural Turn: New Directions in the Study of Society and Culture.* Berkeley and Los Angeles: Univ. of California Press, 1999.

Boron, Atilio. *Empire and Imperialism.* London: Zed Books, 2005.

Braun, Denny. *The Rich Get Richer.* Chicago: Nelson-Hall, 1991.

Brennan, Timothy. "Antonio Gramsci and Post-colonial Theory: 'Southernism.'" *Diaspora* 10, no. 2 (2001): 143–87.

Brint, Steven. "Professionals and the 'Knowledge Economy': Rethinking the Theory of Postindustrial Society." *Current Sociology* 49, no. 4 (July 2001): 101–32.

Brown, Terrance, and Leslie Smith, eds. *Reductionism and the Development of Knowledge*. Mahwah, N.J.: Lawrence Erlbaum Associates, 2003.

Bruhn, Kathleen. "Antonio Gramsci and the Palabra Verdadera: The Political Discourse of Mexico's Guerilla Forces." *Journal of Inter-American Studies and World Affairs* 41, no. 2 (1999): 29–56.

Bryce, Robert. *Cronies: Oil, the Bushes, and the Rise of Texas, America's Superstate*. New York: Public Affairs, 2004.

Burstein, Paul. "The Impact of Public Opinion on Public Policy: A Review and an Agenda." *Political Research Quarterly* 56, no. 1 (2003): 29–40.

———. "Why Do Social Movement Organizations, Interest Groups, and Political Parties Seem to Have So Little Impact on Public Policy?" Paper presented at the American Sociological Association Annual Meeting, Toronto, Aug. 1997.

Bustamente, Jorge A. "Undocumented Migration and National Security." In *U.S.-Mexico Relations: Labor Market Interdependence,* edited by Jorge A. Bustamente et al. Stanford: Stanford Univ. Press, 1992.

Buttigieg, Joe. *Prison Notebooks*. New York: Columbia Univ. Press, 1992.

Byrnes, Dolores. *Driving the State*. Ithaca: Cornell Univ. Press, 2003.

Cameron, Rondo. "England, 1750–1840." In *Banking in the Early Stages of the Industrial Revolution,* edited by Rondo Cameron et al. New York: Oxford Univ. Press, 1967.

Carleheden, Mikael, and Michael Hviid Jacobsen, eds. *The Transformation of Modernity*. Hampshire, England: Ashgate, 2001.

Carroll, William K., and R. S. Ratner. "Between Leninism and Radical Pluralism: Gramscian Reflections on Counter-hegemony and the New Social Movements." *Critical Sociology* 20, no. 2 (1994): 1–24.

Chan, Anita, and Robert J. S. Ross. "Racing to the Bottom: International Trade Without a Social Clause." *Third World Quarterly* 24, no. 6 (2003): 1011–28.

Choate, Pat. *Agents of Influence: How Japan's Lobbyists in the U.S. Manipulate America's Political and Economic System*. New York: Alfred A. Knopf, 1990.

———. *Hot Property: The Stealing of Ideas in an Age of Globalization*. New York: Alfred A. Knopf, 2005.

Chua, Amy. *World on Fire*. New York: Anchor Books, 2003.

Chutintaranond, Sunait, and Chris Baker, eds. *Recalling Local Pasts: Autonomous History in Southeast Asia*. Bangkok: Silkworm Books, 2002.

Collier, G. A. *Basta! Land and the Zapatista Rebellion in the Chiapas.* Oakland: Food First Books, 1994.

Cook, Weston F., Jr. *The Hundred Years War for Morocco: Gunpowder and the Military Revolution in the Early Modern Muslim World.* Boulder: Westview Press, 1994.

Cooper, Frederick. *Colonialism in Question: Theory, Knowledge, History.* Berkeley and Los Angeles: Univ. of California Press, 2005.

Cooper, Frederick, and Ann Stoler, eds. *Tensions of Empire: Colonial Cultures in a Bourgeois World.* Berkeley and Los Angeles: Univ. of California Press, 1997.

Cotter, Cornelius P. "Constitutionalizing Emergency Powers: The British Experience." *Stanford Law Review* 5, no. 3 (1953): 382–417.

Courtemanche, Jeffrey A. "Economic Outcomes in Labor Exporting Regions: A Comparison of the Moroccan Rif and Central Anatolia." Master's thesis, Univ. of Washington, 2000.

Cragg, Wesley, and William Woof. "Legislating Against Corruption in International Markets: The Story of the U.S. Foreign Corrupt Practices Act." In *The Political Economy of Corruption,* edited by Arvind K. Jain. London: Routledge, 2001.

Crozier, Michel, et al., eds. *The Crisis of Democracies: Report on the Governability of Democracies.* New York: New York Univ. Press, 1975.

Crystal, Jonathan. *Unwanted Company: Foreign Investment in American Industry.* Ithaca: Cornell Univ. Press, 2003.

Cuguano, Ottobah. *Thoughts and Sentiments on the Nature of the Slave Trade.* London, 1787.

Cunningham, Hilary. "Nations Rebound? Crossing Borders in a Gated Globe." *Identities: Global Studies in Culture and Power* 11 (2004): 329–50.

D'Anieri, Paul, et al. "New Social Movements in Historical Perspective." *Comparative Politics* 22, no. 4 (1990): 445–58.

DeBrunner, Hans Werner. *Presence and Prestige: Africans in Europe.* Basel: Basler Afrika Biblographien, 1979.

Desker, Barry. "Islam in Southeast Asia: The Challenge of Radical Interpretations." *Cambridge Review of International Affairs* 16, no. 3 (2003): 415–28.

Dillon, Dana. "Maritime Piracy: Defining the Problem." *SAIS Review* 25, no. 1 (2005): 155–65.

Dirlik, Arif, Vinay Bahl, and Peter Gran, eds. *History after the Three Worlds.* Lanham, Md.: Rowman and Littlefield, 2000.

Dixin, Xu, and Wu Chengming, eds. *Chinese Capitalism, 1522–1840*. Houndsmill, England: Macmillan, 2000.

Doran, Michael. *Pan-Arabism Before Nasser*. New York: Oxford Univ. Press, 1999.

Douin, Georges. "L'ambassade d'Elfi Bey à Londres (octobre–decembre 1803)." *Bulletin d'Institut d'Egypte* 7 (1925): 95–120.

Edelman, Marc. "Social Movements: Changing Paradigms and Forms of Politics." *Annual Review of Anthropology* 30 (2001): 285–317.

Edward, Brent Hayes. *The Practice of Diaspora-Literature: Translation and the Rise of Black Internationalism*. Cambridge: Harvard Univ. Press, 2003.

Edwards, Adam, and Pete Gill. "The Politics of 'Transnational Organized Crime': Discourse, Reflexivity, and the Narration of 'Threat.'" *British Journal of Politics and International Relations* 4, no. 2 (2002): 245–70.

Elders, Larry. "How Does Mexico Treat Its Illegals?" *Human Events* 62, no. 13 (Apr. 10, 2006): 17.

Eley, Geoff, and Keith Nield. *The Future of Class in History: What's Left of the Social?* Ann Arbor: University of Michigan Press, 2007.

———. "Scholarly Controversy: Farewell to the Working Class?" *International Labor and Working Class History*, no. 57 (Spring 2000): 1–30.

Elleman, Bruce A. *Modern Chinese Warfare, 1795–1989*. London: Routledge, 2001.

Elman, Colin, and Miriam Fendius Elman, eds. *Bridges and Boundaries: Historians, Political Scientists, and the Study of International Relations*. Cambridge: MIT Press, 2001.

Eltis, David. *The Military Revolution in Sixteenth-Century Europe*. London: I. B. Tauris, 1995.

Equiano, Oladauh. *The Interesting Life of Oladauh Equiano*. London, 1789.

Evans, Peter. "Fighting Marginalization with Transnational Networks: Counterhegemonic Globalization." *Contemporary Sociology* 29, no. 1 (Jan. 2000): 230–41.

Feather, Norman T. *The Psychological Impact of Unemployment*. New York: Springer-Verlag, 1990.

Feldstein, Federico Pablo, et al. "Argentinean Jews as Scapegoats: A Textual Analysis of the Bombing of AMIA." *Journal of Communication Inquiry* 27, no. 2 (Apr. 2003): 152–71.

Feyerabend, Paul. *Against Method*. Chicago: Univ. of Chicago Press, 1993.

Fidler, David P. "Revolt Against or from Within the West? TWAIL, the Developing World, and the Future Direction of International Law." *Chinese Journal of International Law* 2, no. 1 (2003): 29–76.

Floor, Willem, and Patrick Clawson. "Safavid Iran's Search for Silver and Gold." *International Journal of Middle East Studies* 32, no. 3 (Aug. 2000): 345–68.

Forman-Barzilai, Fonna. "Adam Smith as Globalization Theorist." *Critical Review* 14, no. 4 (2003): 391–419.

Freeman, Gary P. "The Decline of Sovereignty." In *Challenge to the Nation State: Immigration in Western Europe and the United States,* edited by Gary P. Freeman. Oxford: Oxford Univ. Press, 1998.

Friedman, Thomas L. *The Earth Is Flat: A Brief History of the Twenty-first Century.* New York: Farrar, Straus, and Giroux, 2005.

Fuk, Kai Cheok. "The Macao Formula: A Study of Chinese Management of Westerners from the Mid-Sixteenth Century to the Opium War Period." Ph.D. thesis, Univ. of Hawaii, 1978.

Gadrey, Jean. *New Economy, New Myth.* London: Routledge, 2003.

Galeano, Eduardo. *Open Veins of Latin America: Five Centuries of the Pillage of a Continent.* New York: Monthly Review Press, 1973.

Galtung, Johan. "A Structural Theory of Imperialism." *Journal of Peace Research* 8, no. 2 (1971): 81–117.

Gates, Henry Louis, and William L. Andrews. *Pioneers of the Black Atlantic: Five Slave Narratives from the Enlightenment, 1772–1815.* Washington, D.C.: Civitas, 1998.

Genovese, Eugene D. "The Political Crisis of Social History." In *Fruits of Merchant Capital,* edited by Elizabeth Fox-Genovese and Eugene D. Genovese, 179–212. New York: Oxford Univ. Press, 1983.

Geyer, Martin H., and Johannes Paulmann, eds. *The Mechanics of Internationalism: Culture, Society, and Politics from the 1840s to the First World War.* London: Oxford Univ. Press, 2001.

Gill, Stephen. *Power and Resistance in the New World Order.* Basingstoke, England: Palgrave, 2002.

Goldstone, Jack A. "East and West in the Seventeenth Century: Political Crises in Stuart England, Ottoman Turkey, and Ming China." *Comparative Studies in Society and History* 30, no. 1 (Jan. 1988): 103–42.

———. "The Problem of the 'Early Modern' World." *Journal of the Economic and Social History of the Orient* 41, no. 3 (1998): 249–84.

———. *Revolution and Rebellion in the Early Modern World.* Berkeley and Los Angeles: Univ. of California Press, 1991.

———. "The Rise of the West—or Not? A Revision to Socio-economic History." *Sociological Theory* 18, no. 2 (July 2000): 175–94.

Gong, Gerrit. *The Standard of "Civilization" in International Society.* Oxford: Clarendon Press, 1984.

Gramsci, Antonio. "Hegemony of Western Culture over the World Culture." In *Selections from the Prison Notebooks,* edited by Quintin Hoare and Geoffrey Nowell Smith, 416–18. New York: International Publishers, 1971.

Gran, Peter. *Beyond Eurocentrism: A New View of Modern World History.* Syracuse: Syracuse Univ. Press, 1996.

———. "Egypt and Italy, 1760–1850: Toward a Comparative History." In *Society and Economy in Egypt and the Eastern Mediterranean, 1600–1900,* edited by Nelly Hanna and Raouf Abbas, 11–40. Cairo: AUC Press, 2005.

———. "Gramsci el principal teorica de la transformacion socialista temprana." In *Poder y hegemonia: Gramsci en la era global,* edited by Dora Kanoussi. Mexico City: BUAP–Instituto Gramsci–IGS, Plaza y Valdes, 2004.

———. *Islamic Roots of Capitalism: Egypt, 1760–1840.* 2d ed. 1979. Reprint, Syracuse: Syracuse Univ. Press, 1998.

———. "Late Eighteenth–Early Nineteenth Century Egypt: Merchant Capital or Modern Capitalism?" In *The Ottoman Empire and the World Economy,* edited by Huri Islamoglu, 27–41. Cambridge: Cambridge Univ. Press, 1987.

———. "Modern Middle Eastern History Beyond Oriental Despotism, World History Beyond Hegel: An Agenda Article." *Cairo Papers in Social Science* 23, no. 2 (2001): 162–99.

———. "Modern World History as the Rise of the Rich: A New Paradigm." *History Compass* 5, no. 3 (2007): 1026–49.

———. *Subaltern Studies, Racism, and Class Struggle: Examples from India and the United States.* Working Paper Series. Pullman, Wash.: Comparative American Cultures, 1999.

Green, Marcus. "Gramsci Cannot Speak: Presentations and Interpretations of Gramsci's Concept of the Subaltern." *Rethinking Marxism* 14, no. 3 (Fall 2002): 1–24.

Greer, Jed, and Kavaljit Singh. "A Brief History of Transnational Corporations." http://www.globalpolicy.org/socecon/tncs/historytncs/html.

Grewal, Inderpal, and Caren Kaplan. "Postcolonial Studies and Transnational Feminist Practices." *Jouvert* 5, no. 1 (2000).

Griffin, Larry K., and Robert B. Korstad. "Historical Inference and Event Structure Analysis." *International Review of Social History* 43 (1998): 145–65.

Gunder Frank, André. *ReOrient.* Berkeley and Los Angeles: Univ. of California Press, 1998.

Haberland, Eike. *Three Hundred Years of Ethiopian-German Academic Collaboration.* Wiesbaden: Steiner, 1986.

Hadari, Zeinabou. "Qur'anic-Based Literacy and Islamic Education: A Basis for Female Empowerment in Niger." Ph.D. thesis, Temple Univ., 2005.

Haigh, Robert W. *Investment Strategies and the Plant-Location Decision: Foreign Companies in the United States.* Westport, Conn.: Praeger Press, 1989.

Hall, Anthony J. *The American Empire and the Fourth World: The Bowl with One Spoon.* Vol. 1. Montreal: McGill-Queen's Univ. Press, 2003.

Hall, Stuart, ed. *The Hard Road to Renewal: Thatcherism and the Crisis of the Left.* London: Verso Press, 1988.

Haller, Mark. "Historical Roots of Police Behavior: Chicago, 1890–1925." *Law and Society Review* 10 (Winter 1976): 303–23.

———. "Illegal Enterprise: A Theoretical and Historical Interpretation." *Criminology* 28, no. 2 (May 1990): 207–35.

Hanna, Nelly. *In Praise of Books: A Cultural History of Cairo's Middle Class, Sixteenth to the Eighteenth Century.* Syracuse: Syracuse Univ. Press, 2003.

Harman, Chris. *A People's History of the World.* Chicago: Bookmarks, 1999.

———. "The Workers of the World." *International Socialism Journalism,* no. 96 (Aug. 2002). Available online at http://pubs.socialistreviewindex.org.uk/isj96/harman.htm.

Harris, Nigel. *The End of the Third World: Newly Industrializing Countries and the Decline of an Ideology.* London: I. B. Tauris, 1986.

Harrod, Jeffrey, and Robert O'Brien, eds. *Global Unions? Theory and Strategies of Organized Labour in the Global Political Economy.* London: Routledge, 2002.

Harvey, David. "The Practical Contradictions of Marxism." *Critical Sociology* 24, nos. 1–2 (1998): 1–36.

Hatchard, John. "States of Siege/Emergency." *Journal of African Law* 37, no. 1 (Spring 1993): 29–36.

Hathaway, Dale A. *Can Workers Have a Voice? The Politics of Deindustrialization in Pittsburgh.* University Park: Pennsylvania State Univ. Press, 1993.

Head, Ivan L. *On a Hinge of History: The Mutual Vulnerabilities of South and North.* Toronto: Univ. of Toronto Press, 1991.

Headrick, Daniel R. *The Tools of Empire: Technology and European Imperialism in the Nineteenth Century.* Oxford: Oxford Univ. Press, 1981.

Heidenheimer, Arnold J., and Michael Johnston, eds. *Political Corruption.* New Brunswick, N.J.: Transaction Press, 2002.

Helleiner, Eric. "Post-globalization: Is the Financial Liberalization Trend Likely to Be Reversed?" In *States Against Markets,* edited by Robert Boyer and Daniel Drache. London: Routledge, 1996.

Herbst, Susan. *Numbered Voices: How Opinion Polling Has Shaped American Politics.* Chicago: Univ. of Chicago Press, 1993.

Hertner, Peter, and Geoffrey Jones, eds. *Multinationals: Theory and History.* Aldershot, England: Gower, 1986.

Hobden, Stephen. *International Relations and Historical Sociology: Breaking Down Boundaries.* London: Routledge, 1998.

Hobsbawm, Eric. *Pre-capitalist Economic Formations.* London: Lawrence and Wishart, 1964.

Hobson, John M., and J. C. Sharman. "The Enduring Place of Hierarchy in World Politics: Tracing the Social Logics of Hierarchy and Political Change." *European Journal of International Relations* 11, no. 1 (2005): 63–98.

Hodges, Donald, and Ross Gandy. *Mexico under Siege: Popular Resistance to Presidential Despotism.* London: Zed Press, 2002.

Holsti, Ole. "Public Opinion and Foreign Policy: Challenges to the Almond-Lippmann Consensus Mershon Series, Research Program, and Debates." *International Studies Quarterly* 36 (1992): 439–66.

Holthoon, Frits Van, and Marcel Van Der Linden, eds. *Internationalism in the Labour Movement, 1830–1940.* Vol. 1. Leiden: Brill, 1988.

Hopkins, A. G., ed. *Globalization in World History.* New York: W. W. Norton, 2002.

Hostetler, Laura. *Qing Colonial Enterprise: Ethnography and Cartography in Early Modern China.* Chicago: Univ. of Chicago Press, 2001.

Huntington, Samuel. "Clash of Civilizations." *Foreign Affairs* 72 (1993): 22–49.

———. *Who Are We? The Challenges to America's National Identity.* New York: Simon and Schuster, 2004.

———. "Why International Primacy Matters." *International Security* 17, no. 4 (1993): 68–83.

Hurewitz, Jacob. *Diplomacy in the Near and Middle East.* Vol. 1. Princeton: D. Van Nostrand, 1956.

Hussain, Nasser. *The Jurisprudence of Emergency: Colonialism and the Rule of Law.* Ann Arbor: Univ. of Michigan Press, 2003.

Indyk, Martin. "The Politics of Patronage: Israel and Egypt Between the Superpowers, 1962–1973." Ph.D. thesis, Australian National Univ., 1977.

Inikori, Joseph E. *Africans and the Industrial Revolution in England.* Cambridge: Cambridge Univ. Press, 2002.

Isaak, Robert A. *The Globalization Gap: How the Rich Get Richer and the Poor Get Left Further Behind.* Upper Saddle River, N.J.: Prentice-Hall / Financial Times, 2005.

Israel, J. I. "Mexico and the 'General Crisis' of the Seventeenth Century." *Past and Present,* no. 63 (May 1974): 33–57.

Jacobson, Kyle Rex. "Doing Business with the Devil: The Challenges of Prosecuting Corporate Officials Whose Business Transactions Facilitate War Crimes and Crimes Against Humanity." *Air Force Law Review* 56 (2005): 167–220.

Jacoby, Neil. *Bribery and Extortion in World Business: A Study of Corporate Political Payments Abroad.* London: Macmillan, 1977.

Jentleson, Bruce W. *With Friends Like These: Reagan, Bush, and Saddam, 1982–1990.* New York: W. W. Norton, 1994.

Johnson, Michael. "International Corruption via Campaign Contribution." Unpublished working paper for Transparency International, 2000.

Joly, Daniele, ed. *Scapegoats and Social Actors: The Exclusion and Integration of Minorities in Western and Eastern Europe.* Basingstoke, England: Macmillan, 1998.

Jones, Geoffrey, and Lina Galvez-Munoz, eds. *Foreign Multinationals in the United States: Management and Performance.* London: Routledge, 2002.

Jones, Richard H. *Reductionism: Analysis and the Fullness of Reality.* Lewisburg, Pa.: Bucknell Univ. Press, 2000.

Jospin, Lionel. *Le monde comme je le vois.* Paris: Ed. Gallimard, 2005.

Kang, David C. *Crony Capitalism: Corruption and Development in South Korea and the Philippines.* Cambridge: Cambridge Univ. Press, 2002.

Kaplan, Robert D. *Imperial Grunts: The American Military on the Ground.* New York: Random House, 2005.

Karam, Azza, ed. *Transnational Political Islam: Religion, Ideology, and Power.* London: Pluto Press, 2004.

Kautsky, John H. *Marxism and Leninism, Not Marxism-Leninism: An Essay in the Sociology of Knowledge.* Westport, Conn.: Greenwood Press, 1994.

al-Khashshab, Isma'il. *Le Diwan du Caire, 1800–1801.* Translated by Andre Raymond and Muhammad 'Afifi. Cairo: IFAO, 2003.

Kingsbury, Benedict. "Indigenous People in International Law: A Constructivist Approach to the Asian Controversy." *American Journal of International Law* 92, no. 3 (July 1998): 414–57.

Kowalewski, David. *Global Establishment: The Political Economy of North/Asian Networks.* New York: St. Martins Press, 1997.

Kposowa, Augustine J. *The Impact of Immigration on the United States Economy.* Lanham, Md.: Univ. Press of America, 1998.

Krueger, Anne O. "Why Crony Capitalism Is Bad for Economic Growth." In *Crony Capitalism and Economic Growth in Latin America: Theory and Evidence,* edited by Stephen Haber, 1–24. Stanford: Hoover Institution Press, 2002.

Kuhn, Thomas S. *The Structure of Scientific Revolutions.* Chicago: Univ. of Chicago Press, 1996.

Lachmann, Richard. "Comparisons Within a Single Social Formation: A Critical Appreciation of Perry Anderson's *Lineages of the Absolutist State.*" *Qualitative Sociology* 25, no. 1 (Spring 2002): 83–92.

Laclau, Ernesto, and Chantal Mouffe. *Hegemony and Socialist Strategy: Towards a Radical Democratic Politics.* London: Verso Press, 2001.

Lambert, Robert. "Labour Movements in the Era of Globalization: Union Responses in the South." In *Global Unions? Theory and Strategies of Organized Labour in the Global Political Economy,* edited by Jeffrey Herrod and Robert O'Brien. London: Routledge, 2002.

Lambert, Robert, and Edward Webster. "Southern Unionism and the New Labour Internationalism." *Antipode* 33 (2001): 327–62.

———. "What Is New in the New Labour Internationalism? A Southern Perspective." Unpublished paper, Leeds Metropolitan University Workshop, May 2003.

Larson, Magali Sarfatti. "Proletarianization and Educated Labor." *Theory and Society* 9, no. 1 (1980): 131–75.

Laurenti, Jeffrey. "Grand Goals, Modest Results: The UN in Search of Reform." *Current History* 104, no. 686 (Dec. 2005): 431–37.

Law, Robin. *From Slave Trade to "Legitimate" Commerce: The Commercial Transition in Nineteenth-Century West Africa.* Cambridge: Cambridge Univ. Press, 1995.

———. "The Politics of Commercial Transition: Factional Conflict in Dahomey in the Context of the Ending of the Atlantic Slave Trade." *Journal of African History* 38, no. 2 (1997): 213–33.

Lawindi, Sa'id. *'Ama'im wa tarabish-misriyun 'ashu fi Baris*. Cairo: Dar Iji Misr, 2000.

Lazonick, William. *Business Organization and the Myth of the Market Economy*. Cambridge: Cambridge Univ. Press, 1991.

Lee, Chung Hee. *Foreign Lobbying in American Politics*. Seoul: American Studies Institute / SNU, 1998.

Leng, Thomas. "Commercial Conflict and Regulation in the Discourse of Trade in Seventeenth-Century England." *Historical Journal* 48 (2005): 933–54.

Lennon, David Charles, and Kathleen Lennon, eds. *Reduction, Explanation, and Realism*. Oxford: Clarendon Press, 1992.

León-Portilla, Miguel. *The Broken Spears: The Aztec Account of the Conquest of Mexico*. Boston: Beacon Press, 1992.

Levine, David, ed. *Proletarianization and Family History*. Orlando: Academic Press, 1984.

Lieberman, Victor. *Strange Parallels: Southeast Asia in Global Context*. Cambridge: Cambridge Univ. Press, 2003.

Lis, Catharina, and Hugo Soly. "Policing the Early Modern Proletariat, 1450–1850." In *Proletarianization and Family History*, edited by David Levine. Orlando: Academic Press, 1984.

Lobel, Jules. "Emergency Powers and the Decline of Liberalism." *Yale Law Journal* 98, no. 7 (1989): 1385–1433.

Lomnitz-Adler, Claudio. *Exits from the Labyrinth: Culture and Ideology in the Mexican National Space*. Berkeley and Los Angeles: Univ. of California Press, 1992.

Lovell, Stephen, et al. *Bribery and Blat in Russia*. London: Macmillan, 2000.

Lugard, Lord [Frederick Lugard]. *The Dual Mandate in British Tropical Africa*. London: Cass, 1965.

Mackenzie, John. "The Continuing Avalanche of Historical Mutations: The New 'New Social Movements.'" *Social Alternatives* 23, no. 1 (2004): 50–55.

Maddox, Robert Franklin. *The War Within World War II: The United States and International Cartels*. Westport, Conn.: Praeger, 2001.

Mangone, Gerald. *A Short History of International Organization*. Westport, Conn.: Greenwood Press, 1975.

Mann, Bruce H. "Failure in the Land of the Free." *American Bankruptcy Law Journal* 77 (Winter 2003): 1–6.

———. *Republic of Debtors: Bankruptcy in the Age of American Independence*. Cambridge: Harvard Univ. Press, 2002.

Manning, Patrick. *Migration in World History*. New York: Routledge, 2005.

———. *Navigating World History: Historians Create a Global Past.* New York: Palgrave-Macmillan, 2003.

———. *Slavery and African Life.* Cambridge: Cambridge Univ. Press, 1990.

Marcus, George. *Lives in Trust: The Fortunes of Dynastic Families in Late-Twentieth-Century America.* Boulder: Westview Press, 1992.

Marshall, Gordon. "Proletarianization in the British Class Structure?" *British Journal of Sociology* 39, no. 4 (Dec. 1988): 498–519.

Marsot, Afaf Lutfi al-Sayyid. *Egypt in the Reign of Muhammad Ali.* Cambridge: Cambridge Univ. Press, 1984.

Martens, Kerstin. "Mission Impossible? Defining Non-governmental Organizations." *Voluntas* 13, no. 3 (Sept. 2002): 271–85.

Marti, Jose. *Inside the Monster: Writings on the United States and American Imperialism.* New York: Monthly Review Press, 1975.

Masters, Bruce. *The Origins of Western Economic Dominance in the Middle East: Mercantilism and the Islamic Economy in Aleppo, 1600–1750.* New York: New York Univ. Press, 1988.

Matar, Nabil. *In the Lands of the Christians: Arabic Travel Writing in the Seventeenth Century.* New York: Routledge, 2003.

———. *Islam in Britain, 1558–1685.* Cambridge: Cambridge Univ. Press, 1998.

———. "The Last Moors: Maghariba in Early-Eighteenth-Century Britain." *Journal of Islamic Studies* 14 (2003): 37–58.

Mayer, Robert. "Marx, Lenin, and the Corruption of the Working Class." *Political Studies* 41 (1993): 636–49.

McAllister, Brad. "Al-Qaeda and the Innovative Firm: Demythologizing the Network." *Studies in Conflict and Terrorism* 27 (2004): 297–319.

McCahill, Michael W. "Peers, Patronage, and the Industrial Revolution, 1760–1800." *Journal of British Studies* 16, no. 1 (1976): 84–107.

McKinley, James, Jr. "A Guide for the Illegal Migrant." *New York Times,* Jan. 9, 2005, 5.

Megill, Allan. *The Burden of Reason: Why Marx Rejected Politics and the Market.* Lanham, Md.: Rowman and Littlefield, 2002.

Mexico-North Research Network, Transnationalism Research Project Database. "On Transnationalism." http://www.mexnor.org/programs/TRP/Ontransnat .pdf.

Mhone, Guy C. *The Political Economy of a Dual Labor Market in Africa: The Copper Industry and Dependency in Zambia, 1929–1969.* Rutherford, N.J.: Fairleigh Dickinson Univ. Press, 1982.

Milward, Alan S. *The European Rescue of the Nation-State.* 2d ed. London: Routledge, 2000.

Moghadam, Valentine. "Gender and Globalization: Female Labor and Women's Mobilization." *Journal of World Systems Research* 5, no. 2 (1999): 301–14.

Morphet, Sally. "Multilateralism and the Non-Aligned Movement: What Is the Global South Doing and Where Is It Going?" *Global Governance* 10 (2004): 517–37.

Morrill, Calvin, Mayer N. Zald, and Hayagreeva Rao. "Covert Political Conflict in Organizations: Challenges from Below." *Annual Review of Sociology* 29 (2003): 391–417.

Morris, Stephen D. "Between Neo-liberalism and Neo-*indigenismo:* Reconstructing National Identity in Mexico." *National Identities* 3, no. 3 (Nov. 2001): 239–55.

Morton, Adam David. *"La resurreccion del Maiz:* Globalization, Resistance, and the Zapatistas." *Millennium: Journal of International Studies* 31 (2002): 27–54.

———. *Unravelling Gramsci: Hegemony and Passive Revolution in the Global Economy.* London: Pluto Press, 2007.

Nash, June. "The Fiesta of the Word: The Zapatista Uprising and Radical Democracy in America." *American Anthropologist* 99 (1997): 261–74.

Negri, Antonio, and Michael Hardt. *Empire.* Cambridge: Harvard Univ. Press, 2000.

Nield, Keith. "A Symptomatic Dispute? Notes on the Relation Between Marxian Theory and Historical Practice in Britain." *Social Research* 47 (1980): 479–506.

Northrup, David. *Africa's Discovery of Europe, 1450–1850.* Oxford: Oxford Univ. Press, 2002.

Nowell, Gregory P. *Mercantile States and the World Oil Cartel, 1900–1939.* Ithaca: Cornell Univ. Press, 1994.

Obeyesekere, Gananath. *The Apotheosis of Captain Cook.* Princeton: Princeton Univ. Press, 1992.

Olney, Peter. "To Renew, Labor Must Look at Its Foreign Policy." *Social Policy* 34, nos. 2–3 (2003–4): 9–15.

Ondrich, Jan, and Michael Wasylenko. *Foreign Direct Investment in the United States.* Syracuse: Syracuse Univ. Press, 1993.

Orozco, Manuel. "Globalization and Migration: The Impact of Family Remittances in Latin America." *Latin American Politics and Society* 44, no. 2 (2002): 41–67.

O'Sullivan, Christopher. "The United Nations, Decolonization, and Self-Determination in Cold War Sub-Saharan Africa, 1960–1994." *Journal of Third World Studies* 22, no. 2 (2005): 103–20.

Ougaard, Morten. *Political Globalization: State, Power, and Social Forces.* London: Palgrave-Macmillan, 2004.

Oweiss, Ibrahim M. *Impediments to Arab Investment in the United States.* IBK Papers, no. 17. Kuwait City: Industrial Bank of Kuwait, 1985.

Paige, Suzanne. *Exporting Workers: The Turkish Case.* Cambridge: Cambridge Univ. Press, 1974.

Parker, Geoffrey, and Lesley M. Smith, eds. *The General Crisis of the Seventeenth Century.* New York: Routledge, 1997.

Passas, Nikos. "The Genesis of the BCCI Scandal." *Journal of Law and Society* 23, no. 1 (Mar. 1996): 57–72.

Passavant, Paul A., and Jodi Dean, eds. *Empire's New Clothes.* New York: Routledge, 2004.

Perle, Richard. "The Strategic Impact of Technology Transfer." In *Selling the Rope to Hang Capitalism,* edited by Charles M. Perry and Robert L. Pfaltzgraff, 3–9. Washington, D.C.: Pergamon-Brassey, 1987.

Persaud, Randolph B. *Counter-hegemony and Foreign Policy: The Dialectics of Marginalized and Global Forces in Jamaica.* Albany: SUNY Press, 2001.

Petras, James. *The Left Strikes Back.* Boulder: Westview Press, 1999.

———. *The New Development Politics.* Burlington, Vt.: Ashgate, 2003.

Phillips, Kevin. *American Dynasty.* New York: Viking, 2004.

———. *The Politics of Rich and Poor.* New York: Harper Perennial, 1991.

Pichardo, Nelson A. "New Social Movements: A Critical Review." *Annual Review of Sociology* 23 (1997): 411–30.

Pocock, J. G. A., ed. *Three British Revolutions, 1641, 1688, 1776.* Princeton: Princeton Univ. Press, 1980.

Pomerantz, Kenneth. *The Great Divergence: China, Europe, and the Making of the Modern World Economy.* Princeton: Princeton Univ. Press, 2000.

Popovic, Sanya. "Review." *Political Science Quarterly* 110, no. 3 (Autumn 1995): 485–87.

Potter, Pitman B. "Origins of the System of Mandates under the League of Nations." *American Political Science Review* 16, no. 4 (1922): 563–83.

Quijano, Anibal. "Coloniality of Power and Eurocentrism in Latin America." *International Sociology* 15, no. 2 (2000): 215–32.

Quintanilla, Mark. "Mercantile Communities in the Ceded Islands: The Alexander Bartlet and George Campbell Company." *International Social Science Review* 79, nos. 1–2 (2004): 14–27.

Rashid, Salim. *The Myth of Adam Smith.* Cheltenham, England: Edward Elgar, 1998.

Reid, Anthony. *Charting the Shape of Early Modern Southeast Asia.* Chiang Mai: Silkworm Books, 1999.

Rhoads, Robert A. "Globalization and Resistance in the United States and Mexico: The Global Potemkin Village." *Higher Education* 45 (2003): 223–50.

Richards, John F. "The Seventeenth-Century Crisis in South Asia." *Modern Asian Studies* 24, no. 4 (1990): 625–38.

Ridley, Ronald. *Napoleon's Proconsul in Egypt: The Life and Times of Bernardino Drovetti.* London: Rubicon Press, 1998.

Ritzer, George. *The Globalization of Nothing.* London: Pine Forge Press, 2004.

Robertson, Robbie. *The Three Waves of Globalization: A History of a Developing Global Consciousness.* London: Zed Press, 2003.

Robinson, William I., and Jerry Harris. "Towards a Global Ruling Class? Globalization and the Transnationalist Capitalist Class." *Science and Society* 64, no. 1 (Spring 2000): 11–54.

Roche, Maurice, and Rik Van Berkel, eds. *European Citizenship and Social Exclusion.* Aldershot, England: Ashgate, 1997.

Roman, Richard, and Edur Velasco Arregui. "Worker Insurgency, Rural Revolt, and the Crisis of the Mexican Regime." In *Rising from the Ashes? Labor in the Age of Global Capitalism,* edited by Ellen Meiksins Wood, Peter Meiksins, and Michael Yates, 127–41. New York: Monthly Review Press, 1998.

Romero, Matias. *Mexican Lobby.* Lexington: Univ. Press of Kentucky, 1986.

———. *A Mexican View of America in the 1860s: A Foreign Diplomat Describes the Civil War and Reconstruction.* Cranbury, N.J.: Associated Univ. Press, 1991.

Rose, Fred. "Toward a Class-Cultural Theory of Social Movements: Reinterpreting New Social Movements." *Sociological Forum* 12, no. 3 (1977): 461–94.

Rosenblum, Marc R. "Moving Beyond the Policy of No Policy: Emigration from Mexico and Central America." *Latin American Politics and Society* 46, no. 4 (2004): 91–125.

Rubies, Joan-Pau. "Oriental Despotism and European Orientalism: Botero to Montesquieu." *Journal of Early Modern History* 9 (2005): 109–80.

Ruggie, John Gerard. "Multilateralism at Century's End." In *Constructing the World Polity*, edited by John Gerard Ruggie. London: Routledge, 1998.

———, ed. *Multilateralism Matters*. New York: Columbia Univ. Press, 1993.

Sahlins, Marshall. *How "Natives" Think: About Captain Cook*. Chicago: Univ. of Chicago Press, 1995.

Sassens, Saskia. *Cities in a World Economy*. London: Pine Forge Press, 2000.

———. "The De Facto Transnationalizing of Immigration Policy." In *Challenge to the Nation State: Immigration in Western Europe and the United States*, edited by Christian Joppke. Oxford: Oxford Univ. Press, 1998.

Schedler, Andreas, et al. *The Self-Restraining State: Power and Accountability in the New Democracies*. Boulder: Lynne Rienner, 1999.

Schmenner, Roger W. "Geography and the Character and Performance of Factories." In *Industry Location and Public Policy*, edited by Henry W. Herzog Jr. and Alan M. Schlottmann. Knoxville: Univ. of Tennessee Press, 1991.

Schneider, William, Jr. "Technology Transfer and U.S. Foreign Policy." In *Selling the Rope to Hang Capitalism*, edited by Charles M. Perry and Robert L. Pfaltzgraff, 83–87. Washington, D.C.: Pergamon-Brassey, 1987.

Schroeder, Paul W. "The Transformation of Political Thinking, 1787–1848." In *Coping with Complexity in the International System*, edited by Jack Snyder and Robert Jervis. Boulder: Westview Press, 1993.

Schwartz, Stuart B. "Expansion, Diaspora, and Encounter in the Early Modern South Atlantic." *Itinerario* 19, no. 2 (1995): 48–59.

Scott, Andrew M. *The Revolution in Statecraft: Informal Penetration*. New York: Random House, 1965.

Scott, Peter Dale. *Deep Politics and the Death of JFK*. Berkeley and Los Angeles: Univ. of California Press, 1996.

Seigel, Micol. "Beyond Compare: Comparative Method after the Transnational Turn." *Radical History Review*, no. 91 (Winter 2005): 62–90.

Senghaas, Dieter. *The Clash Within Civilizations*. London: Routledge, 2002.

Sexton, Jay. "Toward a Synthesis of Foreign Relations in the Civil War Era, 1848–1877." *American Nineteenth Century History* 5, no. 3 (2004): 50–74.

Sfakianakis, John. "The Whales of the Nile: Networks, Businessmen, and Bureaucrats During the Era of Privatization in Egypt." In *Networks of Privilege in the Middle East: The Politics of Economic Reform Revisited*, edited by Steven Heydemann, 77–100. New York: Palgrave-Macmillan, 2004.

Singerman, Diane. "Egypt." *Current History* 107 (Jan. 2002): 29–36.

Sinjela, Mpazi, and Robin Ramcharan. "Protecting Traditional Knowledge and Traditional Medicines of Indigenous Peoples Through Intellectual Property Rights: Issues, Challenges, and Strategies." *International Journal on Minority and Group Rights* 12 (2005): 1–24.

Sklair, Leslie. *The Transnational Capitalist Class.* Malden, Mass.: Blackwell, 2001.

Sklair, Leslie, and Peter T. Robbins. "Global Capitalism and Major Corporations from the Third World." *Third World Quarterly* 23, no. 1 (2002): 81–100.

Sklar, Holly, ed. *Trilateralism: The Trilateral Commission and Elite Management for World Management.* Boston: South End Press, 1980.

Slaughter, Anne-Marie. *A New World Order.* Princeton: Princeton Univ. Press, 2004.

Smith, Dwight C., Jr. "Paragons, Pariahs, and Pirates: A Spectrum-Based Theory of Enterprise." *Crime and Delinquency* 26 (1980): 368–86.

Sonbol, Amira. *The New Mamluks: Egyptian Society and Modern Feudalism.* Syracuse: Syracuse Univ. Press, 2000.

Sorenson, Georg. *The Transformation of the State: Beyond the Myth of Retreat.* Houndsmill, England: Macmillan/Palgrave, 2004.

Stavrianos, Leften. *Global Rift: The Third World Comes of Age.* New York: Morrow, 1981.

Stearns, Peter. *Consumerism in World History: The Great Transformation of Desire.* New York: Routledge, 2002.

Steensgaard, Niels. "The Seventeenth-Century Crisis and the Unity of Eurasian History." *Modern Asian History* 24, no. 4 (Oct. 1990): 683–97.

Steiner, Ivan. "Primary Group Influences on Public Opinion." *American Sociological Review* 19 (June 1954): 261–67.

Steinmetz, George. "Regulation Theory, Post-Marxism, and New Social Movements." *Comparative Studies in Society and History* 36, no. 1 (1994): 176–212.

Stern, Steve J. "Feudalism, Capitalism, and the World-System in Perspective of Latin America and the Caribbean." *American Historical Review* 93, no. 4 (1988): 829–72.

Suri, Jeremi. *Power and Protest: Global Revolution and the Rise of Détente.* Cambridge: Harvard Univ. Press, 2003.

Teivainen, Teivo. *Enter Economism, Exit Politics.* London: Zed Press, 2002.

Thachuk, Kimberley. "Corruption and International Security." *SAIS Review* 25, no. 1 (2005): 415–28.

Thompson, E. P. *The Making of the English Working Class*. New York: Vintage Press, 1963.

Thornton, John K. *Africa and Africans in the Making of the Atlantic World, 1400–1800*. Cambridge: Cambridge Univ. Press, 1998.

———. "The Role of Africans in the Atlantic Economy, 1450–1650: Modern Africanist Historiography and the World-Systems Paradigm." *Colonial Latin American Historical Review* 3, no. 2 (1994): 125–40.

Tibebu, Teshale. "On the Question of Feudalism, Absolutism, and Bourgeois Revolution." *Review: A Journal of the Fernand Braudel Center* 13, no. 1 (Winter 1990): 49–152.

Tolchin, Martin, and Susan Tolchin. *Buying into America: How Foreign Money Is Changing the Face of Our Nation*. New York: Times Book, 1988.

———. *Selling Our Security: The Erosion of America's Assets*. New York: Alfred A. Knopf, 1992.

Tonelson, Alan. *The Race to the Bottom: Why a Worldwide Worker Surplus and Uncontrolled Free Trade Are Sinking American Living Standards*. Boulder: Westview Press, 2000.

Twain, Mark. *The Gilded Age*. Hartford, Conn.: American Publishing, 1873.

Ungar, Sheldon. "Misplaced Metaphor: A Critical Analysis of the 'Knowledge Society.'" *Canadian Review of Sociology and Anthropology* 40, no. 3 (August 2003): 331–48.

Unger, Craig. *House of Bush, House of Saud: The Secret Relationship Between the World's Two Most Powerful Dynasties*. New York: Scribner, 2003.

Vellinga, Menno, ed. *The Political Economy of the Drug Industry: Latin America and the International System*. Gainesville: Univ. Press of Florida, 2004.

Weeks, Emily M. "About Face: Sir David Wilkie's Portrait of Mehemet Ali." In *Orientalism Transposed: The Impact of the Colonies on British Culture*, edited by Julie F. Codell and Dianne Sachko Macleod. Aldershot, England: Ashgate Publishing, 1998.

Wehler, Hans-Ulrich. *The German Empire, 1871–1918*. Dover, N.H.: Berg, 1985.

Weakliem, David L., and Casey Bosch. "Alienation in the United States: Uniform or Group Specific Change?" *Sociological Forum* 21, no. 3 (2006): 415–38.

Weinbaum, Marvin. *Egypt and the Politics of U.S. Economic Aid*. Boulder: Westview Press, 1986.

Weiss, Linda. "Explaining the Underground Economy: State and Social Structure." *British Journal of Sociology* 38, no. 2 (1986): 216–34.

―――. "Is the State Being Transformed?" In *States in the Global Economy: Bringing Domestic Institutions Back In,* edited by Linda Weiss. Cambridge: Cambridge Univ. Press, 2003.

Wilkins, Mira. "Foreign Companies in the U.S., 1945–2000." In *Foreign Multinationals in the United States: Management and Performance,* edited by Geoffrey Jones and Lina Galvez-Munoz. London: Routledge, 2002.

―――. *The History of Foreign Investment in the United States to 1914.* Cambridge: Harvard Univ. Press, 1989.

Wilkins, Mira, and Harm Schroter, eds. *The Free-Standing Company in the World Economy, 1830–1996.* Oxford: Oxford Univ. Press, 1998.

Wills, John E., Jr. "Maritime Asia, 1500–1899: The Interactive Emergence of European Domination." *American Historical Review* 98 (Feb. 1993): 83–105.

Windler, Christian. "Tributes and Presents in Franco-Tunisian Diplomacy." *Journal of Early Modern History* 4, no. 2 (2000): 168–99.

Wolfowitz, Paul, ed. *Managing the International System over the Next Century.* New York: Trilateral Commission, 1996.

Wong, R. Bin. "The Search for European Differences and Domination in the Early Modern World: A View from Asia." *American Historical Review* 107 (Apr. 2002): 447–69.

Wood, Ellen Meiksins. *Empire of Capital.* London: Verso Press, 2003.

―――. *The Origin of Capitalism: A Longer View.* London: Verso Press, 2002.

Wood, Ellen Meiksins, and Neal Wood. *A Trumpet of Sedition: Political Theory and the Rise of Capitalism, 1509–1688.* New York: New York Univ. Press, 1997.

Wood, Geoffrey, and Chris Brewster. "Decline and Renewal in the British Labour Movement: Trends, Practices, and Lessons for South Africa." *Society in Transition* 33, no. 2 (2002): 241–57.

Woodiwiss, Michael. *Organized Crime and American Power.* Toronto: Univ. of Toronto Press, 2001.

Woodward, Douglas P., and Norman J. Glickman. "Regional and Local Determinants of Foreign Firm Location in the United States." In *Industry Location and Public Policy,* edited by Henry W. Herzog Jr. and Alan M. Schlottmann. Knoxville: Univ. of Tennessee Press, 1991.

Woolf, Stuart. "The Construction of a European World-View in the Revolutionary-Napoleonic Years." *Past and Present,* no. 137 (Nov. 1992): 72–101.

Worth, Owen. "The Janus-Like Character of Counter-hegemony: Progressive and National Responses to Neo-liberalism." *Global Society* 16, no. 3 (2002): 297–315.

Worth, Owen, and Carmen Kuhling. "Counter-hegemony, Anti-globalisation, and Culture in International Political Economy." *Capital and Class*, no. 84 (2002): 31–42.

Yasumuro, Kenichi. "Japanese Multinational Location Strategies." In *Foreign Multinationals in the United States: Management and Performance*, edited by Geoffrey Jones and Lina Galvez-Munoz. London: Routledge, 2002.

Zaalouk, Malak. *Power, Class, and Foreign Capital in Egypt: The Rise of the New Bourgeoisie*. London: Zed Press, 1989.

INDEX

Rise of the West paradigm: corporations and, 3; description of, x–xiii; eighteenth century study and, 79–80; as an end of revolution, xxviii; Eurocentrism of, xi–xii, xiv, xxix–xxx; great power unilateralism in, 206n. 40; liberalism and, xxi, xxiii–xxiv; Marxism and, xxi, xxiii–xxiv; New Liberalism and, 59; periodization to other areas of the world, 16; periods of crisis and, xv, 182; preservation of, 1, 59, 186; social history and, 185; Third World and, xii–xiii; transnationalism and, 5

Risk Society, 26–27, 28–32

Robertson, Robbie, 195n. 9

rocket technology, 168

Rose, Fred, 197n. 2

Rubies, Joan-Paul, 202n. 9

rule by civilization, 107, 112

rule by law, 107, 112–15

rule by state of emergency. *See* state of emergency rule

rulers: accountability and transparency from, 31; bilateral relations and, 61; class conflict and, 24; in contemporary history, xxvii; crimes against humanity and, 114; fear of their subjects, xxviii; nation-state sovereignty and, 48; New Men and, 72–73; personal safety of, xxvii; position of strength for, 129; primitive accumulation facilitated by, 116; public opinion polls and, 133; symbiotic relations among, 71; world policeman and, 128

ruling classes: collaboration by, 72; core, 148–49, 176; cultural hegemony and, 41; European goods for, 71–72; factory relocation and, 163; foreign, xxix; Industrial Revolution and, 80–81; interests of, 87–88, 192n. 7;

liberation of mass populations and, 18; luxury goods and, 16–17; Mexican immigrants and, 173, 174–77; multilateralism and, 145, 185; periphery, 176, 184; political, 155; power elites, 192n. 7; privacy for, 216n. 16; proletarianization and, 74; provincial, 86–87; rank in, 104; redistribution to, 184; rights of, 89; Rise of the Rich paradigm and, xxv; security and, 79; treaties and, 87–88; tribal-ethnic states and, 57–58; United States, xxviii; Westerners as, xiv; world, xiv, 192n. 7. *See also* Third World ruling classes

rural to urban migration, 10

Russian Empire, 87, 93

Russian Revolution, 51, 101

Russian Road states, 56–57, 90–93, 94, 154

Rust Belt, 151

Rwanda, 114

al-Sadat, Anwar, 118–19

Sahlins, Marshall, 206–7n. 42

Said, Edward, 207n. 42

sales, 62–63

San Andreas Peace Accords, 33–34

San Francisco Conference (1945), 106

SAPs (Structural Adjustment Programs), 134–38

Sarajevo, 100

Sa'ud dynasty, 12

Saudi Arabia, 58, 151, 159, 162

Saul, John, 209n. 1

Schiller, Daniel, 212n. 30

Schiller, Herbert, 212n. 30

Schmidt, Arthur, 176

Schneider, William, Jr., 168

scholarship, 98–99, 200n. 29

unilateralism, 106, 206n. 40

unions. *See* trade unions

United Auto Workers, 160

United Kingdom: alliance with the U.S., 56; capitulation treaties with, 94–95; Chinese in, 11; Egyptian independence and, 118; Emergency Powers Act, 129; European Union and, 13; feudalism in, 75–76; foreign lobbyists from, 151; as the great power, 103; Industrial Revolution in, 73, 80–81, 205n. 34; mandate system, 108; Marxism on, 20; moral economy protests, 72, 73; Palestine Mandate, 108, 109; peerage, 75, 81, 205n. 34; proletarianization in, 61, 74–78, 204n. 29; ruling classes, 80–81; state of emergency rule and, 129–30; working class in, 75, 77. *See also* British Empire

United Nations, 115, 121, 156

United States: Amerindian peoples and, 83–84, 206n. 38; automobile industry, 5, 160, 166, 169–70, 178; Bill of Rights, 130; capitalism of, 38; core culture of, 161, 179–80; crisis in, xv, 185, 186–87, 191n. 1; debtors in, 81, 205n. 35; defense of corporate interests by, 4; deindustrialization of, 72, 149, 151, 165; dynastic families in, 104; electoral system, 141; executive decrees in, 130; foreign influence in, 153, 184–85; foreign investment in, 7–8, 159, 216n. 16; foreign lobbyists in, xxviii–xxix, 149–62, 186; foreign-owned debt, 7; Gill on, 34–35; as the great power, 103; Hispanization of culture in, 179–80; imperialism, 58; increasing power of the state in, 31; industry lost overseas, xxix; industry relocation in, 149, 151, 160–61,

162–66; international law and, 112, 115, 210n. 11; Iranian Islamism and, 198n. 7; Japanese investment in, 159–60, 164; liberal hegemony, 35; Middle East policy, 83, 205n. 37; Midwest, 217n. 18; New Social Movements in, 31–32; Northeastern, 160; organized crime in, 120–21, 211n. 19; Peruvians in, 10–11; Pinochet Coup and, 37–38; power of, xxix, 192n. 7; recognition of Israel, 110; Rise of the Rich paradigm and, xxii, xxviii, 148–51; Rise of the West paradigm in, 186; ruling classes of, xxviii; Saudi Arabia and, 58; Southern, 151, 160–61, 164–65; Southwestern, 151, 164–65; state of emergency rule and, 129, 130, 144–45; stratification of, 183; Structural Adjustment Programs, 134–38; Thatcher and, 54; underclass, 144; unequal power of, 96; United Kingdom alliance with, 56; United Nations criticism by, 115; world history textbooks in, 196n. 23; as world policeman, 101, 128–29, 148

United States–Mexico Bi-National Immigration Commission, 175

unskilled immigrants, 174–75

Unwanted Company: Foreign Investment in American Industry (Crystal), 216n. 16

upper class, 127. *See also* ruling classes; the Rich

urban areas, 165–66

urban studies, 44–45

USAID, 211n. 18

use value, 66

USS *Pueblo*, 161

USSR. *See* Soviet Union

utopian teleology, xxiii